Your Digital Undertaker

EXPLORING DEATH IN THE DIGITAL AGE IN CANADA

SHARON HARTUNG

 FriesenPress

Suite 300 - 990 Fort St
Victoria, BC, V8V 3K2
Canada

www.friesenpress.com

www.digitalundertaker.ca

Technical editing by Irma Tadic
Front Cover and Infographics editing by Vincent Murakami

This book is a personal story and journey navigating the deathcare and estate planning industry. The intent of the book is simply to encourage adult Canadians to consider the importance of creating a will and estate plan, and engage qualified estate professionals in doing so. The author does not warrant or guarantee the accuracy or currency of any information provided herein. The laws in a province/territory or jurisdiction change and are potentially different than what was presented here. The author is not providing advice, and you are encouraged to seek qualified professional advice authorized in your jurisdiction for your specific situation.

ISBN
978-1-9994501-5-1 (Hardcover)
978-1-9994501-4-4 (Paperback)
978-1-9994501-6-8 (eBook)

1. BUSINESS & ECONOMICS, PERSONAL FINANCE, MONEY MANAGEMENT

Distributed to the trade by The Ingram Book Company

To Karen and Ryder, who along with my favourite orange GPS tracker, walked, talked and listened for miles as I worked through the material.

First it was: the book, the book, the book,
Then: the speech, the speech, the speech,
Then back to: the book, the book, the book.

SHOUTOUTS

Writing a book was a new adventure for me but just like every project I've been on, it would not have been a success without the tremendous support of family, friends and colleagues. I have been lucky to have so many people cheer me on, offer help and I want to thank the following people who went above and beyond the call of duty:

Ron Laudadio who was my go-to for bouncing ideas,
Peter Martin for our many discussions on the taxation of estates and for introductions to his network in the estate industry,
Dr. Sara M. Johnson who challenged me to get it academically right but client readable,
Calvin Fong whose knowledge of the estate world is mesmerizing,
Kathleen Cunningham who introduced me to the network of digital practitioners in STEP Global,
Margaret A. Lanthier whose insight to philanthropy is amazing,
The Byte Bright Mastermind group who challenged me to push the envelope.

I would also like to thank the following people who took the time to help me understand specific topics and the business of publishing: Alysha To, Beth Bell, Chuck Grossholz, Diana Philip MacLaren, Douglas Gibson, Dr. Blaize Horner Reich, Fan Chun, Heather Martin, Isaac "Ike" Shanfield, Kathy Stivin, Quinton Pullen, Sarah Dale-Harris, Treva Anderson and Wanda Morris.

And the following people who assisted me in preparing the manuscript for publication: Dani Kent, Deborah Stinson, Irma Tadic, Pam Beck and Vincent Murakami.

Table of Contents

Foreword

When I was at the height of my information technology career, I would imagine a day when I would have the time to write a book. It was something fun to think about, and a welcome distraction from my amazing and busy tech career. Now well entrenched in my entrepreneurial life, I feel as energized as I did at the beginning of my military career or whenever I finished a project for an IBM client. In the last several years, I've engaged with a whole new group of people in the deathcare and estate industry, who have enthusiastically embraced me, and to whom I say: thank you for helping me navigate the complex world of estates.

So why this book and why now – simply because I let my life take me where it did. The direction of my life changed when my mother died. Death affects everyone; it is inevitable – certain, in fact. Death affected me, I was not immune. It literally stopped me in my tracks, forced me to face grief in a way that I'd never experienced before and handed me a troubled project I was not expecting. As I worked my way through my mom's estate project, I began to realize that, somehow, we generally still haven't figured out how to talk about death. There is shock and so many revelations when dealing with the death of a loved one. It is really time to figure out how to have a better conversation about death.

The subject of death and how to prepare for it is a very important subject which touches us all. Baby Boomers, I encourage you to get your affairs in order, because it is hard enough in the digital age for the next generation to keep up and you might even find it is a liberating and uplifting experience. Generation Xers, for you, it means going through the death journey with mom and dad, and learning from it. Millennials and Generation Zers, it will likely mean a total rethink of how you want to approach death, the same way you are rethinking how you want to work, socialize, get around and communicate.

You think your life is simple. It is not. Your life is complicated and that's what makes you special. You may have grown up on the farm with one family, one set of parents, or lived in the same city with all your relatives. That world as a norm is almost gone. Families are now dispersed across the province, the country and the globe; your possessions span multiple locations, your relationships are complicated and there is a growing demographic without children, or those who are single by choice, divorce or death. If there was an old recipe for death that your parents used, it likely won't work for you today if you have gone even partially digital. If it does work, it might only work if you have a will, an estate plan, have talked to your beneficiaries and the executor, and have left enough information in an estate binder.

This book shares my personal journey and attempts to "crack the code on death" by looking at it from a completely different lens – the project management and digital lens. Technology is the new player at your estate planning table. Let this book change the conversation and inspire you to get your affairs in order in the digital age and then get on with spending more time with those you love.

It's my hope after you've read this book that you, as a consumer, can engage with the deathcare and estate industry more confidently – by asking more informed questions and becoming better prepared. Perhaps you'll even be moved to using technology, such as social media, to collectively raise Canadians' knowledge of estate planning and estate administration through your experiences. With a more enlightened and engaged Canadian estate client like yourself, combined with technological innovation in the digital age, perhaps estate planning and estate administration will get just a little bit less overwhelming and easier to navigate over time, making the whole subject of death, which is always emotionally charged, easier to deal with and talk about.

Chapter 1
Death Never Comes At a Good Time

I remember thinking it was morbid when I heard that my grandparents had prearranged their funerals. Who does that? When you're in your twenties and starting life on your own, looking for spare change in all your pockets to see if you have enough to go out on a Friday night, anything to do with death is far from your mind. That didn't change when I was in my thirties and trying to find my way in a new career in my new home of Vancouver with new friends. Funeral planning started to make sense in my forties, when I began thinking it was being proactive, but I couldn't imagine where I would find the time as my job became a 24/7 obsession. I remember wondering if it was because my grandparents were organized and hardworking people, determined to always do the right thing. Still, I thought it odd.

My opinion changed on a beautiful spring morning, a Friday, when RCMP officers came to my front door. I had no idea what they wanted, didn't really hear their first question and hoped to send them on their way. Then it dawned on me why they were there. They had come to tell me my mother had died. I thought it was very respectful that they were giving me notification in person, which I had always assumed was just a TV thing. They encouraged me to call family and friends for support. I struggled to organize my thoughts. I was lost, with no idea where to begin. I didn't know the first thing about what my mother would have wanted. We had never talked about it.

After making all the necessary phone calls, I quickly had more suggestions than I could possibly handle. I remembered attending my grandmother's and grandfather's funerals, each at a family gathering, with a service, a graveside ceremony and a wake. It all seemed to go so smoothly. Having project management experience, I was intrigued by the planning that must have been involved. I called the same funeral home and they booked an appointment for Monday. I wanted to drive there for a meeting right that minute. Wasn't this an emergency? Shouldn't we be mobilizing? The adrenaline was kicking in. I had a hundred questions. Someone had recommended cremation, so I figured I should start with that. The funeral director promised to e-mail me information and a price list. Ultimately, the close family members I contacted also became overwhelmed, withdrew and wanted to figure things out later. I had to do something, so I chose a date for a memorial at my house that was several weeks down the road.

When I awoke Saturday morning in a post-adrenaline rush stupor, I faced the e-mail from the funeral home. The words seemed to blur on the screen. Why is it not making sense? What is wrong with me? Gradually a wave of panic emerged as I read the list of details required. I knew my mother's maiden name, but where were her parents born? What was her health card number? Her Social Insurance Number? I had no idea. I decided to work from a hard copy, thinking it might make better sense on paper. There, at the bottom of the e-mail, were the prices – approximately $4,500 for cremation with no service. I knew my mother didn't have that kind of money. Who has that kind of cash on hand? The rest of the day was spent in a haze, trying to make sense of how my mother died and how to get access to her condo. She had passed away suddenly, unexpectedly and alone.

Sunday morning brought more phone calls, e-mails and people stopping by. In the middle of the command post that I had set up in my dining room to try to bring a sense of order to this situation, I remembered when my friend's dad died. She had arranged things with a low-cost crematorium company that offered simple cremation services. I checked their website, which looked straightforward, and they seemed to want less information. Funny how the need to provide less information was suddenly more appealing to me. I left a message and they called me back in a couple of hours. An appointment was arranged.

By this point, I had also stumbled over a number of websites offering information, such as the Government of Canada website called After a Death,[1] the Government of British Columbia website called Wills and Estate Planning[2] and the Canadian Bar Association British Columbia Branch article called What Happens When You Die without a Will?[3] Pretty soon, searching for information on how to deal with my mother's death in Canada, and specifically in British Columbia, also became overwhelming. Law firms, financial institutions, trust companies, funeral homes, government agencies, charitable and not-for-profit associations all offered some sort of "what to do" or executor checklists. I realized that they were all just recommendations for every possibility, and I needed to start a list of things that were specific to my mother's situation in the province where she died.

Over the next few hours I also learned that cemetery arrangements are separate from funeral services. Who knew? Funeral homes generally handle the cremation or burial, and the services or memorial events. Cemeteries take care of the resting place, either for burial or memorialization, although more are getting into the complete funeral/memorial service option. We figured out that because my grandparents were in separate cemetery burial plots, we could inter (bury) a cremation urn with my mother's ashes (cremated remains) in the same plot as one of her parents, and booked an appointment at the cemetery.

When Monday came, I cancelled the funeral home appointment and met with a representative from the low-cost cremation company at my house. He told me not to worry about the missing information about my mother, that he could get it. He told me I could pay later and asked if I wanted to choose an urn. I selected a metal blue one with carved seagulls because my mother collected bird pictures and it reminded me of her. He asked me how many death certificates I needed – one was included. I had no idea, so I ordered five. It turned out five death certificates for her estate was too many, and I ended up using only two but, in fact, I could have lived with one, as I could have acquired another later. He went over a list of things I needed to do using a checklist he left with me, which included applying for the Canada Pension Plan death benefit.

I tried to focus on everything he told me, but much of it just washed over me. I did remember that it was important to keep the cremation certificate (called a *disposition permit* in British Columbia), required by law for the interment. He said he would call before dropping off the urn with my mother's ashes. The final bill came to $1,395, which was $3,000 less than the funeral home package. After he left, I felt a bit better that some of the pieces were coming together.

On Tuesday, when I arrived at the cemetery, I thought that all I had to do was provide some identification and pay, but there was much more to be done. Fortunately, I had brought the deed for the burial plot and a probated copy of my grandfather's will, both of which were required. I had to get approvals from my brothers for our mother's urn to be interred in either her father's or her mother's grave. The cemetery staff would set up a tent over the gravesite with some chairs. Family members could say a few words and some earth would be put in the grave before a worker completed the burial. The total cost was $500 plus taxes and a nominal British Columbia Consumer Protection Fee, which I thought reasonable. I also selected a marker – the cemetery term for a bronze plate with name, birth date and death date – to be added to the bottom of her parents' marker, for an additional $750.

Wednesday brought panic. I had finally accessed my mother's condo and collected any papers that looked important. As I started going through them, I found a piece of paper with pricing for a burial. It looked like she had done some preplanning, but there was no date and no funeral home name. There was a funeral home near where she lived, so I called them. Their search found her name, but what showed up was the name of the funeral home that had assisted with her parents' plans. I thanked them, but worried for weeks that I had chosen cremation when she might have wanted to be buried.

The memorial took place on a beautiful, warm, sunny afternoon, on the third Sunday in May. I had called friends and neighbours to be room fillers as I had no idea who might show up. After two box store runs, one for food and one for flowers, and a grocery stop, I had everything I needed. And, of course, everyone brought a large quantity of some form of comfort food – meat balls, kebobs, blueberry scones, Nanaimo bars with extra icing and marshmallows (because they need more sugar) and so on. A cousin had rallied the family and we had a full house. It was amazing to see how many calories a group of mourners could consume. We had cleared out my house to accommodate everyone, but the earliest to arrive decided the event was going to be in my backyard. I kept things simple. I put my mother's urn with some favourite photos on a glass side table, we brought the platters of food outside, and I asked that we spend a moment remembering my mother. I delivered the eulogy that I had hoped reflected the woman she was. My cousin offered his shoulder as a prop, and I think I permanently impressed squeeze marks into his shoulder as I read my prepared words. It seemed to go over well. My brothers gave me hugs before I dashed into the house to start the dessert platters. I wanted to save everyone from having to say anything, as I could feel the emotion swelling up like a massive ball in my chest and didn't want to lose it in front of everyone.

My take away is this: leaving your family to decide what happens to your body and organize your funeral/memorial is like asking someone to plan your wedding and reception but giving them no details, no budget, a very tight timeline, and then never really knowing if you would have liked it or not.

And that was the easy part. After that, things got much worse.

While the memorial service and the graveside ceremony completed the tribute to my mother, it marked the beginning of a

2-year process of sorting out her estate. It was a process that was made far more complicated because, as far as I could tell from a search of the British Columbia Wills Registry database and a thorough search of her condo, my mother didn't have a will. As her daughter, I could make the funeral arrangements, but the process of dealing with her estate was completely shut down until I was legally assigned to act as her executor. This obstacle could have been easily avoided had she made a will in which she named me or one of my siblings – or anyone, for that matter – her executor. Had she taken the time to do that, I could have started the wheels turning immediately.

Instead, I found myself taking a self-taught crash course in provincial will legislation, studying the 90-plus pages of British Columbia's *Wills, Estates and Succession Act* ("WESA," pronounced *way-saw*).[4] This is the provincially legislated statute that sets out who can apply to be executor and who gets what if there is no will in the province of British Columbia. With her parents and siblings having predeceased her, my mother's situation called for my brothers and myself to agree on who was going to apply to be the executor. Because I was the only one who lived in the province of her death, we agreed I should do the job. I had the paperwork drawn up, sent it around to my brothers to sign and submitted it to the court. Nothing, however, is ever simple when someone dies without a will. It took 9 months, the same amount of time it takes to conceive and bring a life into this world, just to get to the same starting point as the executor named in a will.

During that frustrating time, I did as much as I could – hiring a lawyer, explaining the situation, collecting a list of all her assets and compiling relevant information. But every institution I encountered needed a copy of the court document allowing me to act as the executor. I also had to pay several thousand dollars in expenses out of my own pocket, which would only be reimbursed once things were settled.

Some personal context is important here because death never comes at a good time, not for the deceased and not for the family and friends left behind, who are dealing with their own challenges. In my case, heavy rains that year triggered several months of a long, muddy, messy and expensive drainage project that left my yard looking like a disaster scene. I was coming off a cancer scare surgery and had taken extended time off work to rethink my career after almost 30 years in information technology.

I was lucky. I realized early on that sorting out my mother's estate was like running a project, with a start date and an end date. I've managed projects throughout my career, first as an aerospace engineering officer with the Royal Canadian Air Force and then as an executive with IBM, working with clients in both the public and private sectors. However, I certainly hadn't done anything like this before, so it was new to me. The start date was when she died. The end date, presumably, would be when whatever liabilities she had were taken care of, her final taxes filed and her assets distributed.

I did what I always do when beginning a new project – I got organized. I started by keeping track in a simple spiral notebook documenting who I talked to and what we discussed, and created a log to capture what I needed to figure out or solve. I drew up a cost tracking spreadsheet to record the expenses incurred and set up a directory on my computer with subfolders for all the scanned documents. My project plan had to be updated every time I discovered something new or realized something else needed my attention. In the beginning, this was a daily occurrence, but eventually it meant weekly updates. When the volume of papers started growing, I created a binder for each of the major categories that I needed to keep track of as things progressed. I collected all my mother's important documents at the condo. It took almost 2 weeks to go through all the papers – sorting them, trying to figure out what bills needed to be paid, what debts she had and what she owned.

Dealing so intensely with my mother's death became a very emotional experience for me. I wondered if there was more I could have done during her life, as I came to understand the challenges she never shared with me. Sadness shadowed my life for a long time. Longevity runs in my family, so her death caught me completely off guard. Our last visit wasn't the best as it had been delayed a week, so she wasn't in the best of moods, but she seemed physically fine. I had taken my 94-year-old great aunt along for this particular visit. When I inadvertently gave her the "time to go" signal, to which she promptly leaped up and put on her jacket, I used it as my excuse to leave. That decision is burned into my brain, a guilt loop on endless replay.

It was the mechanics of managing the project that kept me from breaking down or being overwhelmed. Making daily entries in the chronology, detailing what I learned, who I had talked to and what I had done gave me a sense of satisfaction that tasks were being accomplished, problems were being solved and the project was moving forward.

It also became a very useful tool to summarize what was happening for my brothers, who were supportive, although I expect they rolled their eyes every time they received yet another "Sharon Estate Project Update" in their e-mail inboxes. As I've come to learn through talking with dozens of other people, family harmony is often not the norm. Strained relationships usually worsen when an estate is up for grabs. My brothers assured me they had no expectations as beneficiaries. They both knew my mother had little means and recognized the challenges that I had to face.

While everyone I had to deal with – from government agencies like the Canada Pension Plan staff, to bank personnel and funeral industry people – were empathetic, helpful and accommodating, there were many bumps in the road. After receiving permission from the courts to act as the executor, called an *administrator* in the province of British Columbia, the piece of paper I received from the court was the equivalent of a probated will. Fortunately, the courts waived any requirement for me to post a bond, which can be required in situations where there is no will (*intestate*). However, after going to the bank to shut down my mother's credit card, I discovered the document had a significant error. After another appointment with the lawyer, who followed up right away, the court corrected the document promptly, but this still added another month to the timeline.

Once I received the corrected copy, I had to apply to be appointed the executor for my grandfather's estate. My mother had been my grandfather's executor and inherited the condo when he died, but for reasons that remain unclear, the paperwork never got finalized at the Land Titles Office. The court had to recognize me as her backup executor so that I could work with the Land Titles Office to move ownership of the condo from his estate to hers. That added another 2 months and incurred more legal fees. During that entire time, I had to keep paying her monthly condo expenses, insurance, electricity and other ongoing incidental costs because the bank, realizing their client had died, had stopped all her automatic payments.

In hindsight, I should have booked a meeting with the bank manager or asked if she had dealt with someone in particular at the bank on a regular basis. I should have gone down there with the death certificate and explained the situation – that I was her daughter and was waiting for the court to appoint me as the administrator. I should have realized that the bank's client, my mother, was still the bank's client, alive or deceased. They could have continued to pay these bills from her frozen account, and they could have released payment for funeral expenses from her frozen account. The bank obviously has procedures they would need to follow with any such request, but as I understand, these are some of things that can be done, depending on the discretion given to the bank manager and corporate policy. Building that relationship with the bank manager would have helped other things down the road as well. When the court finally did grant me administrator rights, it took months to have the bank transfer the funds, and not without reengaging the lawyer to talk to the bank twice.

As a professional in my day job, I would not have hesitated to do client cold calls and relationship building. I really had to ask myself later why I didn't do it with my mom's bank as I would have done at work. Well, there wasn't really an answer. Everything was new about this death experience (grief does funny things to a person) and I felt paralyzed because I didn't have that critical piece of paper, even though I had other documents like the death certificate and had engaged a lawyer.

I soon realized that I needed help from professionals who had expertise in estate administration. If there are things like unpaid debts and taxes, the executor is expected to get them paid. When I asked about hiring an experienced estate accountant, my lawyer recommended a firm he had worked with many times. In my professional life, I like to stack my project teams with people who come with strong referrals and ideally have worked together successfully before. It reduces confusion and improves communication. It can also save time and money, because people who have solved problems together have usually worked out the dynamics of their relationships in complex environments. One of the firm's estate and trust accountants was assigned to my file and, over the next year and a half, I spent more time with him than any of the other people I interacted with over my mother's estate.

Because my mother had not filed income tax for several years, he helped me collect the necessary information and completed the paperwork for filing her returns with the Canada Revenue Agency. Also, because her income was low, she was eligible to receive Goods and Services/Harmonized Sales Tax ("GST/HST") rebates. We applied for them and that money went into the estate bank account to help pay for the various professional services I had hired. We figured out that my mother had not claimed her child-rearing years when she had applied for Canada Pension Plan entitlements. A follow-on application fixed the payments retroactively, with that money also going into the estate bank account. The estate accountant then helped complete my mother's T1 Individual Tax Form (Terminal Return), which covered the time between January 1 and the date of her death, and also filed a T3 Estate Income Tax Form when her assets were finally sold. Ultimately, the professional estate accounting services and tax advice I received from this firm more than paid for itself.

I learned a lot of things. I came to understand, unlike the United States, Canada has no estate tax. However, in Canada, we have probate tax (often called *fees*) and income tax on things such as capital gains, and the taxation of registered plans, that are the deceased person's final tax obligations upon their death. I assumed the estate would receive the full Canada Pension Plan death benefit of $2,500 to cover the cremation. I discovered that, at the time of her death, $2,500 was the maximum benefit and was prorated based on how much a person paid into their Canada Pension Plan throughout their work life. My mother received slightly more than half: $1,266. I learned that it's not a good idea to die at the end of the month. Had my mother died one day later, she would have received one more month of Canada Pension Plan and Old Age Security payments. The payments for the following month had to be returned, adding another task to the project plan. Like everything else that changes, I understand that in the future, the Canada Pension Plan death benefit is proposed to be a lump sum, the same for everyone.[5]

Over time, I gradually became more comfortable with the project and started to understand what worked and what didn't when dealing with the estate professionals, financial institutions and government agencies. Sending a short agenda before each meeting and e-mailing a summary of the discussion with a list of who was doing what made a big difference. I came to realize that if I didn't initiate meetings, weeks and months could pass with nothing happening. I would never have done that in my job, and learned to always ask when we should meet again and to set up the next session right away.

Soon my entire project management consulting skill set began to emerge. I drew diagrams and created charts to understand the business flow, created decision trees for each of the processes I encountered, and began to ask questions such as: What is probate and how does it work? What is the tax process upon death and how many tax forms do I have to fill out? It became a welcome distraction to my grief and cleared up my foggy headedness.

That didn't prevent my journey from hitting potholes. My mother co-owned (in joint tenancy) a rental property with *rights of survivorship* with another person, which essentially means that if either person dies, the survivor gets full title. The entire property was transferred to the surviving owner outside her estate, but her estate was responsible for paying the taxable capital gains on her half of the property. This meant her estate and beneficiaries got nothing and I was again out of pocket for the tax bill for several months. I learned a valuable lesson. The way property ownership is set up becomes paramount on the death of one of the owners, so get it right before you or someone you love dies, because it affects who ends up with the property and what taxes may have to be paid by the estate.

There were plenty of other bizarre details that just wasted time. My mother had one credit card, which had less than $200 owing on it. To avoid additional expenses, I felt I needed to pay off the balance right away and close the account. I made an error, however, and underpaid, for which the credit card company started to charge interest. After paying to fix it, her monthly statement showed a $0.99 overpayment for almost a year, even after the card had been cancelled. What I've learned since is that one should consider first informing the credit card company that the person has died, and then investigating if they had credit card insurance coverage or other insurance coverage that pays off the balance in the event of death – because if you pay off the balance and/or cancel the card without explanation, you might accidentally cancel any insurance coverage the now deceased account holder had in place.

There were also things I should have known, but didn't. This was, after all, my first death project. For instance, most provinces permit executors to be compensated for their time. In British Columbia, it's a maximum of 5% of the probated estate value, but that value is prorated by the complexity of the estate. While that sounded good, I learned that the amount paid is taxable income and that in paying the executor, the estate must act like an employer and file the proper documentation with the government. The executor receives a T4 slip and must file income tax for the amount. I questioned whether it was worth the paperwork hassle to take the fee, given that my mother's estate was so small. With a myriad of tasks to do, I opted not to claim the executor's fees. To this day, I'm not sure if I made the right decision, as I've learned through my business experience, "free" doesn't necessarily mean valued.

Because her condo stood empty for over a year while waiting for the paperwork to be finalized, the insurance company didn't want to extend the coverage. Apparently, insurance companies don't like insuring domiciles left empty for long periods of time. I eventually found an understanding insurance broker who negotiated a special risk policy that cost more, provided less coverage and required arranging for regular visits to the condo. There was other nonsense too, like the fact that someone started parking in her spot, so that each time the place was checked, more phone calls had to be made.

The condo was built in the 1980s. The main building had been kept up and was clean and tidy, with beautiful landscaping, but it was outdated inside, with worn carpets, creaky stairs and furniture in the public areas that could have been my grandparents' cast-offs. There was another unit in the building identical to my mother's, right down to the original light fixtures and white carpet, that had languished on the condo market for over a year with no buyer in sight. After conferring with a cousin who works in real estate, I realized updates were necessary to sell the unit.

This was a decision made while I was still waiting for the executor paperwork to come through and it was one that caused more than a few sleepless nights. As the eventual executor, anything I did would be my responsibility and potentially at my expense. If I messed something up, I'd have a problem. I drew up a budget, documented the work and reviewed things regularly with my brothers who, as the beneficiaries, were the key stakeholders in this subproject. Being reasonably handy, I opted to save costs by doing some of the painting, moldings and other less complicated tasks myself, but I hired professional bonded companies to do the big jobs like flooring and plumbing. The simplest choice would have been to do nothing and sell the unit as it was. But I concluded, based on the market, that the condo might go unsold for years, during which time the estate would be responsible to pay the condo fees, insurance and other costs. In all, it took several thousand dollars to get the unit in shape to sell. I put it on the market after getting my executor appointment by the court, as administrator, and it sold within several weeks. It was a gamble that paid off.

My mother also owned a small cottage in Ontario, bought in the early 70s. This meant hiring another lawyer in that province and more estate expenses. Fortunately, the Government of Ontario recognized the British Columbia proof of probate which gave me authority to sell the cottage. This is not always the case; there are jurisdictions where you pretty much go through a second probate process. This is especially true for properties owned in other countries, like the United States. As it turned out, that was the easy part; then came the capital gains tax nightmare.

A capital gain is the taxable difference between the amount paid when a cottage is built or bought and the amount received when it is sold, minus the cost of upgrades, such as adding a bathroom. When settling an estate, a cottage is deemed to have been sold at fair market value on the day of the owner's death. In my case, I could prove my mother had paid $7,800 for the land back in the day, but who keeps 40-year-old construction receipts? Luckily, in 1994, the federal government allowed individual income tax submissions to document the cost base of non-primary residences, including cottages, declaring the price paid for the property and all the upgrade expenses incurred until then. Who keeps 20-plus-year-old tax returns? After dozens of wasted nights spent finding, taping and counting whatever building receipts I could find among her effects, I somewhat miraculously found her 1994 income tax documents. They had been tucked away in a box of papers in a crawl space under a relative's house.

To make things even more complicated, my mother never got around to settling the financial aspects of her long-ago divorce. As the executor, I suddenly became my mother's representative in a fresh round of negotiations many years after she and her ex-husband had parted company. Beyond creating an interesting new family dynamic, it added many more weeks to what should have been a simple estate disbursement.

I was fortunate to find that my mother's digital life didn't really need much closing down. With one piece of paper written in her beautiful and legible handwriting, outlining her e-mail account information and password, that was pretty much it. Her technology collection was simply one computer she had nursed for many years past its expiry date for her hobbies and writing. After I told her a story many years ago about a colleague at university who had lost his thesis due to a computer crash back in the early days of personal computing, she carefully backed up her files on CDs which were neatly filed and dated. The most she ever asked me to do was check the settings on her computer, set up a printer and pick up printer paper. Of all the user help desk support I've provided over the years, a tech role which I fell into outside work only because friends and family didn't really understand what I did for a living, she was my easiest digital client in life and death. If my mother had been the social media mogul that most people seem to have become today to stay connected, or even had gone digital with her basic life management such as utilities, paying bills and condo fees, my job as the executor would have taken on a whole other level of digital undertaker.

How did a woman who lived a relatively simple and modest life come to have such a complicated estate? I now have several spiral notebooks containing hundreds of pages of records about meetings, phone calls and e-mails with lawyers, accountants and all the other people and agencies I encountered in the process of settling her estate. Dying intestate (without a will) made everything many times far more complicated and unsettled, adding layers of difficulty that could have been easily avoided.

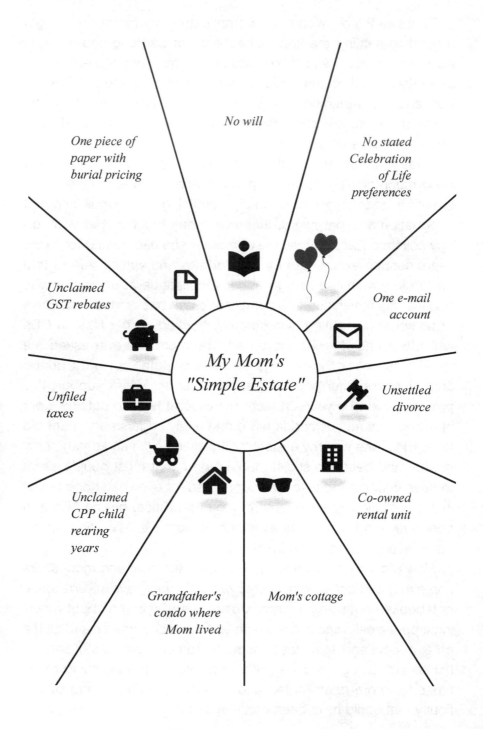

No will

One piece of
paper with
burial pricing

No stated
Celebration
of Life
preferences

Unclaimed
GST rebates

One e-mail
account

My Mom's
"Simple Estate"

Unfiled
taxes

Unsettled
divorce

Unclaimed
CPP child
rearing
years

Co-owned
rental unit

Grandfather's
condo where
Mom lived

Mom's cottage

Every issue I encountered added time and costs. In my professional life, I would have called this estate administration a troubled project. I couldn't give the recovery project a fun name and hold team building events. There was no cool project logo and no celebratory closeout party.

Just when I thought I was free and clear, the Canada Revenue Agency came back into my life. Twelve months earlier, a full year after my mother's death, I had asked my estate accountant to apply for a tax clearance certificate. I don't know exactly why it took so long, but a year later, the government had several questions they wanted answered before issuing the certificate, which meant calling in the estate accountant again. It wasn't a big deal; it was resolved by resending information that had already been sent. But still…

It took a little more homework to find that, as the executor, you shouldn't distribute the estate to the beneficiaries until the clearance certificate is in hand. Otherwise, you risk being held liable for any additional taxes. I mistakenly assumed, more than a year and half after my mother died, that I was sure I had done all that was required. I proceeded with beneficiary signoff and had dispensed the remainder of the estate. I didn't think it was practical or reasonable to delay any longer and incur more costs. So, there I was incurring more expense retaining the estate accountant to get us through this final hurdle.

In retrospect, I don't feel any differently about my mother; I am not mad or disappointed that I had to deal with all of this. She didn't ask for much while she lived. I feel a sense of closure in being able to do something for her after death, and giving her the same effort and diligence I would have given my professional clients. While my project management and consulting instincts kicked in and saved me, I also feel lucky to have good friends and family who rallied to help.

When the cemetery e-mailed me a photo of the completed marker, I asked if I could come in for some pre-planning myself. I took a tour with the cemetery person I had previously dealt with. I learned that she came from the family funeral business in Asia. I asked her what the difference was between what happens in

Asia and Canada. She explained that in Asia, the families get very loud and animated when it comes to trying to decide what to do, whereas in Canada everyone is pretty polite. I said that is probably because all the fighting happens back at home before they come to the cemetery. She laughed.

I found myself oddly fascinated with the tour, and a bit stunned. My grandparents had paid next to nothing for their burial plots back in the 1980s. The going rate at this Vancouver Lower Mainland cemetery was $20,000-plus, with a plot for an entire family going for $1 million. We had developed a bit of a banter at this stage of the tour when I realized this galactic pricing was far beyond my realm of reality. She joked that at least you don't have to pay property taxes. I laughed – now that's funny. There were other less expensive memorial areas and niches, including a nice one next to a pond, and she explained other mausoleums were being added in the future. Clearly, Vancouver real estate prices have hit cemeteries too.

Fortunately, because I was in the military, there was a significant discount for veterans and I purchased a plot that can hold one burial or two cremations, pre-paying for the interment. I will deal with the marker later, but I documented that I would like to have pictures engraved on it. I asked her if someone can supply their own marker, to which she replied yes, if it met the specific sizing requirements. I figured that down the road, one of my nephews ought to have a 3D laser printer and be able to handle that.

I can also tell you that walking into a funeral home is a completely different experience when you are not in mourning or grieving. The options are clear, embarrassingly simple and the terminology really isn't that difficult. I went back to the original funeral home I had called when my mother died. Like most, they have three standard packages for burial and three packages for cremation. And, of course, there are lots of extras to select from, such as memorial items. I asked about cremation and there it was: the $4,500 cremation with no service package that I had seen before, along with a $10,000 cremation with service option, and the works at $13,000. Ultimately, I just bought a funeral plot and have it written in my will that I want a low-cost crema-tion. I like to think my grandparents would be proud.

Chapter 2
Getting Your Affairs in Order – Building Your Death Project in the Digital Age

The Digital Age We Are Living In

We are living in the digital age and are affected by it, whether or not we choose to adopt technology or anything digital in our personal lives. The digital age, often referred to as the information age, is a period that, I think we can all agree, began in earnest with the widespread use of the World Wide Web or internet. The way we communicate and engage socially has been transformed, from physical letters to e-mail to social media.

Digitization and automation have also critically affected the consumer marketplace and the traditional workplace. For example, in the retail sector, many "stores" you know have moved from traditional brick and mortar storefronts to online stores.

This digital age has been evolving around us for a while. The accepted stereotype of people over the age of 65, is that this age group is less tech savvy. But internet usage statistics in Canada paint a different picture. According to a Statistics Canada study (2010),[6] Canadians over 65 years old: 90% use e-mail, 63% search online for medical or health-related information and 45% use the internet for electronic banking.

Is Dying in the Digital Age That Much Different Than Dying in the Non-Digital Age?

Here's the spoiler alert right out of the gate: in general, dying in the digital age, in many respects, is exactly the same as dying in the non-digital age. The main reason for this is that laws play into what happens when you die. Laws will continue to evolve over time to deal with new situations and complexities or specific cases. Current law is the starting point. The digital age might be new, but the concept of law applying to any age is not. Laws were applied and updated in response to the Industrial Revolution; it will happen for the digital age as well, and for whatever future era important enough to be named, such as the Robotics Age, the Virtual Reality Age or the Artificial Intelligence Age.

Consider this oversimplified example: an online store is still a store. Some of how the store is run is covered by business law(s), whether it is a physical store or an online store in the jurisdictions where it operates. Obviously, the e-commerce store has something new, a different channel to customers than a physical store. There are new laws or updated laws required to deal with the online aspects. Consider, for example, that privacy laws and computer usage laws have been introduced or updated as a result of the use of the online technology of that store, and multiple laws might be involved, depending on which jurisdictions this online store operates in. The point here is that everything wasn't necessarily newly written because of online stores – just those aspects that were required to deal with the new or innovative piece.

The point of this simple example is to say that dealing with your digital estate means dealing with your estate, which now also includes digital aspects. Much of the traditional planning aspects of estate planning and estate administration still apply, with a digital twist. Learning what is the same is the best starting point. From there, layering on an understanding about what is different in dealing with the digital aspects will help ground your overall understanding of this new age and its impact on estate planning and estate administration.

It will probably come as a bit of relief to many of you that, to a certain extent, some things are constant, such as the current laws that govern wills, succession, estate planning and estate administration (although they do evolve over time). This means, in order to contemplate your digital life and how your life in the digital age will be impacted by death, you'll need to understand how the current laws, traditional estate planning and estate administration, and the deathcare and estate industries that support it, already work today and how they apply to the physical world of your belongings. There are two basic ways that the current laws catch up to something like technology: (1) new law is created in the form of legislation (*e.g.*, acts, statutes, regulations) which is passed by a government within a jurisdiction;[7] and (2) for common law jurisdictions, case law (often called *judge-made law*) which is made through precedent-setting decisions.[8] And that, my friends, takes some learning beyond just a keen sense of curiosity.

How Do We Get There from Here

This book will share with you what I've learned about how the deathcare and estate industries generally work in Canada, in my quest to deal with my mother's estate. Before we get into your digital life and the digital things you might own, we need to get comfortable with the basics and some of the terminology in the deathcare and estate spaces. In this chapter, I will offer a point of view on how to approach the deathcare and estate Industries by looking at them through a project management lens. By doing so, perhaps you too can bring all that knowledge from your job or former career to your own estate planning journey. In Chapters 3 to 6, I'll share what I've learned about the funeral business in Canada, wills, trusts, executors and advance care plans.

Chapter 7 cuts to the heart of the matter on the digital front with a look at your digital life and what there is to know about digital death and its afterlife. Chapter 7 will also address your digital life on a micro level, because there are differences worth highlighting with respect to the digital possessions you might own when you die. I'll get into more detail in Chapter 7 on what those digital things you own are called: *digital assets* or *digital property*.

Chapter 8 goes into tax territory, because even digital assets get taxed and there is no digital escape from the tax man. Chapter 9 covers philanthropy and touches on how even charities have been affected by the digital age with new emergent *charity tech* organizations and crowdfunding.

Chapter 10 brings it all together. I'll summarize by sharing my starting set of questions called Your Digital Undertaker Question Matrix. I created this summary for myself as an easy reference to what I've learned along my journey exploring the deathcare and estate industry.

The key learning for me, to navigate this new space, is that to understand your digital life and what happens on death, you really need to begin by understanding what happens to your physical assets that are not digital. For example, if you own something digital that has value, such as cryptocurrencies or cryptoassets, it is taxed upon death in the same manner that something physical, like gold, art or stocks, might attract tax. To really understand your estate in the digital age, you need to understand what an estate is in the first place.

Your Digital Undertaker Book Structure

A work breakdown structure ("WBS") is a critical part of a project manager's toolkit for creating a project schedule and a supporting project plan. If a project manager doesn't see a WBS, as in this book, they might break out into a cold sweat, so I included an alternative view of the table of contents, just to be cool with the project management crowd.

Your Digital Undertaker
Work Breakdown Structure
(For Project Managers)

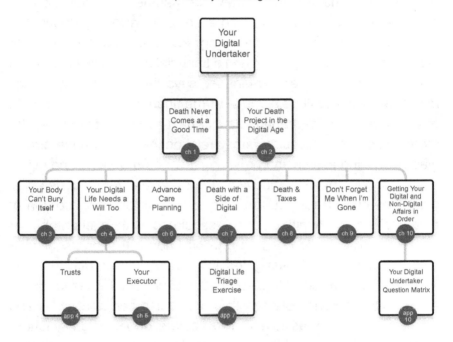

First Order of Business: Getting Comfortable with the Term "Estate Planning"

Who, you might ask, has an estate anyway? The word *estate* may seem too Downton Abbey for the 21st century. But you don't need to own fox hounds to have an estate because if you own a home in a major Canadian city and a decent vehicle, you're probably already worth hundreds of thousands of dollars upon your death. (Likely more than a million if that city is Toronto or Vancouver.) Then there are your investments, pensions and insurance policies. Plus, all your possessions (personal property and digital assets). Who has an estate? You do, of course, as long as you own all those things in your own name.

So, this is where *estate planning* comes into play. But what do the words actually mean? There are as many definitions of estate planning[9] as there are professionals who call themselves estate planners. When a legal advisor says they will help you with estate planning, they usually mean they can handle the legal aspects, such as drafting a will or drafting a power of attorney document, or drafting a trust deed or providing advice on the legal and risk elements of an estate plan. When a financial advisor, like a certified financial planner or wealth manager, says they will help you, they might mean they will help you with the financial planning aspects of your money under management, which can include holistic elements, such as discussing family relationships, insurance strategies, assessing assets and providing advice on options and risks.

An accountant or tax advisor may use the term to describe what they can do for you in terms of the tax planning portion of estate planning. A gift planner associated with a charitable or non-profit organization might be talking about the legacy or philanthropic aspects of gifting. An insurance advisor may use the term to describe term life insurance, permanent life insurance or the various insurance options to meet your other estate planning requirements (such as taxes, risks, estate equalization or charitable giving).[10] A funeral home director brings a whole other set of considerations to the table. My view of estate planning includes personal planning too – arranging your health and financial backup plans while you're living.

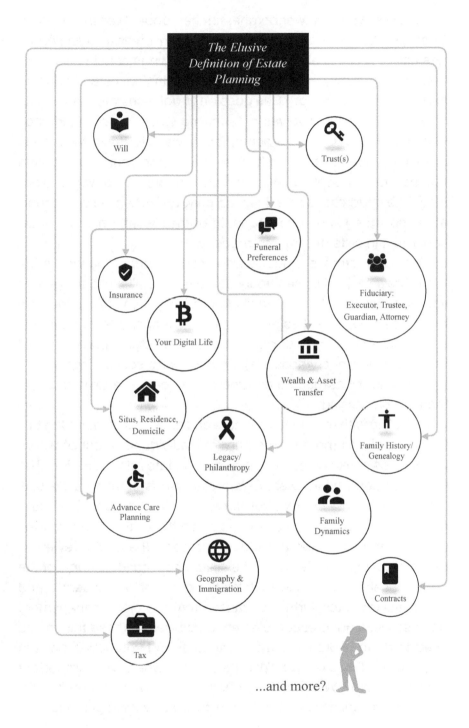

The Elusive Definition of Estate Planning

Will

Trust(s)

Funeral Preferences

Insurance

Fiduciary: Executor, Trustee, Guardian, Attorney

Your Digital Life

Wealth & Asset Transfer

Situs, Residence, Domicile

Legacy/ Philanthropy

Family History/ Genealogy

Advance Care Planning

Family Dynamics

Geography & Immigration

Contracts

Tax

...and more?

Christine Van Cauwenberghe, in her book *Wealth Planning Strategies for Canadians*, describes the term *wealth planning* as referring to an umbrella of processes, including financial planning, tax planning, family law issues, disability planning, estate planning and insurance planning.[11] She goes on to define estate planning as "the process which involves determining what sort of inheritance you need to leave your dependants, or want to leave for others, even if they are not financially dependent upon you."[12] She points out that "most people take a haphazard approach to wealth planning. They address isolated issues only, and often do not understand how the various components of their wealth plan must be consistent in order to operate properly."[13]

One quick term we probably also need get out of the way is the term *assets*, which I'll use throughout to refer to all those things that you own, whether they are tangible or intangible, whether they are real property (*e.g.*, real estate) or personal property (*e.g.*, your personal possessions, art), or digital assets (*e.g.*, digital photos, social media accounts or cryptoassets). Property has a specific legal definition, and not all assets are considered property. The term *assets* is more encompassing.

In dealing with my mother's estate and as part of researching this book, I spoke to more than a hundred individuals, most of whom had their own take on estate planning or estate administration. The best definition I heard was: *Estate planning is creating a deliberate and thoughtful strategy for transferring wealth*. Deliberate and thoughtful because you have considered the options, determined the pros and cons, set a budget, accessed the costs, reviewed tax implications, understood the risks and engaged appropriate professional help. I'd like to take the concept of deliberate and thoughtful one step further because, from a project management perspective, a good estate plan encompasses all those things you need to do to avoid leaving the executor and your loved ones in a quandary. For example: Will they know where your important documents are? Will they know how to shut down monthly subscriptions to online services? How to close your digital life, like your social media accounts? What happens to your pets? These, I believe, are all part of estate planning. They are all part of what you need to do to get your affairs in order.

The idea of getting your affairs in order can be uplifting. Particularly if you consider who you are getting your affairs in order for – your loved ones and beneficiaries. I know from personal experience that the least stressful path to getting one's affairs in order, knowing your loved ones will be taken care of and your wishes will be respected when you're gone, is to remove most of the emotional upheaval by treating your death the same way you would a kitchen renovation. Make it a project – Your Death Project.

Preparing for Death like a Project: Your Death Project

Treating death like a project reduces the inherent emotional reaction to it being a sensitive and morbid subject. No one wants to admit they are going to die. You've probably heard the expression *I'm not going anywhere*. Those who work in the deathcare and estate industry told me people avoid dealing with death out of some vague superstitious notion that to do so will somehow bring it on. The thinking is this: if we ignore it, it won't happen. The allure of this kind of magical thinking is powerful.

We all have a deadline, excuse the pun, but because we just don't know when it is, everything else in life comes first – routine tasks at work and at home override dealing with something that you don't want to happen and that, with some luck, probably won't occur until some unknown future point in time.

Another reason is blissful ignorance. Most people are simply unaware that if they die without providing their survivors with a detailed guide to follow (including at the very least a will), it could potentially cripple their family's ability to function. Just to jolt you a bit, if you were to die tomorrow without planning your estate and could somehow come back to watch things unfold, you likely would be:

- disturbed by how much gets spent at your funeral on things you don't care about;

- horrified to watch your loved ones fighting over your money and your house;

- even more horrified to watch the time spent by your loved ones arguing over trivial things;

- aghast to watch your estate spend all your money on those fights in court over money and trivial things;

- angry about who is rooting through your personal belongings;

- dismayed when prized possessions get thrown out accidentally;

- mortified at the cost of the debate about where you were considered to have lived;

- frustrated with yourself for not leaving your passwords because the executor was unable to access your digital files;

- outraged at what gets paid out in taxes because you didn't leave enough information nor plan; and

- even if you did some estate planning, surprised by how your family reacts to your last wishes because you chose to leave everything to charity or left money in a trust for your pets.

Within the technology industry, project management has been applied and is used to help organizations and clients achieve their business goals and technology objectives. Project management is applied to everything from launching new products and creating new software, to creating new client solutions. Treating your individual death like a project, Your Death Project, can help avoid all that – or at least most of it.

What Is a Project?

You might already have your own examples because you helped your kids or grandkids do their class project or your spouse/partner turned your growing "honey-do list" into a weekend project. A project is about tackling something new, getting something specific done which likely produces a result, usually within a time period – to the extent that it has a start date and an end date. A project normally operates within an agreed-upon scope that sets out what the ultimate goal is. Projects usually involve coordination of people, have some degree of uncertainty (at the outset you may not be entirely sure about the challenges involved), and require the use of resources. A project is not something you do regularly, like mowing the lawn or doing the dishes.

If you are looking for a more formal definition of a project, check out the Project Management Institute ("PMI"),[14] a global organization which certifies project managers and sets standards for the project management profession. The Government of Canada has a project management website with publications, guidance and resources provided by the Treasury Board of Canada Secretariat, that deals with the application of project management. In their view, "project management is about improving the likelihood of success of time-limited initiatives by applying certain practices."[15]

Your Death Project

Whether it is Digital or Not!

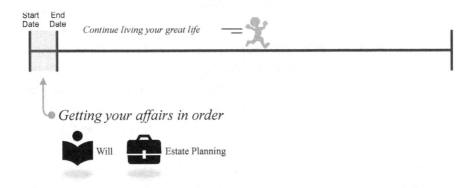

What Are the Projects?

- *Your Death Project* – The first project is to get your will and estate plan complete. Your estate plan may result in the creation of documents or actions you decide to take to get your affairs in order as part of the planning process (*i.e.*, updating beneficiary designations, insurance, trusts, power of attorney, tax planning, funeral pre-planning, advance care planning).

- *Your Executor's Death Project* – There is another project, which the executor will be responsible for in order to administer your estate and implement your legacy wishes. This project will start after you die.

Your Death Project: Review your Affairs
• Every 5 years
• When major life events unfold
• When laws change
• When you move
• When your wishes or intentions change
• ...or whenever you want

Regardless of whether you've ever led a project at home or at work, you probably already know a lot more about being a project manager than you realize. If you have ever asked friends and family to help you move, you were the *de facto* project manager. You lined up the people you needed to help, set out the time it would take, arranged the truck rental, made sure the boxes had labels showing their contents/the rooms they should go in, and finally, you ordered the pizza.

Because it was your move, you intrinsically understood the project. This is important because in business, a project manager needs to understand the project they are working on. This is called *domain knowledge*. As no one knows your life better than you do, you are inherently qualified to be the project manager of your death project. Your life is your domain. One of the key aspects of your domain knowledge is that you are the only one who truly knows what your wishes and intentions are, what you are trying to achieve and what you want to see happen for the final distribution of your assets.

A project manager confirms the scope of the project, draws up a plan and assembles a team to do the work. He or she then follows through on the project plan, making sure tasks get done. The project manager manages the team, updates the project schedule, communicates with stakeholders (those interested in the project's outcomes, which in this case would be the executor, your family and your beneficiaries), and deals with any issues and risks as they arise. The main outcome or deliverable(s) of your death project is minimally a will, ideally an estate plan, and hopefully an associated estate binder.

Although you may not know much about funerals, wills and filing taxes at death, there are plenty of qualified estate professionals who can explain what you need to know in simple terms, provide you with options, and communicate the issues and risks involved. That said, you'll need to be actively involved throughout and be able to engage effectively with the estate professionals you hire. This means asking plenty of questions and taking lots of notes because, while you will be dealing with many professionals, *you* will be the project manager, not them. You may, as many people do, expect a legal advisor to draft a suitable will, with you playing a passive role in developing it. This is not desirable. You might have checked the box, and have a piece of paper called a will, but if you are deeply engaged in the process with the legal advisor, by asking questions, researching, and doing homework, it can result in estate planning documents that better align to your ultimate wishes, intentions and objectives.

Who's on First
The Roles in Your Death Project

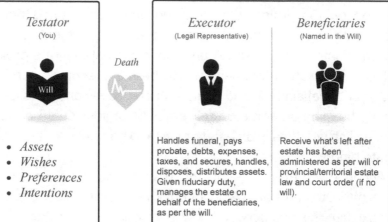

Your Death Project
Estate Planning

Testator
(You)

Will

- *Assets*
- *Wishes*
- *Preferences*
- *Intentions*

Death

Your Executor's Death Project
Estate Administration

Executor
(Legal Representative)

Handles funeral, pays probate, debts, expenses, taxes, and secures, handles, disposes, distributes assets. Given fiduciary duty, manages the estate on behalf of the beneficiaries, as per the will.

Beneficiaries
(Named in the Will)

Receive what's left after estate has been administered as per will or provincial/territorial estate law and court order (if no will).

Roles, titles, terms, rules and laws are defined by applicable province, territory or other jurisdictions.

Project Management Applied: Planning Your Death Project in the Digital Age

A professional project manager in a business setting will use processes or a project management system to manage and bring a project to completion. You could call these *tools* or simply questions, and collectively consider them a project management *checklist* or *toolkit*. Having used project management practices for most of my career, I created a checklist which includes six basic project management concepts that I used to explore the death topic and deal with professionals in the estate industry. I boiled things down considerably and simplified concepts so that anyone can put them to use. I call this starter set of questions Your Digital Undertaker: Project Management Checklist.

Obviously, most professional project managers have more than six basic project management tools at their disposal. A professional project manager would use their organization's project management system, or procure one commercially. These systems often include processes, templates, software, information repositories and tools. The goal here isn't to make you an expert – it is to help you manage Your Death Project with some relevant starting questions.

To garner the value of project management on Your Death Project, I will be bringing this checklist of the six questions and applying them to each chapter. Although they are generic questions, they were selected and adapted to logically progress through any estate planning topic. We'll start with the basic question of *what's in scope*, then evaluate the *options & trade-offs*, progress to clarify *preferences and costs*, understand if *professional advice* is available, investigate the *risks* and finally consider how to *communicate* what was planned. I'll culminate, in the last chapter, with a summary, in the form of a question matrix, of these exploration questions for easy reference down the road.

Your Digital Undertaker
Project Management Checklist

- ✔ Scope
- ✔ Options & Trade-Offs
- ✔ Preferences & Costs
- ✔ Professional Services
- ✔ Risks
- ✔ Communication

Your Digital Undertaker:
Project Management Checklist

1. Scope: *Why are you doing this?*

To succeed, a project manager needs a clear answer to the question Why am I doing this? Scope sets out what it is you want to accomplish – your goal(s). Ultimately, the goal(s) may be different for everyone, just as your wishes and intentions are very personal to you. Among the reasons might be to achieve the peace of mind that comes from knowing that when you die your intentions will be met, your wishes fulfilled, the people you love will be provided for and the executor and family will not be left with an expensive, complicated puzzle.

That said, getting your affairs in order means different things to different people, so the scope of Your Death Project may be entirely different than it is for someone else, and could be as simple as gaining the knowledge that comes from understanding what you can and can't do under the law. You may want a big church funeral service with a choir, followed by a graveside gathering and a catered memorial service. Someone else may want a quiet family focused memorial with the ashes scattered at the cottage or cabin by a few select friends. Deciding what your goals are will define the scope so you can appropriately allocate resources to get things done well and on budget. Want a starting point to consider what should be in an estate plan? The Government of Canada has a simple Estate Planning Checklist,[16] which outlines the benefits of estate planning and considerations for inclusion.

2. Options & Trade-Offs: *What are the pros and cons?*

There is no right way to do anything; there are only options and associated pros and cons. Considerations such as cost, risk and convenience will influence decisions made on any project. Knowing about the options and trade-offs is very important. If you go to a funeral home and ask about cremation, they will explain their service, but it may not be in their interest to tell you that there are other companies that have basic, low-cost cremation services.

However, shopping around to get a better price might not be something you are prepared to do and the one stop, all-inclusive package deal that the funeral home offers might be appealing. Options, options, options; there are always conflicting objectives in any project. The triple constraints of scope, time and cost need to be balanced. If you change one of the constraints – suppose you want things done quickly – it will affect one or both of the other two. It could cost more or it might not be done to your satisfaction.

3. Preferences & Costs: *What do you need and what's it going to cost?*

Once you have made a decision on which options you would like to pursue after considering the trade-offs, the next logical step is documenting the specific preferences (requirements) and calculating costs for the selected options. What do you need to achieve your clearly scoped out "getting your affairs in order," and what are the requirements that make up that scope? In project management terms, requirements and cost management means deciding exactly what you need and what it's going to cost – the individual and quantifiable components that make up the total project scope. It is about tracking the decisions you make and accounting for any changes as they come up. Each preference (requirement) comes with a cost attached that contributes to the overall project cost.

Requirements and cost management are also about setting a budget and sticking to it, which is far easier said than done. It doesn't take much for a project to go off the budget rails when requirements are underestimated or changed. Changes in requirements are normal and to be expected and the project manager handles them through change requests. The more you learn about Your Death Project, the more you may want to amend your original plans. Just remember, everything is connected; if you set a budget and want to stick to it, spending more on one thing (a high end casket) means you might have less to spend somewhere else (the gravestone).

4. Procurement of Professional Services: *Your body can't bury itself!*

Procurement management means managing whatever outside help you need to complete a project – the products and services you will purchase or hire. This means researching what you need, getting quotes and making decisions about what to buy and who to buy it from, then making sure they follow through. While you know your life and your wishes better than anyone else, you might not know what you *don't know* when it comes to wills and estate planning. And this is tricky territory. For example, many of the laws involved in estate planning (*e.g.*, will law, estate law and family law) in Canada are legislated by province or territory, not federally; meaning every province and territory has a different set of laws and rules.

If you have a brother in Ontario, a sister in Newfoundland and you live in British Columbia, the estate rules that apply to each of you could be different. And if your cousin lives in Québec, laws are very different as they follow civil law[17] versus the other provinces/territories that follow common law. How the Canada Revenue Agency views your estate via the *Income Tax Act*,[18] a Canadian federal statute, might differ from how it is seen by family law or estate law in your province or territory. If you are coupled up but not formally married, Canada Revenue Agency's definition of a common-law partnership may differ from your respective province or territory.

To keep organized on the names, roles and titles of the various professionals or practitioners involved in estate planning and/or estate administration in your province/territory/jurisdiction, I'll refer to them in this way:

- *Legal advisors* – the legal professionals that are authorized to practice law in a specific province/territory. For example, lawyer, solicitor, barrister (litigator), notary (Québec), notary public (if authorized in your province/territory).

- *Tax advisors* – the tax professionals that are recognized and authorized to provide tax advice. For example, tax accountant, tax lawyer.

- *Insurance advisors* – the insurance professionals that are licensed to sell insurance products. For example, insurance broker, insurance agent.

- *Financial advisors* – the financial professionals that are recognized, certified and authorized to provide financial advice within the financial sector. For example, certified financial planners, wealth managers, investment advisors, portfolio managers.

- *Funeral and deathcare professionals* – Licensed funeral directors, licensed embalmers, and pre-need salespersons.[19]

- *Estate advisors* – lots of titles here, often a specialty related to estate planning or estate administration within a specific profession.

There are a variety of other estate planning and estate administration roles I encountered in my exploration journey, such as gift planners, trustees, trust officers, executors, appraisers, auctioneers, and certainly any number of other professionals depending on what asset they are dealing with (*e.g.*, real estate agents, real estate lawyers).

Each of the professional estate roles are typically governed by multiple elements such as laws, professional associations, the financial and estate industry/sector, or companies they are associated with. When engaging deathcare and estate industry professionals, similar to other industries, you'll want to understand that they are accredited, authorized or certified to provide the advice they are providing, that the advice is within their scope of practice, that they are licensed or have a designation if they are required to do so, and are current with any professional or practitioner association or the company they are associated with.

As I took on the administrator role for my mother's estate, I was surprised to learn that fiduciary appointments, like that of an executor or a trustee, even considering this role might be filled with a son or daughter like myself, are subject to the same laws and rules as a professional who might do it as a job.

Qualified estate professionals can help you overcome these challenges and navigate the confusing deathcare and estate industry landscape. At the very least, I encourage you to consider engaging a legal advisor to draw up a will – I did. Get someone trustworthy that you can work with, perhaps a recommendation from your own network of friends and family. Go in with your eyes wide open. The deathcare and estate industry is expanding almost as rapidly as the population is aging and it is targeting you, trying to convince you that you need to purchase their specific products or services. Be especially skeptical of fear mongers – those who will try to convince you that you need a specific product or service to avoid a particular issue – they might cite probate hassles, for example, instead of looking at your estate planning situation in its entirety. A holistic approach is better.

Also, because the deceased's body is not going to dispose of itself, you will also need the services of a funeral home or cremation operation licensed in your province/territory. As you'll see in the following chapters, arranging these things well in advance can save thousands of dollars that might be spent by grieving survivors who aren't thinking clearly when expensive options are put in front of them.

5. Risks: *What are the risks? What are the backup plans?*

At the start of a project, a good project manager will try to identify potential risks – essentially, things that could go wrong and derail the project – and think about possible backup plans (risk mitigation strategies and plans, in project management speak) to deal with them if the event occurs. For example, if you enjoy hiking, there is always a risk of getting lost or encountering unanticipated challenges. To mitigate the risk, you might have prepared a backup plan, such as letting someone know where you were going, bringing a map or carrying extra water and supplies in case you had to wait it out.

For Your Death Project, some risks are obvious: muck it up and your estate's assets might get tangled up in court as the beneficiaries duke it out. Furthermore, your estate may end up paying more in taxes. Essentially, you need to identify the things that could possibly lead to your wishes being ignored or overlooked – and come up with a plan to deal with them.

Now keep in mind, even the best estate planning can result in a situation where there are unintended consequences. One can't possibly forecast every scenario, because no one knows exactly when they are going to die. Life and other events may introduce unexpected factors that affect the execution of that plan. Having said that, on the spectrum of "do nothing" to "doing something," your estate planning can increase the odds of success that your wishes will be met.

Remember, there is no one right way to do anything; there are only options and associated pros and cons. That's important to know if you feel that an advisor is only providing you with one solution. It might be a great question to ask them if there other solutions or options. What are the pros and cons of each? On the other hand, that doesn't mean everything is randomly the same in terms of risk and cost either. In fact, there are options which are better than others, and that only investigation, research or advice from professionals will help you discover. What are the risks involved of doing it one way or another?

Skilled estate professionals can help you avoid unnecessary risks that could unravel or impact your estate planning. You'll want to find the estate professionals who can put all the options on the table or who are willing to refer you to a specialist in a specific area if that's where the planning process takes you. If your financial advisor is not aware of multiple estate options, such as insurance, you might not realize that's something to consider for covering tax costs or dealing with equalization issues that otherwise might burden your family. Similarly, if your legal advisor isn't up to speed on the benefits that a trust can offer, you might miss an opportunity to protect yourself and your survivors further down the road. Do your homework, ask lots of questions and weigh the risks.

6. Communication: *It's on a need-to-know basis and someone needs to know!*

Some think of communication as being on a need-to-know basis, and you don't need to know. They couldn't be more wrong. Nothing can derail a project more quickly than poor and ineffective communication. If the people involved in the project don't know what each other is doing, it can lead to misunderstandings, hurt feelings and cost overruns (usually through duplication of effort or neglecting to do something important because you thought someone else was all over it). If all the stakeholders in the project (in the case of Your Death Project, this would be the executor, your family, and your beneficiaries) don't have a clear understanding of why you did what you did, it can lead to family fights and costly, drawn out estate litigation battles. The same goes for the estate professionals that you engage for Your Death Project and creating your estate plan.

Think of it this way. Ever had someone give you a gift or organize a surprise party? While you were grateful and appreciative, you wished they had discussed it with you beforehand because it wasn't what you wanted. Expect the same thing to happen if you don't give the executor, family and close friends clear preferences on what you want done for your funeral arrangements. If you don't clearly communicate your wishes, it is then left up to your survivors to decide what they think you would have wanted, and your funeral could end up with an expensive, over the top service, even if you are the kind of person who truly hates having a fuss made over them. This doesn't mean full disclosure, either. If you are concerned about sharing exact dollar figures of your financial holdings, it can be a general, high level discussion about your wishes and intentions, with no details mentioned. The point of the conversation would be to help manage expectations and reduce some of the surprises or confusion that can occur in a vacuum after you're gone.

Communication with the person you name in your will as the executor is especially important – they will be your voice and act on your behalf after you die. Be sure to talk things through with them beforehand, while you're around to answer any questions. Also, your funeral wishes should not be a guessing game, given how time sensitive the information will become.

Communication is about the right information, at the right time, to the right people. For example, in a business project, a project manager might communicate to the project governance committee of executives in a specific manner, with a focus on risks and the overall budget. At the project team level, the project manager might spend more time helping their team understand how specific design decisions affect the project budget and perhaps pointing out the rewards of meeting milestones in a timely manner. Both of these stakeholders have different communication needs to effectively contribute to the project goals, but what information or how the information is shared or when it should be provided can differ. When you evaluate the stakeholders in Your Death Project, for example your beneficiaries, you might decide some of the beneficiaries are too young to handle the information or you might be concerned about what they will do if they know the information in advance. These can all factor in to the way you choose to communicate. What you share about your estate plan will completely depend on what you are trying to accomplish and the stakeholders themselves.

Most of the communication I've outlined is communication from yourself to others about your wishes and your plans. There is another kind of communication some families engage in within the estate planning process that involves the stakeholders upfront. It specifically involves engaging the beneficiaries in a series of conversations to solicit their input to the estate plan or wealth transfer. It might surprise you to find out what they think, they might have suggestions that make sense or they might even push back on what you are proposing.

The closing point on communication: unlike a project while you're living, there is no handover from yourself for Your Death Project other than the conversations you had in advance of your death, and the documentation and paperwork you left behind. Hopefully, someone knows where it is and what it means. A verbal conversation to cover your wishes need only happen once. It doesn't need to be the topic of every Sunday dinner or summer BBQ.

Part of Communication Is Sometimes about Documenting

The possibilities here are endless, and the answer I heard many times when I asked what documentation one should keep for an estate plan was *it depends*. From a project management perspective, I'll say this: project managers are expected to keep good project records for many reasons, such as traceability on project decisions, tracking of project requests and changes, communicating success, capturing and approving expenses, managing the project budget and keeping the project plan up to date so people can continue to progress on their milestones. And frankly, it is just easier to update a set of documents on a regular basis than starting from scratch or scrambling when the information is requested. Worst case, the executor will have to try to find all the appropriate documentation about your assets and reverse engineer your life so they can deal with your estate.

I did come across the term *an estate binder* multiple times. It is simply a binder, folder, index, directory or box of important papers that an executor will need to do his or her job, over and above the legal documents, such as the will. A quick online search will give you many ideas of what to put in it, as well as many others who want to offer you a prepared book or checklist. When you are dealing with your estate advisor, you may want to ask for their suggestion as they might already have one published by their firm or professional association. CARP calls this binder or file "The 'If Something Happens' Binder,"[20] and they offer a free download of a "Where to find key info for YOUR NAME MONTH YEAR" template, which lists what they recommend should be in it. CARP, formerly known as the Canadian Association of Retired Persons, is a non-profit organization that advocates on behalf of older Canadians.[21]

Minimally, it should contain the paper trail or listing that supports the executor in determining what your assets are and where they can be found. It can also contain copies or pointers to insurance documents (*e.g.*, life insurance policies, critical illness insurance, long term care insurance, credit card insurance, annuity contracts, segregated funds) and pension plans, as well as information about your home, home insurance policy and utility bills – all those payments that the executor might need to keep paying for a while and then eventually close down. Putting all that important information in one place will require some consideration about how to keep it safe and secure, as well. If you are concerned about confidentiality and privacy and not comfortable with including photocopies of such documents, statements or account numbers, then at least leave the name of the institutions you deal with, the address of those institutions, the applicable contact person to call and contact information, such as a phone number.

In Passing

An important thing to remember is that every life is unique. Your situation and circumstances are different than anyone else's. As such, Your Death Project to get your affairs in order will be different for you than it will for your family, neighbours, co-workers or friends. Estate and family laws also differ by province/territory. What works for someone in Manitoba may not be right for their child in Nunavut.

Bear in mind that if you own a business or are in a business partnership, you will likely have a separate and equally important death project to address those concerns. Regardless, taking on Your Death Project just makes sense.

There are ripple effects, too. To undertake a project like this is like doing an inventory of your life, because you need to know exactly where you're at, what relationships are important and relevant to you, what debts you are carrying, what and where your assets are (your property, your investments, your house, your vehicles, your art and collectibles), and how to allocate who gets what and why. It could lead you to discover that you are better off than you realized.

This can also be an uplifting experience. Taking stock of your life, your relationships and your assets can clarify how and where you are spending your time and money. It might open your eyes to what you're missing. We are all consumed with our daily lives and immediate concerns. Stepping back to look at the big picture can help you focus on what's truly important. It can be life changing in a very positive way.

Chapter 3
Your Body Can't Bury Itself

There are plenty of good reasons not to think about your funeral. For one, it probably hasn't come up with the boys at poker night or with the gals from your book club. Maybe you considered it when a family member or friend passed away, thinking it should be something you make time for, but then you put it out of your mind when life got busy again. You probably have many more pressing demands on your time and attention. Besides, who feels comfortable thinking about – never mind discussing and planning – their own funeral?

The good news in planning your funeral is that it is about as easy as planning a vacation. To get started, you just need to ask yourself two simple questions, neither one of which requires getting up off the couch.

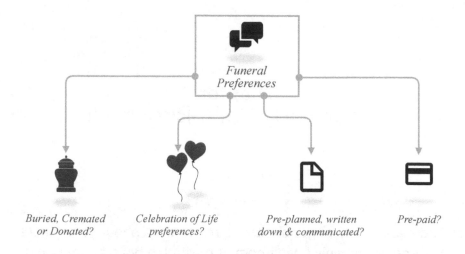

Buried, Cremated or Donated?   Celebration of Life preferences?   Pre-planned, written down & communicated?   Pre-paid?

What Are Your Funeral Preferences?

1. Buried, Cremated or Donated?

In Canada, the funeral business offers two basic choices for the "disposition" (of your body): cremation or burial. What and how it can be done is governed by laws in your province/territory. Burials include the traditional burial (as in a cemetery plot in the ground) or whole body placement in a mausoleum, a crypt or tomb burial options, as permitted in your province or territory. For example, in British Columbia, the funeral and cremation legislation and rules are covered by the *Business Practices and Consumer Protection Act*[22] and the *Cremation, Interment and Funeral Services Act*.[23] Another term you'll come across is *interment* or *inter*, generally meaning burial or entombment, of either the whole body or cremated remains.

Over the past 50 years, cremation has overtaken burial as the most common choice for what to do when someone dies.[24] The reasons behind the popularity of cremation are not surprising: it's simpler and usually much less expensive. With cremation, the question then becomes: what to do with the ashes (the funeral business calls these the *cremated remains*)? Urns can be purchased for a couple of hundred dollars to thousands. However, you don't even need to purchase an urn, you can use just about anything from a sewing basket to a fishing tackle box, to something you've made; people often use containers that have some sentimental value. It just needs to be rigid and large enough to hold the cremated remains. If you don't bring a container or purchase an urn, the cremated remains will normally be given to you in a cardboard box.

The urn can then be displayed on someone's mantle, placed in a plot just like a casket burial, or inserted into a memorial wall at a cemetery in what's called a *columbarium niche*[25] or some mausoleums that also have niches.[26] Some cemeteries offer burial sites that can hold one casket and one urn, instead of side-by-side burial, so there could be an option to inter your urn with another family member. It's an intriguing alternative and will only become more popular as the cost of new plots escalates in space limited city cemeteries.

If you're intrigued by the idea of saving money, cremation at an independent low-cost crematorium is a consideration. Depending on where you live, basic cremation packages usually include registering the death, transferring the body after death, providing a combustible container, cremation, and the provincial/territorial cremation certificate (called a *disposition permit* in B.C.), plus putting the cremated remains in an urn. The savings can be substantial. In terms of the cremation container, you can also make your own – they must be combustible for obvious reasons (*e.g.*, cardboard, plywood), leak proof and rigid. You'll want to confirm in advance with the crematorium or funeral home that their establishment will accept your design.

You could also arrange to have your cremated remains scattered. You'll want to confirm that the province/territory that you live in allows this and whether a permit is required. This information is easily found online on the provincial/territory government website (for example, in Ontario, you can find it on the Government of Ontario website under "Arrange a Funeral, Burial, Cremation or Scattering" – Consumer Protection Ontario[27]). Your city or municipality could also have by-laws or regulations, especially if you want to be spread out over a waterway or a park, so you should seek permission.

Traditional burial is a bigger deal and usually a more expensive option than cremation, though it needn't be complicated. If you opt to be buried, you need to start with a casket. If you need a concrete vault or a liner to protect the buried casket, it can add to the interment (burial) costs. Whether or not you need one will depend on the by-laws of the cemetery. From a project management perspective, the cost of a burial and funeral will depend completely on what preferences are selected, from the casket to the celebration selected, right down to if food is catered or not. All these choices add to the overall cost.

You can buy your casket from third-party and online suppliers. Just make sure the funeral home you plan to use is prepared to accept it. Just like with the cremation container, you can also make your own burial casket. Again, you'll want to contact the funeral home or cemetery to determine if they will accept it, and if so, what the requirements are. This is becoming more common than you think, and there is a growing movement of DIY caskets and/ or families decorating their chosen casket as part of their grieving rituals.

Finally, you will need the burial plot, which is a separate cost from the funeral arrangements. You can go simple and inexpensive with a basic burial, perhaps at a less popular or more remote location, or you can spend thousands on a big city, prime real estate location. Traditional burial costs include items like the purchase price of a plot, the opening and closing fees (digging out and filling in the grave), perpetual care and purchasing and installing a marker or headstone with an inscription.[28]

Whole Body Donation to Science

Medical schools need cadavers to train the next generation of doctors and researchers.[29] By donating your entire self to medical science, you'll be doing a good thing for society, although there could be fees for dealing with things such as transporting your body to the university. Not every university medical school may be amenable to this, so check first.[30] There is no reason why your family and friends can't hold a memorial service so your life can still be celebrated. Now this is something you have to plan in advance and apply to be part of their program – your family can't make this choice for you after your death. To manage expectations, even if you have been accepted into the program, there are a variety of reasons why your body may not be accepted at the time, even with the pre-planning.

Organ Donation

Bear in mind that whole body donation is different than organ donation. If you do wish to donate some of your body parts, that will likely make you ineligible for the medical school donation; schools generally don't want bodies with missing parts. Speaking of which, donating organs and tissue after death is so easy to arrange that, excepting those whose religious beliefs prevent it, it's difficult to understand why more people don't. Some provinces/territories make organ donation an option when you renew your driver's licence or health card. How it's arranged varies from province to province, territory to territory, so go online and check.[31] You can usually do it in a couple of minutes, about the same amount of time it takes to change your social media status – and it could save someone's life.

2. Celebration of Life: How Do You Want Others to Celebrate Your Life?

Celebration preferences, also referred to as *memorialization rituals*, brings us to the big question: do you want a ceremony to mark your passing, be it a funeral service, memorial, prayer service, wake, church service, gathering, private family event, regimental funeral, ceremonial public event or celebration of life? Or just a good old party at the cottage where your family and friends get together and cry a little, laugh a little and tell their stories about you? Maybe you would rather people quietly remember you in their own way with no service, at your request?

As with all things, how death is marked is a personal choice. Some couples like big formal weddings that cost more than the down payment on their dream home. Others go small and simple. Some elope. Similarly for death, there is no right way; there is only what is right for you and your family and friends. Celebration of life events are for the people left behind, to help them grieve and find closure, if such a thing is ever truly possible, by mourning your death and celebrating your life. If you have lived a good life and touched the lives of many people in a positive way, they will want to gather together to give you a good send-off. They may need it more than you. Think about what your family and the people who are important to you would want. That said, your religion, culture or community sometimes also influence what will happen.

The next steps, after answering questions 1 and 2, require you to actually get off the couch, but these next two questions (have you pre-planned and have you pre-paid) are still relatively simple:

3. Pre-Planning: Have You Written It Down and Shared It?

The ability to make sound decisions usually flies out the window when emotions are running in overdrive, as when someone dies. Based on my experience with my mother, the concern that I had not honoured her funeral wishes impressed upon me how important it is to make your personal wishes known to the people you will leave behind, and most importantly – the executor. Telling your family and friends can help manage expectations, leaving no doubts about what you want. Telling the executor is especially important because he or she is the one responsible for making the arrangements. Logistically, if the executor knows about your pre-arrangements and knows where to access the documentation, they can get on with planning your funeral. Otherwise, they could end up in a family debate which will only introduce time delays.

For example, if you plan to donate your organs or your whole body, make sure your spouse/common-law partner/adult children/executor know about it. It's not something that should come as a surprise to them, or something they should discover only after you've been embalmed. The benefits of planning ahead (or pre-planning, as the deathcare industry puts it) can't be understated. Beyond sparing the people you leave behind the hassle of making decisions on the fly when they are highly stressed, it can save your estate a lot of money, even if you opt to go all out.

Best practice is to write down your after death preferences and give a copy to those who will follow through on your wishes or instructions. Many funeral homes have pre-arrangement kits to fill out to guide you through the process. Regardless of format, you will enhance the chances of having it your way when you die if you write it all down in a document that can be easily found and referred to by the executor and family after you're gone.

I learned it is really also important to leave some specific information about your health and body, as it affects disposition. For example, a pacemaker and any implanted medical devices (such as radioactive brachytherapy seeds) will need to be removed. The medication you are taking can affect the body and, as such, affect the embalming process. If you are making pre-arrangements, these are good questions to ask the organization you are dealing with on what should be noted.

3.1 *What You Do in Life Can Also Affect How Things Go When You Die*

Police departments usually have protocols in place to work on funeral services with the families of fallen officers. The Canadian Armed Forces have a process they follow that's online, called What Happens after a Canadian Armed Forces Member Dies.[32] If you are a former forces member, there are pre-planning options at some funeral homes and cemeteries, so remember to identify yourself. Canada's National Military Cemetery at Beechwood in Ottawa has eligibility requirements posted on its website.[33] Veterans Affairs Canada has a funeral and burial program called the Last Post Fund that ensures those eligible receive dignified funeral and burial services.[34] How you die is also a factor (*e.g.*, on duty or killed in action versus not) in terms of the options.

There might also be death benefit options available to your family to fund the funeral, depending on where you worked, who your employer was, what benefits you contributed to or how you died, such as: Canada Pension Plan ("CPP") death benefit,[35] Québec Pension Plan ("QPP") survivors' benefits,[36] Crime Victim Assistance program in your region, Driver's Insurance policy, Veterans Affairs Canada, Workers' Compensation Board (or equivalent) in your province/territory, the RCMP,[37] or a death benefit associated with your insurance coverage or other benefits at work.

If money is a concern for low income families to cover funeral expenses, it is worth checking what support is available from your local government. For example, the British Columbia Ministry of Social Development & Poverty Reduction webpage states: "A supplement may be provided to pay *necessary funeral costs* of any person who dies in B.C. if the estate of the deceased person or any responsible person has no immediate resources to meet these costs."[38]

4. Have You Pre-Paid or Made Provisions for the Expenses?

Pre-planning[39] can be done at a funeral home and a cemetery, or with an independent crematorium. Basically, the idea is to make your selections, then pay for them outright or by instalments. These pre-arranged funeral contracts[40] often involve a trust or an insurance policy so that if that business fails, the money will still be reserved for you. There are also insurance policy options available, the proceeds from which are dedicated to your funeral costs.

Ultimately, the reason people use funeral homes is that they offer simple, one-stop shopping. A funeral home can take care of everything from the death certificates to getting your obituary published in the local paper or online. Along with their core business of attending to the body, preparing it for visitation and providing celebration of life services, they often provide additional amenities such as travel support, grief support, and fraud insurance. The major benefit is that everything is integrated and you are likely getting a funeral director who knows how to help your family and survivors navigate through this sensitive and emotionally charged time. They are the professionals who do this as a job or career. If you consider how few people actually pre-plan, their ability to marshal all that is required upon a death in such a short period of time is quite admirable.

You can and should shop around and exercise all the due diligence you would with any other business (*i.e.*, check references, Better Business Bureau). By provincial/territorial regulations, funeral homes are supposed to provide price lists of all the supplies and services they sell.[41] As with every other sector of the consumer marketplace, prices can vary. As with other industries, the funeral/memorial business is dominated by large, multi-national conglomerates. Meanwhile, the number of independent funeral homes and cemetery operations, like the number of family farms, is dwindling. To get a feel for the players and options, talk to a low-cost crematorium business, a family run or independent funeral home and a national funeral home chain.

Even simpler, start shopping online. Most funeral businesses, from the low-cost crematoriums to the full service funeral homes or cemeteries, have websites and online links to their pre-planning information.[42] If you are not sure what is available in your province/ territory, some have their own funeral associations, for example:

- Ontario Funeral Service Association: "Important Consumer Information" and "Find a Funeral Home";[43]

- Bereavement Authority of Ontario: "Search for Licensed Establishment, Consumer Information, and Search for Licensed Individual";[44]

- British Columbia Funeral Association: "What Should You Know When Planning A Funeral";[45]

- Federation Des Cooperatives Funeraires Du Québec: "Why Make Your Prearrangements With the Cooperative";[46]

- Nova Scotia Board of Registration of Embalmers and Funeral Directors: set of resources called "For Consumers";[47]

- Funeral and Cremation Service Council of Saskatchewan ("FCSCS"), although their mandate is to set standards for the funeral profession in the province of Saskatchewan: set of resources "For Consumers" that covers topics such as "Contracts & Your Rights" and "Pre-Planning Your Funeral";[48]

- A (national) Funeral Service Association of Canada ("FSAC/ASFC"), which is an industry member organization, with a mission to "promote the ritual of memorialization through leadership, education and public awareness";[49] and

- As I mentioned at the outset, your provincial/territorial government website likely also has some good starting point information (*e.g.*, Government of Ontario – "What to Do Following a Death").[50]

As you might expect with other significant purchases, ask your family, friends or colleagues for referrals or information on who they might have dealt with. You might be pleasantly surprised to find your community group or religious affiliation has options or recommendations or even a program they run. There are also independent associations and societies. For example, in British Columbia, there is a non-profit organization called the Memorial Society of British Columbia.[51] Finally, don't forget to investigate if your family, parents or grandparents made pre-arrangements or where they might already be interred. There may be additional services or spaces that are already available for you to use.

There is another lesser known method which the Canada Revenue Agency recognizes. It is a saving vehicle called an Eligible Funeral Arrangement ("EFA"),[52] that allows your contributions (to pay for future funeral and cemetery services) to grow tax free. Only licensed funeral home professionals are qualified to set them up and there are contribution limits and other rules. Be aware that tax rules change regularly.

It's Your Funeral

Key questions on your funeral preferences.

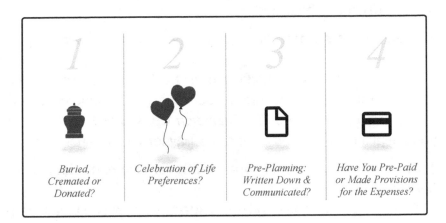

1	2	3	4
Buried, Cremated or Donated?	*Celebration of Life Preferences?*	*Pre-Planning: Written Down & Communicated?*	*Have You Pre-Paid or Made Provisions for the Expenses?*

Your Digital Undertaker:
Project Management Checklist Applied to Chapter 3

1. Scope: *Why are you doing this?*

The advantages of pre-planning are obvious. You spare your survivors or executor the pressure of deciding what to do in a highly emotional situation, while arranging to get what you want at a price you're comfortable paying. You'll also be paying in today's dollars, as opposed to what it may cost decades or more from now.

2. Options & Trade-Offs: *What are the pros and cons?*

The only way to find out about funeral options is to talk to the funeral industry. In addition to a detailed description of what you have ordered, you might also consider providing some notes on what you didn't order, so that the executor or family can consciously change or add to what happens.

There may be other considerations as well. For example, if you want to travel with the cremated remains by air, you'll want to use a non-metal container so they can scan it, and ensure you have the provincial/territorial/jurisdictional disposition certificate as it will have a number that corresponds to the tag placed on the cremated remains container. Again, these are all questions you can ask of the crematorium and the transportation carrier you are using, and of course, if you are going out of country, there are a lot more questions to be asked.[53]

3. Preferences & Costs: *What do you need and what's it going to cost?*

The Government of Canada webpage called "Making a Will and Planning Your Estate"[54] recommends looking at the funeral section of the publication called *The Canadian Consumer Handbook*[55] if you are planning to pre-plan and pre-pay for your arrangements.

4. Procurement of Professional Services: *Your body can't bury itself!*

Funeral services can only be provided by a licensed business in your province/territory. If you consider that some of the laws/rules are put into place to protect you as a consumer, it is worthwhile having a look at what rights you have in your province/territory. For example in Ontario, according to the Consumer Protection Ontario webpage,[56] as a consumer under the *Funeral, Burial and Cremation Service Act, 2002*[57] you have a right to ask the Bereavement Authority of Ontario[58] or the Government of Ontario if the bereavement related business has a license in good standing.

5. Risks: *What are the risks? What are the backup plans?*

Talking about your funeral isn't easy. Start the conversation the same way you started all the big decisions in life. Like any major decision, research and dialogue will inform your thoughtful decision-making process. Don't forget to write down your research and certainly tell someone about your decisions. You can refine or change your mind down the road.

6. Communication: *It is on a need-to-know basis and someone needs to know!*

Failure to communicate might mean things get done in ways you might not have wanted and could cost way more than you would have spent. Good communication now will prevent somebody from saying that you would turn over in your grave if you knew what was spent at your funeral. All the pre-planning in the world can be for naught, if your family or executor aren't aware of your wishes, those pre-arrangements, or get upsold at the other end.

In Passing

In my opinion, the funeral business and deathcare industry is ripe for a transformation. Think of the technology startups that impacted the taxi business, the hospitality or hotel sector, or the online tech giants who shook up retail sales. While it has yet to see that kind of consumer driven, technology enabled revolution, the deathcare industry is overdue for similar significant changes. The increase in popularity of low-cost cremation and burial, and the evolution of the endless choices for a celebration of life, may be the thin edge of the wedge of that change. Another trend to watch: eco-friendly (green) burials in which non-embalmed bodies are buried in compostable ways. Obituaries have already gone online and this is only the beginning of the world of digital memori- alization possibilities. While Baby Boomers may be content to see themselves off the same way their parents did, their Millennial chil- dren, who have already forsaken newspapers, landline telephones and cable television, will surely have their own ideas about how best to make their earthly exits.

Chapter 4
Your Digital Life Needs a Will, Too

You've got the theme now. Before your digital life can have a digital afterlife, you need to understand how your regular life gets covered by estate planning components, such as a will. Personally, I had always been aware of the basic need for a will, probably because when I joined the military at 18, they gave me a will kit to fill out. But until I had to deal with my mother's estate, I never truly understood just how practically important that physical legal document was, in terms of giving me the power as her executor to act right away.

Furthermore, my experience as an executor helped me to realize that conversations or other additional information, like an estate binder, would have been really helpful in filling in all the other pieces of information in dealing with her estate administration. The fact that my mother didn't have a will wasn't the whole problem; it was only half the story. If my mother had a will, I would have still had many of the same challenges. She may have not known what she didn't know when it came to estate planning – what happened upon her death with the way her joint ownership of the rental property had been set up, or her cottage being in a different province/territory, would pose challenges and add costs to the estate administration. Neither did I, for that matter, even though I have always had a will. After you die, the rubber hits the road when the executor who is named in the will picks up where you left off and has to deliver on your will.

What Is a Will?

It is a legal document that you sign in front of witnesses that sets out how you want your estate to be distributed among the people you care about, your beneficiaries, when you die. Believe it or not, this legal document can also cover your digital life and digital assets. The Canadian Bar Association offers the public a one-page checklist called *CBA Legal Health Check – Preparing a Will*.[59]

3 Good Reasons for a Will

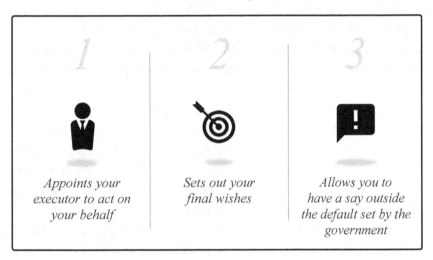

1	*2*	*3*
Appoints your executor to act on your behalf	*Sets out your final wishes*	*Allows you to have a say outside the default set by the government*

Three Good Reasons for Making a Will

The will:

- sets out your final wishes for who gets what from your estate. Ideally, you have communicated your wishes and preferences using the good old *five Ws and the how* – along the lines of *who* gets *what*, *when*, *how*, *where* and *why* (your intentions);

- appoints the executor, who is your estate representative – the person who is legally authorized and recognized to act on your behalf after you're gone. The will gives the executor powers to administer your estate, pay your final taxes and make distributions to your beneficiaries (ideally, you have also identified a backup or alternative executor); and

- allows you to have a say in the distribution of your final assets, instead of the government's default set out by the provincial/territorial legislation if you die without will.

The best reason I heard for making a will is that it is the only legal document, if found and valid, other than your birth certificate, that is sure to be used. You may never get a driver's licence, never sue or be sued, never get arrested or do anything that requires a legal advisor or a legal document. But you will die; if you have a valid will, it will get used. A will, after all, is just a piece of paper until you die; how it survives your death is what really matters.

Your will also identifies who you want to act as your estate or legal representative when you are no longer around. The title of that person can vary by province/territory. Most often the role is referred to as an *executor* or *trustee*, but for the purposes of this book, I'll call the person who administers your estate the *executor*. I have devoted the entire next chapter to what that executor role involves and some considerations when selecting someone, from a project management perspective. What you are called, by the way, is the *testator* (the one who writes the will) or in British Columbia, the person making the will is called the *will-maker*.[60]

There is no shortage of estate planning books that already stress in much greater detail what can go wrong if you don't have a valid will in place when you die. Despite this, many Canadians don't. Most surveys claim that the number of Canadians without wills is at about 50%.[61] That number might even be greater if you include people who haven't updated their will in so many years that it no longer reflects their situation or wishes. Even the Government of Canada has weighed in on the question on their webpage called "Making a Will and Planning Your Estate."[62] They point out: "You're not legally required to prepare a will. However, if you don't have a will, the laws in your province or territory will determine how your estate is divided."

Dying without a Will

Dying without a will is called dying *intestate* or an *intestacy*, with the emphasis on *test*, because your survivors will feel like they are facing a final exam in a subject for which they never studied. If you die without a will, then someone will have to apply to the probate court to be the executor. The provincial/territorial estate legislation outlines who can apply to the court and what that person is called. In British Columbia, this statute is called the *Wills, Estates and Succession Act* ("WESA") and the person who gets appointed by the court in an intestate estate is called an *administrator*. In addition, who gets the estate itself is also spelled out in Division 1 of WESA (Distribution of Estate When There Is No Will).[63]

In Ontario, the statute is called *Succession Law Reform Act*[64] and in New Brunswick, the statute is called the *Devolution of Estates Act*.[65] There is also an interesting federal law, called the *Escheats Act*, where the Government of Canada "is entitled to any land or other real or personal property by reason of the person last seised or entitled thereto having died intestate and without lawful heirs."[66] The estate law in each province/territory dictates who might be considered a *lawful heir* when someone dies without a will and when one can stop searching the family tree for heirs. *Escheats Act* – it sure sounds like someone is getting "cheated" out of something if you die without a will.

Dying intestate means letting the government decide who is eligible to get what, and you might not be particularly happy about who the government considers your beneficiaries to be.[67] This is a great opening question to ask your legal advisor. Who gets your estate by default when you don't have a will? The answer to that question differs by province/territory/jurisdiction. For example, depending on the province/territory, your common-law partner may be treated differently than a married spouse if you die without a will. If you die without a will, your married spouse might not get everything either.

If you have minor children and/or qualified dependents and die intestate, a government official called the Public Guardian and

Trustee (or equivalent in your province/territory) could be appointed by the court to step in and manage their government-decided inheritance.[68] This might be a bit of an issue if you expected someone else to take care of the money, like your spouse/ common-law partner or the other parent. This situation only gets more complicated if you have a blended family with children and step-children from different partners. If that's not enough, consider this family member: Who gets Princess the Persian cat or Max the pure bred boxer dog? With no instructions in a will, there is a great chance they could be dropped off at a local animal shelter.

Generic Will Creation Process

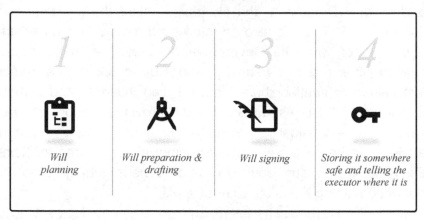

1	*2*	*3*	*4*
Will planning	*Will preparation & drafting*	*Will signing*	*Storing it somewhere safe and telling the executor where it is*

* *Roles, titles, terms, rules and laws are defined by applicable province, territory or other jurisdictions.*

What Is the Generic Will Creation Process?

Let's assume that the preceding paragraphs successfully convinced you to get a will or you already planned to get one. The next logical question is: What is the process to getting a will done? There are four generic steps in the will creation process, namely, *will planning*, *will preparation and drafting*, *will signing*, and *storing it somewhere safe*. As with everything so far, it is completely dependent upon the laws and processes in your province/territory/

jurisdiction, so consider this process just the gist of what happens in Canada.

Step 1: Will planning is collecting all the information about your life situation including relationships, and analyzing all of your estate (finances, assets including ownership rights and where they are, and this includes your digital assets). It can also include capturing your final wishes, preferences and your intentions. Through the will planning step, which is often done in conjunction with estate planning, you can engage estate professionals to provide advice on the various estate planning options to meet your wishes and planning objectives.

Step 2: The actual preparation of your will, which includes engaging legal advice, reviewing your situation, providing instructions, and the actual creation of the document itself, which is referred to as *drafting*, which is done by yourself or with a legal advisor who is authorized to practice law in your province/territory.

What is required to create a valid will is set out by will legislation in your province/territory. For example, although different in content, in New Brunswick,[69] Nova Scotia[70] and Yukon,[71] the will legislation is called the *Wills Act*. Just as the deathcare industry uses the term *disposition* of your body, you'll also hear the term *disposition* of your estate used in the legal context of your will.

Step 3: Signing the will with all the necessary witnesses and meeting any other provincial/territorial requirements for a valid will. You'll hear this signing process referred to as *executing* a will, meaning you are signing it in front of witnesses and bringing the will to life.

A valid will is the original with the original ink signatures. The original is so important that, for integrity purposes, even the staples shouldn't be taken out, as removing them can bring the will's validity into question. If you need to add to or change your will, it is recommended you re-engage a legal advisor.

To get started on estate administration upon your death, the executor will need the original version with the original ink signatures, because photocopies or scanned copies just won't do. The original is also what the court will need to approve the will as valid in a process called *probate* (if probate is required for your situation). In dealing with third parties, such as the bank, depending on the amount of money involved, the executor will likely need to produce either the original will or *proof of probate* from the court.

Step 4: Put the original will in a safe place where you won't spill any coffee on it and tell the executor exactly where it is and how to get it. What's a safe place? You may think a safety deposit box at your bank is a great idea, but can the executor get access to it when you die? This is a good question to ask the bank manager. Ditto for the in-home safe. I've heard of people storing their wills in their freezers, thinking that it must be emptied after they die. Yikes! The best thing to do is discuss where to store your will with your legal advisor when you're creating it; perhaps they have an option for their firm to store it.

Ideally, in this last stage, you also register the location of your will with a wills registry, if such a registry exists in your province/territory. In British Columbia, the Vital Statistics Agency manages the wills registry which records the location of a will.[72] I found a reference in the Ontario legislation called *Estates Act*[73] where, it appears, you can leave your original will at the office of the local registrar of the Supreme Court of Justice, covered in Section 2 of the Act called "Depository for the Wills of Living Persons."[74] If you live in Ontario, this is worth investigating as an option for storing your will.

Québec has what appears to be an efficient system, where the legal advisors in the province, called *notaries*, are authorized to draft a specific kind of will called a *notarial will*.[75] The notary's office or firm keeps the original notarial will and registers the will in a registry managed by The Notaries Association of Québec (Chambre des notaires du Québec).[76] Notarial wills in Québec do not need to be probated; other types of wills do. This system in Québec hopefully reduces some of the frantic searching for one's will in that province.

One Other Consideration: Laws That Could Apply to Your Will and Estate Plan

Other laws might apply to your estate, and these can include other provincial/territorial laws, Canadian federal laws, or other countries and their laws. A few examples:

1. If your assets reside in another jurisdiction and/or you are considered to have lived there.

2. Your estate is also covered by laws that apply to other legislation such as: family law, insurance law, dependent relief rights law, spousal property rights law, beneficiary designation law – all which can vary by jurisdiction. For example, if your will doesn't make adequate provisions under family law, the court could consider spousal claims and/or dependent relief claims.

There are other laws within Canada that could apply, depending on your situation. For example, in Canada, if you are a member of the Indigenous Peoples of Canada and have property, there are additional considerations such as the *Indian Act*.[77]

Laws That Could Interact and Apply To Your Life & Estate Plan

Provincial/Territorial

- Will Law
- Estate & Succession Law
- Trust Law
- Probate Law

Lots of estate surprises

#*!?

- Income Tax Act
- Other Canadian Laws
- Other Jurisdictional Laws
- Other Jurisdictional Taxes

Provincial/Territorial

- Family Law
- Beneficiary Designation Law
- Dependant Relief Rights Law
- Spousal Property Rights Law
- Insurance Law

Roles, titles, terms, rules and laws are defined by applicable province, territory or other jurisdictions.

Who Can Draft My Will?

In terms of drafting a will, you can draft it yourself, or you can engage a legal advisor as authorized or licensed in your province/ territory to draft it. No one else can prepare or draft your will, as this is considered the practice of law which is governed by legislation in your province/territory. Regardless of whether you draft a will yourself or hire a legal advisor, I think what gets lost in translation when preparing a will is that it is not simply a process of slapping your personal information and wishes into a template or a kit. The process should involve an analysis of your life, your assets, your relationships, understanding your wishes and intentions, under- standing the laws that impact your estate and getting advice on estate planning options that take into consideration your specific situation, and creating a roadmap (plan) for those things that will meet your wishes, including a will.

1. Do-It-Yourself

A growing number of people are taking control of their legal lives by representing themselves in divorces and other legal proceedings. It reflects a desire to have a greater control in all aspects of our lives. Those who want to draft legal documents themselves are seeking resources and/or obtaining kits from a variety of bookstores and retailers, such as Self-Counsel Press – Business & Legal Publisher.[78]

You could draft a do-it-yourself will for a fraction of the cost of securing a legal advisor. The internet is certainly willing to help. If you search "write your own will," thousands of results will pop up. However, the real cost of that will won't be realized until after you have died. If applicable in your province/territory, probate is the court regulated process that your will may need to go through to confirm that it is valid. Your downloaded will kit might not serve you well if it turns out to be invalid or the wrong template (*i.e.*, from the U.S. or another country).

I would be remiss if I didn't mention the simplest do-it-yourself will there is, namely the *holograph will*. This simply means sitting down with a pen and paper (a typewritten or computer generated copy won't do) and writing out your entire will in your own handwriting. It will still need to meet the provincial/territorial legislation requirements to be valid (*e.g.*, it will need to be properly witnessed). If you plan to use this type of will, you'll also want to confirm that a holograph will is actually valid for use in your province/territory, as it is not universally recognized.

If you feel confident about taking the do-it-yourself route, consider some rigorous homework to make sure the template or the will kit you are using is valid in your province/territory, and appropriate for your situation. Perhaps consider taking your do-it-yourself kit and making an appointment with a legal advisor to review it.

2. Hire a Legal Advisor

A legal advisor's value is their expertise in reviewing your life circumstances and advising you within the framework of the laws that apply to your situation. An estate legal advisor will also take instructions from you and draft a will that meets the provincial/territorial requirements of a will. There is another important value they can bring to the table as professionals – they can provide options to minimize risks in your estate plan and advise you on any challenges that your wishes might have for the executor when they are tackling estate administration.

If you don't already have a legal advisor who has estate and will expertise, ask for a referral or talk to people you respect. Who handles their legal affairs and, specifically, who handled their estate plan and will drafting? Provincial/territorial law societies are another good resource. Some examples:

- The Law Society of Ontario provides an online directory where it's easy to search on "Wills, Estates, Trust Law,"[79] or further refine the search by city. The Law Society of Ontario also has a Law Society Referral Service.[80]

- The Nova Scotia Barristers' Society has a search feature to look up a specific lawyer.[81] Their website also directs you to the Legal Information Society of Nova Scotia for a lawyer referral.

- The Canadian Bar Association website has a "Find-A-Lawyer" webpage where you can select location (*i.e.*, any city in Canada) and area of law (*i.e.*, one of the dropdowns is "Wills, Estates and Trusts").[82]

- Another resource is the Society of Trust and Estate Practitioners ("STEP"), a global organization with a Canadian chapter, which has a public directory for finding a member in your area by searching by city/town.[83] In addition to legal advisors, STEP has a listing of all its member practitioners in the estate profession and has recently launched a new public site called *You Can Talk to a TEP*.[84]

Legal advisors charge for will drafting services in a variety of ways, including hourly rates and flat rates. That is something you'll want to know upfront. And if cost is a concern, it will be up to you to ask the legal advisor if there are ways to reduce expenses. Go in prepared so that you can reduce the chance of wasting their time and your money. Ask in advance of the first meeting with the legal advisor what documentation you need to bring. Ask if they have a checklist or a list of questions for you to complete in advance. Some of the information could include:

- a fact sheet detailing your current and past family situations, the full names, other names used, addresses and relationships to yourself, your immediate family and those with whom you have significant relationships;

- copies of documents that outline your legal relationships, such as a marriage licence, prenuptial or marriage agreement, cohabitation agreement, separation agreement, divorce settlement, adoption records, child custody arrangements;

- a chronology of where you live, have lived, plan to live, where you hold/held citizenship and/or residency;[85]

- a chronology of where you work, have worked, hold or held work permits/visas;

- a list of intended beneficiaries by full legal name, relationship to you and addresses;

- a list of specific assets you intend to gift to specific people;

- your wishes and intent in terms of how you want your estate distributed;

- a list of your digital assets and your wishes for them;

- a list of trusted estate representatives and alternatives – executor, trustee, guardian;

- a list of all your financial assets, including investment accounts, registered accounts, joint assets, assets with beneficiary designations, pension contracts, insurance policies, real property, businesses, partnerships and assets in other provinces/territories and other countries;

- a list of personal property of financial, sentimental or historical value;

- names of family pets and preferences on how you want them cared for;

- charitable or philanthropic wishes;

- funeral wishes and pre-arrangements; and

- a copy of your previous will.

Don't, however, let that list overwhelm you. You should still go see a legal advisor even if you don't have all this information in hand. He/she can tell you what they need and what they don't, based on your situation. The important thing is to start the process. Outlining your wishes and preferences might seem obvious, but another important part of the process will be explaining your intentions about those wishes.

Where Do Trust Companies Fit In?

Now that most members of the Baby Boomer generation have, to a large extent, sorted out their retirement plans, and Gen Xers are starting to look down the road of life, estate planning has become a growth industry. Banks, financial institutions, trust companies and wealth management firms are offering an ever increasing line of estate planning products.

There are advantages to engaging a trust company early in the will and estate planning process, especially if you are going to name the trust company as the executor of your will or as a trustee of your trusts. Now you might get the benefit of estate planning, including will planning, but you will still need to engage a legal advisor to actually draft your will(s) and/or trusts. The trust company may have a referral recommendation.

However, this option could be overkill, pun intended, if your estate is a simple one without a large amount of money and assets, and with few complicated situations, such as blended families or dependent survivors who will need to be provided for in the long term. However, if things are complicated, it's an option worth considering. For example, if you are setting up trusts for yourself or others, a trust company could be a good call as a starting point.

Your Digital Undertaker:
Project Management Checklist Applied to Chapter 4

1. Scope: *Why are you doing this?*

A will is considered the basic building block of an estate plan. In terms of additional information and resources, one worth mentioning is that many provincial/territorial/jurisdictional government websites have information about wills and estate planning:

- The Government of British Columbia has a Make a Will Week focus and website.[86]

- The Government of Alberta has a Wills in Alberta website.[87]

- The Government of Ontario has information on Wills, Estates and Trusts on the Ontario Ministry of the Attorney General website.[88]

- The Government of Manitoba among its resources, has a publication called A Guide to Farm Estate Planning.[89]

The point of these examples above is to further illustrate that researching the topic of wills and estate planning can start right at home with your provincial/territorial government, law societies and community organizations. If you are not a big fan of searching online, you can call or go to a local government service centre and ask for this information.

2. Options & Trade-Offs: *What are the pros and cons?*

A lot of what you'll find when getting your will drafted is finding out what you didn't know. If you don't know where to start the conversation with a legal advisor, start with this question: What's my default? What happens if I die without a will? Perhaps the answer will motivate you to communicate your wishes and pursue getting a will drafted.

3. Preferences & Costs: *What do you need and what's it going to cost?*

Exactly what you need and what you will pay to have an estate plan prepared, and a will and/or trust drafted, varies by situation. If you lead a simple life with few complications, a simple will could cost much less than it might for someone who has had several life partners, has many dependents and owns multiple properties in different geographies. No one wants to be surprised about costs, so don't hesitate to ask those questions upfront as you begin the process.

4. Procurement of Professional Services: *Your body can't bury itself!*

The Government of Canada webpage Making a Will and Planning Your Estate says:

> It's a good idea to get professional legal help when you make a will. This will help you make sure all your documents are prepared and witnessed properly. Be prepared to pay legal fees. It's a good idea to make a will, even if you're not sick or don't seek legal advice.[90]

When hiring a legal advisor in wills and estate planning, here are a few questions to ponder:

- Are they authorized or licensed to draft wills and/or trusts (depending on your needs)?

- What's their expertise in preparing wills and trusts?

- Are they recognized by the law society in their province/territory as having an estate specialty?

- Do they draft probate submissions and advise on estate administration?

- How do they stay current on will and trust law?

- Have they set up trusts for clients?

If you are in a financial pinch, find out if using a notary public[91] is an option, if they are authorized in your province/territory to draft wills. Check to see if there are *pro bono* legal services in your area by checking online, with your local community centre, senior's centre, or if you are lucky enough to have a university close by with a law school, see if they might have student legal services under the supervision of a qualified legal advisor. There is a website called Pro Bono Students Canada that operates in a number of law schools in Canada and provides "legal services free of charge to low-income citizens and not-for-profit organizations."[92] Many of the provincial/territorial government websites also have information on wills and estate planning.

5. Risks: *What are the risks? What are the backup plans?*

You also can't control what people might do after you're gone. A will can be challenged for specific reasons accepted by the court. A good question to ask your legal advisor is to enquire what risks apply to your situation. Beneficiaries may even fight over stuff that has no dollar value, like who gets Dad's old, broken watch.

Also, don't wait until it's too late. If you put off making a will until you are unwell or in failing health, there could be a greater risk of people questioning your legal capacity. Disputes could cause delays, add costs and extend the estate timeline. This also invariably could mean bringing in more expensive experienced estate professionals to deal with court challenges.

6. Communication: *It's on a need-to-know basis and someone needs to know!*

Reading your will should not be like a reality TV show's big reveal. Telling key people now what's in your will, and why, might help manage expectations after you're gone. Ultimately, communication is tied into risk management.

Good communication could also minimize misunderstandings. For example, if you have named a friend as a guardian of your minor child, it might come as a surprise to your sister or brother. A conversation or a letter might help put that decision in context and reduce unintended hurt feelings. The thing to always keep in mind is that you won't be around after death to smooth things over.

Of course, these are not easy conversations to have, and you might also determine in the end that some conversations should not happen in advance. How best to tell people is up to you, depending on how your relationship dynamics work. The point is that you take the time to consider the stakeholders and determine what is appropriate for your situation and the beneficiaries involved.

In Passing

In the business context, I am all about process improvement and implementing automation that improves a business process. This can ultimately cut costs and increase client value by bringing innovation to the table. I also think that the estate industry and the firms that support it should continue to leverage and embrace the benefits from some of the transformative innovations we have seen in other knowledge-based professions. The Canadian government is also considering how to leverage technology to better serve us as Canadians in the estate space. One hopeful example, as reported by the *Ottawa Citizen* in an article called "Death Notifications Receive Digital Make-Over,"[93] is the federal government commission of a report on recommendations to streamline administration of death notification among levels of government.

Finally, just around the corner is the entrepreneurial innovation and transformative leap-frogging where clients will ask in the future (if they haven't already): What about electronic wills? Can I put my will on a will blockchain? Just like a pet trust, can I set up a social media, blog or virtual reality trust to maintain my digital afterlife? And wait until artificial intelligence is applied to client data collection and estate advisory services.

Appendix to Chapter 4:
If There's a Will, There is a Way – Trust You Will

The other thing to consider while getting a will made is setting up a trust, or trust relationship. Trusts have some advantages worth considering. For example, you can set up a trust in a will so that the trustee has the power to disperse installment payments instead of a lump sum. There are several trusts recognized by the Canada Revenue Agency for those over 65 years of age or for other qualified individuals. They can provide protection in addition to a power of attorney document and a will.

You might think that trusts are only for the wealthy. However, setting up a trust relationship is another option in estate planning that's well worth considering. I've included this quick overview of what I've learned. In many respects, setting up a trust is no more complicated than creating a will.

Just when I thought the average person probably didn't know anything about trusts, imagine my surprise when I found out one of my neighbours had put her house in a trust. If you are a dog owner like myself, over time you get to know the other dog owners in the neighbourhood. One day while out on my regular route, my neighbour stopped to chat and she asked me about the book I was writing. To my amazement, she went on to say she knew all about trusts, and even described how they are actually a relationship with a trustee. A number of years after she retired as a school teacher, she realized she needed to get her affairs in order, had done a substantial amount of research and had come to the conclusion that putting her house in a trust managed by a trustee was what she needed to do. She didn't have family that lived nearby, so she wanted to make sure that someone would help her move into an extended care home and take care of all the details of selling her house, if she needed to move at some point.

You might not realize it, but trusts are everywhere. If you own a mutual fund in Canada, it was likely set up as a trust in which you are a beneficiary.[94] If you receive income from, or sell some or all of the mutual funds, you would have received a trust tax slip (T3).[95] If you have done any pre-planning for your funeral, whether for the cemetery and/or funeral arrangements, and pre-paid for these services, the money was likely put into a trust. If you have a Registered Retirement Savings Plan ("RRSP"), Registered Retirement Income Fund ("RRIF"), Registered Disabilities Savings Plan ("RDSP") or a Registered Education Savings Plan ("RESP"), it is treated by Canada Revenue Agency as a trust (see "Types of Trust" on the Canada Revenue Agency website for a complete listing[96]). If you bought or sold real estate, you might be familiar with the point in the transaction when the funds were held in trust, likely by a legal advisor or his or her firm, as they were being trans-ferred from buyer to seller.

Although there is no one definition of a trust, they are described along these lines:

- A trust is a recognized relationship in which you (the *settlor*) transfer the title of your property from yourself to the trustee, who now holds the title for the benefit of beneficiaries.

- Most people think a trust is a standalone concept, like a bank account or a trust account held by a bank. It is not. A trust is a relationship in which you appoint a trustee to look after property for you, according to terms you set out. The title of the property transfers to the trustee from you. The document itself that outlines this relationship is often referred to as the *trust deed*, *trust instrument* or *trust inden-ture*. To keep it simple, I'll call it the trust deed.

- There are laws (provincial/territorial/jurisdictional and federal) that govern their usage and how they are taxed (*e.g.*, Canada's *Income Tax Act*). The trustee complies with the trust deed and the laws in the province/territory/jurisdiction.

- According to *Waters' Law of Trusts in Canada*: "In broad terms, the contemporary tax-planner might say that the trust is a means of managing wealth for the benefit of one or a number of persons."[97] Waters' book does provide several definitions that are considered the best among common law lawyers, but for our introductory purposes, the contemporary tax-planner view is just right.

- If you are looking for more information, you might find the article called "Trusts Explained" by the Society of Trust and Estate Professionals ("STEP") helpful.[98]

- The province of Québec does recognize the trust concept, but their definition in the Québec civil code is different than what I have described above.

There are two basic types of trusts – trusts that are created (settled) while you are living (they are called an *inter vivos trust)* and trusts that come into effect (become settled) after your death (called a *testamentary trust* through your will).[99]

Inter Vivos Trust
vs.
Testamentary Trust

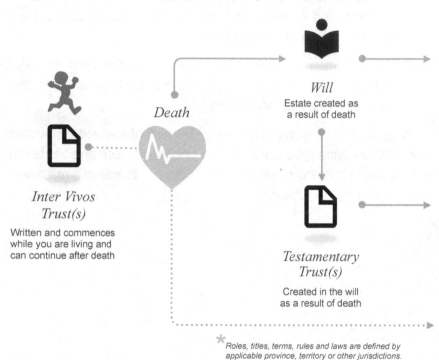

Will
Estate created as
a result of death

Death

*Inter Vivos
Trust(s)*

Written and commences
while you are living and
can continue after death

*Testamentary
Trust(s)*

Created in the will
as a result of death

*Roles, titles, terms, rules and laws are defined by
applicable province, territory or other jurisdictions.*

A will and a trust have two important things in common: (1) they are both considered trusts; and (2) they are both methods for you to give gifts to beneficiaries. They just accomplish it in different ways. A gift in a will can only be given on death. A gift in a trust can be given while you are living (*inter vivos trust*) or after you have died (*testamentary trust* through a will). Think of a will as a set of instructions to the executor to provide gifts for beneficiaries as a one-time transfer or transaction after he or she arranges the funeral, settles your debts, pays expenses and winds down other activities associated with estate administration. A testamentary trust in the will sets instructions and powers for what gifts are to be transferred to the newly created testamentary trust that continues on after the estate is closed. The point of most inter vivos trusts and testamentary trusts is to last for a longer term, as opposed to an estate. Trusts are private relationships, whereas a will becomes a public record when you die.

The role of executor in most cases is temporary. The executor administers your estate for the specific purpose of closing down your life and disposing of your assets. When you put assets into a trust, the trustee looks after it according to instructions set out in the trust deed, normally over a period of time. The executor and trustee are both subject to the rules, obligations, and responsibilities on how they must act under the *Trustee Act* in a province/territory/jurisdiction. The role of the executor is to take your estate to estate termination. The executor might also have a separate role as a named trustee of a testamentary trust – this is an additional role. These roles are covered in Ontario and Manitoba under trust legislation called *The Trustee Act*, but these are two separate statutes specific to each province/territory.[100]

To compare wills to trusts, think of it in these simplistic terms:

Example 1: *Options for dealing with an investment portfolio*

- A will – Give my entire investment portfolio to my spouse when I die.

- A testamentary trust deed in a will – When I die, put my entire investment portfolio into a testamentary trust and pay the income it generates annually to my spouse (a *life interest*) as long as my spouse is living. When my spouse dies, give the entire investment portfolio (the *capital*, the remaining interest) to my nieces and nephews.

Example 2: *Options for dealing with a house*

- A will – I leave my house to my children.

- A testamentary trust deed in a will – Put my house into a testamentary trust and have the trustee look after it so that my spouse can live there as long as they want or while they are alive. When they die or no longer want to live there, give my house to my children.

An inter vivos trust deed – Put my house in a trust, look after it for me while I am alive and living in it; if I become incapacitated, sell the house and pay for my independent or advance care living needs, and when I die, give the remainder to charity.

Example 3: *Options for dealing with gifts for children/grandchildren*

- A will – Divide all my remaining money and give equal amounts to my grandchildren.

- A testamentary trust deed – When I die, take all remaining money and put it into a trust for the benefit of my grandchildren to pay for any extra education expenses that are not covered by RESP Trusts.

Inter Vivos Trust

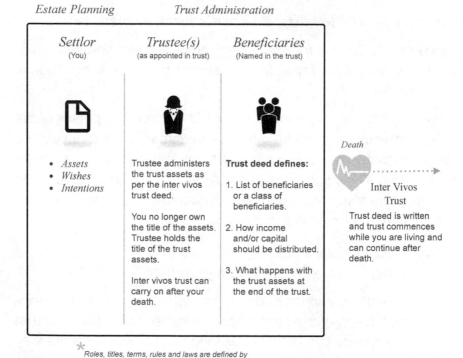

Estate Planning   *Trust Administration*

Settlor (You)	Trustee(s) (as appointed in trust)	Beneficiaries (Named in the trust)

- *Assets*
- *Wishes*
- *Intentions*

Trustee administers the trust assets as per the inter vivos trust deed.

You no longer own the title of the assets. Trustee holds the title of the trust assets.

Inter vivos trust can carry on after your death.

Trust deed defines:

1. List of beneficiaries or a class of beneficiaries.

2. How income and/or capital should be distributed.

3. What happens with the trust assets at the end of the trust.

Death

Inter Vivos Trust

Trust deed is written and trust commences while you are living and can continue after death.

* *Roles, titles, terms, rules and laws are defined by applicable province, territory or other jurisdictions.*

Testamentary Trust

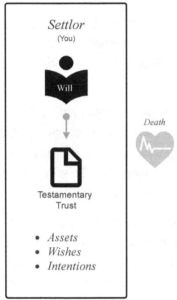

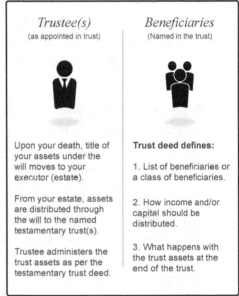

Estate Planning

Settlor
(You)

Testamentary Trust

- *Assets*
- *Wishes*
- *Intentions*

Death

Trust Administration

Trustee(s)
(as appointed in trust)

Beneficiaries
(Named in the trust)

Upon your death, title of your assets under the will moves to your executor (estate).

From your estate, assets are distributed through the will to the named testamentary trust(s).

Trustee administers the trust assets as per the testamentary trust deed.

Trust deed defines:

1. List of beneficiaries or a class of beneficiaries.

2. How income and/or capital should be distributed.

3. What happens with the trust assets at the end of the trust.

Roles, titles, terms, rules and laws are defined by applicable province, territory or other jurisdictions.

Different Situations, Different Trusts

Trusts can be set up for a variety of reasons and situations. The Canada Revenue Agency also has several trusts that they recognize and have specific tax treatments for qualified beneficiaries. As with all trust options, there are lots of choices, pros and cons, risks, transaction costs to set up, costs to administer and tax implications. There is obviously expertise, and current knowledge of provincial/territorial statues and laws, and the *Income Tax Act*, that are required to draft any trust. Just like drafting a will or preparing an estate plan, you'll need qualified estate advisors for drafting your trust(s). Engage appropriate estate professional advice on whether a trust is appropriate for your estate plan. Here are just a few examples of how trusts might be used:

- **Family trusts:** Set up for a family to transfer income and capital in a structured manner to other family members. Has been used for tax planning and a variety of different objectives in family wealth management planning.[101]

- **Trusts to protect yourself:** An option for incapacity planning in which you set up a trust for yourself while you are living, in which the trustee administers your assets. This is called an *alter ego trust* ("ALT").[102]

- **Trusts to protect yourself and your spouse:** An option for incapacity planning in which you set up a trust for yourself and your spouse/common-law partner while you are living, in which the trustee administers your assets. This is called a *joint spousal or common-law partner trust* ("JPT").[103]

- **Trusts to protect your spouse:** If your spouse/common-law partner is not well or you have concerns that they could be taken advantage of after you're gone, a trust in which a trustee looks after the assets is an option to consider. This is called a *spousal or common-law partner trust*.[104]

- **Education trusts:** These can be used by family members (*i.e.*, parents, grandparents), a related person or anyone having an interest in a child they want to make provisions for. They can be set up for other purposes, such as starting a business. The other obvious choice is the Canada Revenue Agency recognized RESP trust.[105]

- **Trusts to protect your loved ones:** There is a trust recognized by Canada Revenue Agency called a *qualified disability trust* ("QDT"),[106] which has specific rules defined by the Canada Revenue Agency. This is not the only way to make provisions for a disabled person. You can work with an estate professional to determine what is right for your situation and what works in your province/territory.

Some Myths and Reasons Trusts Get a Bad Rap

1. *People hide their money in asset protection trusts, normally off-shore trusts, to avoid tax.* There are legal asset protection trusts. There are laws that address what you can and can't do when setting up these kinds of trusts. You can't do this fraudulently and there are ramifications when it's uncovered. Trusts are subject to the laws of the land. You also can't hide your money from creditors in a trust. If you put your money in a trust purposely to hide from creditors, the trust could be voided.

2. *You need a lot of money to put in a trust.* Not necessarily. It depends on what you are trying to accomplish. If you want a trustee to just distribute the capital of a trust to beneficiaries, without any concern for its growth, then any amount can be put into a trust – just keep in mind there will be some fees to create the trust, transaction fees to set it up and ongoing annual maintenance fees. However, if you want the annual income of the trust assets to support beneficiaries while preserving most of the capital, then you're going to need a larger starting point. Trust companies have structured setup costs and ongoing management fees. If you are serious, you'll want to shop around. You will also want to get tax advice, because transferring assets into a trust can trigger tax consequences.

3. *Trusts are no longer worthwhile because the tax law changed.* In 2016, how trusts are taxed did change significantly. Previously, any income or capital that remained in the trust and was not disbursed to the beneficiaries, was taxed at graduated rates just like an individual. The change means that a trust is now taxed at the top graduated tax rates (highest tax rate) on what remains in the trust. However, there is a nuance here worth considering: any income or capital that is given to a beneficiary in a particular year is taxed in the hands of the beneficiary, at the beneficiaries' individual tax rate, which would likely be lower than the highest tax rate. Any income or capital gain not paid out and remaining in the trust is taxed at the highest rate.[107]

4. *A trust is a voice beyond the grave.* Yes, but so is a will, to a certain degree. And what's wrong with that? It's your money and property, and if you want to set it aside for a specific purpose in a specific way, that's your choice.

Chapter 5
Leaving Your Executor the Physical and Digital Keys to Your Kingdom

Maybe you think that naming someone as the executor is a way for you to bestow on him or her an honour, like asking them to be best man or maid of honour at your wedding. However, all they have to do for that gig is get an outfit, arrange a pre-wedding party, corral guests to the rehearsal dinner, make a little speech and help out on the big day. Assuming the duties of executor is a whole different scenario.

The Government of Canada refers to the executor role as the *estate representative*[108] and *legal representative*,[109] and the term varies by province/territory/jurisdiction. For example, in the Northwest Territories, the role is known as an *executor* or *executrix*.[110] In Ontario, the role is called an *estate trustee*.[111] And in Québec, the role is called a *liquidator*.[112] I'll refer to this role as the executor.

Naming someone to be the executor means signing them up to step into your shoes and shut down operations for your life on earth. A project that could take years to sort out. He/she will have to deal with not just your beneficiaries (who may not even be talking to each other), but with funeral providers, legal advisors, financial advisors, tax advisors, the provincial/territorial/jurisdictional courts, and the Canada Revenue Agency (and the provincial tax department, if you live in Québec). They may also have to deal with your company pension plan administrator, Canada Pension Plan or Québec Pension

Plan, your financial advisors, mortgage holders, appraisers, auctioneers, insurance companies, real estate agents and sorting out your digital life. Quite likely, they will be the one stuck with the job of cleaning out your fridge and garbage can. Some honour.

Your Death Project
Hand Over to Your Executor

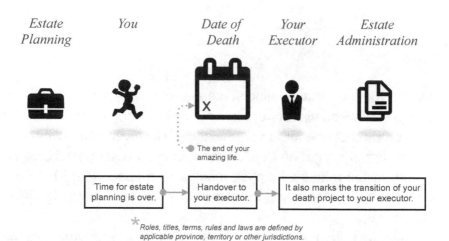

| Estate Planning | You | Date of Death | Your Executor | Estate Administration |

The end of your amazing life.

| Time for estate planning is over. | Handover to your executor. | It also marks the transition of your death project to your executor. |

Roles, titles, terms, rules and laws are defined by applicable province, territory or other jurisdictions.

Given all the potential snags and snares, from a project management perspective, you are going to want to choose an executor who is up for the challenge of this project. Their project being the administration of your estate (closing down your life after you have died). The size and complexity of your estate can be a factor in choosing the right person for the executor role. Furthermore, as we now live in the digital age, that too will affect the executor's role. If you have an e-mail account or do online banking then you, too, have a digital life. The executor will follow your dwindling paper trail and now they will also have to follow your digital trail. I'll start first with the basics of the job of executor, and in Chapter 7, I'll layer on the digital aspects of the role.

Think about it in business or project management terms. If you were running a company or project, would you hire this person to manage a project that your team depended on? You want someone who is good with both numbers and people. Someone who can be counted on. Someone who isn't work shy, who doesn't show up late and leave early. Someone who is not easily frustrated by complex situations or difficult people. They should be someone you would trust with your life, because that is exactly what you are doing – entrusting them with the assets you've accumulated during your lifetime.

What Is the DNA of a "Good" Executor?

Are They Capable?

Are They Willing?

Are They Ready?

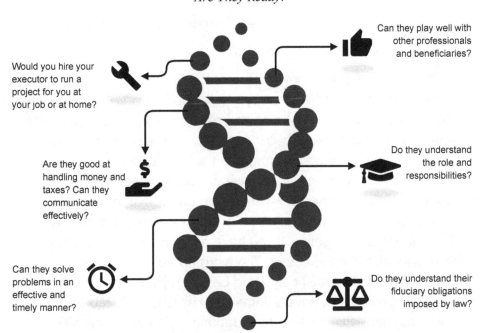

Can they play well with other professionals and beneficiaries?

Would you hire your executor to run a project for you at your job or at home?

Are they good at handling money and taxes? Can they communicate effectively?

Do they understand the role and responsibilities?

Can they solve problems in an effective and timely manner?

Do they understand their fiduciary obligations imposed by law?

The Executor Has a Fiduciary Duty Governed by
Jurisdictional Laws

The executor has what is called a *fiduciary duty* to act in the best interests of the beneficiaries of the will. The word *fiduciary* is both an adjective and a noun. As an adjective, it describes a relationship of absolute trust. As a noun, it represents the person (in this case, the executor) in whom that trust is placed. He/she is your fiduciary, the one you trust unconditionally to execute your wishes in the distribution of your estate. This responsibility is a heavy one and requires that the executor act in good faith, honestly, without a conflict of interest and to operate within the powers they have been given. Along with what's in the will, the executor's responsibilities[113] and obligations are governed by laws, the most important laws being:

- estate law (which varies from province to province, territory to territory);

- trust law (which also varies by province/territory); and

- tax law (federal and provincial).

The law that covers how the executor should go about their job is generally referred to as *trustee legislation* with the executor as the *trustee* – the person who holds powers of administration for the estate. It gets confusing, because the term *trustee* is often associated with someone who manages a trust relationship. However, it also refers to the executor, as they are the trustee of a trust relationship called the estate. Most people don't think of an estate as being a trust, but it is considered as such for tax purposes by the Canada Revenue Agency. If you have a will, read the first sentence that talks about the executor. The word *trustee* is in there.

The main difference I could find between estate law and trustee law is that estate law covers items such as what constitutes a valid will, what happens in intestate situations (dying without a will), and who can be appointed to the executor role. Trustee law sets out the rules concerning how an executor must execute their duties as trustee of the estate and the default powers assigned to them.

The Government of Canada has a webpage that provides a list of resources on estate law for each province and territory.[114] It says: "Estate law, including wills, Powers of Attorney and probate fees, is governed by the provinces and territories."[115]

The beneficiaries have the legal right to hold the executor accountable in how they carry out their fiduciary duties. The executor's liability could get really personal should the estate expenses not be approved by the court. And here's another potential pitfall: if the executor distributes the assets from the estate before getting a Canada Revenue Agency clearance certificate, he/she could be liable for any income taxes owing.[116]

What Are You Asking the Executor to Do? What's Involved?

To provide a sense of how long an executor may have to spend on settling an estate, there is a term the estate industry refers to as *the executor's year.*[117] Basically, it's the grace period after a death before the beneficiaries can really start making noises and pestering the executor about the status of their inheritance. A year is a long time, but even a simple estate can take much longer to close out and obtain the required clearance certificate.

The executor's responsibilities start the day you die, beginning with the funeral arrangements. In the confusion of it all, however, the family often goes ahead and makes the arrangements, regardless of whether or not one of them is the executor, which may be problematic. Most people don't know that it is the legal responsibility of the executor, unless specified otherwise in the will, or determined by your province/territory.

Similar to the estate planning information that is available on your provincial/territorial government websites, these websites also contain information for the executor about their responsibilities, probate and what to do when someone dies. Many financial institutions and trust companies provide an executor's kit or checklist that itemizes tasks you'll be asking your chosen executor to take on during estate administration. Sources of information about the executor role don't stop there. There are a number of estate companies, funeral homes, societies and not-for-profit organizations that also publish information for the executor. If you think the executor will use one of these checklists, you'll want to alert them to confirm whether it applies to the province/territory where you died.

Highlights of What the Executor Can Be Expected to Do

The specific tasks and the time to do these tasks will completely depend on your life situation and the laws in the province/territory you live, and other jurisdictional laws, if applicable.

First, the executor must locate your will. Ideally you have secured your will in a safe location and the executor knows exactly where it is and how to access it. The executor is not just searching for any old will – they must search for your last original, valid one.

The second order of business is protecting your estate: your assets, such as your property, including real property, personal property, valuables, collectibles, your pets and your digital assets. That can mean changing the locks on the doors, securing the contents appropriately, and handling/dealing with unique items (*e.g.*, firearms, prescription medications). It is part of the estate now and needs to be protected against possible damage or loss or misuse. Insurance premiums also must be kept up-to-date and insurance policy(s) changed to reflect a vacant status if the dwelling is no longer occupied.

The third order of business is collecting all the information about your assets and figuring out which ones fall under the will (and/or are subject to taxation under the estate). The executor will need all this information for many reasons, but there are four main ones: probate, tax preparation, determining if there is outstanding debt, and lastly, for final distribution to the beneficiaries.

Now there is one point that probably needs a bit of clarification: the executor will need to know which assets are in your estate (as covered by the will), which is within their job description. There may be assets you own that fall outside the will (and outside of your estate). It can be a bit confusing because during estate planning, everyone will include all your assets into the planning process.[118] What is lost, though, is that after you die, some assets will pass outside the will (pass outside the estate), such as assets that have rights of survivorship and insurance policies, and registered plans where beneficiaries are named and are recognized in a province/ territory. In theory, that is someone else's job to worry about. Most people think it is the executor's job. Joint assets can be tricky, as some might pass outside the estate, but the taxes related to them might still be the responsibility of the estate, which is something the executor would have to deal with. This topic is beyond the scope of this book, but a good discussion to have with your estate professionals on who is responsible, after you die, to chase down insurance policies, and deal with assets that are outside your will (estate), and therefore could be outside the scope of the executor's job description.

If the executor has to do massive searches and hire professionals to figure out your assets, this may only delay other steps in the process, such as probate, and add to the cost of estate administration. One interesting site I came across was the OmbudService for Life & Health Insurance ("OLHI").[119] In addition to a tool that lists all the Canadian life and health insurance companies, they have a link called "Search for Policy of a Deceased," with information on how to search for the lost life insurance policy of a deceased person. Their site lists the criteria upon which they will conduct a search, which includes producing evidence that the policy exists. Now, this might be one last ditch resource for a beneficiary who is searching for your insurance policy, but there is no convenient spot to search online for the rest your assets – you would have had to create that yourself prior to death and have left a list for the executor, ideally in an estate binder.

What Does Your Executor Do with All Your Possessions?

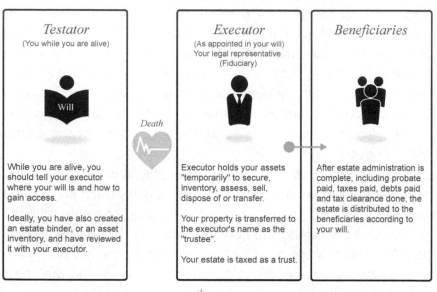

Estate Planning   *Estate Administration*

Testator
(You while you are alive)

Executor
(As appointed in your will)
Your legal representative
(Fiduciary)

Beneficiaries

Death

While you are alive, you should tell your executor where your will is and how to gain access.

Ideally, you have also created an estate binder, or an asset inventory, and have reviewed it with your executor.

Executor holds your assets "temporarily" to secure, inventory, assess, sell, dispose of or transfer.

Your property is transferred to the executor's name as the "trustee".

Your estate is taxed as a trust.

After estate administration is complete, including probate paid, taxes paid, debts paid and tax clearance done, the estate is distributed to the beneficiaries according to your will.

Roles, titles, terms, rules and laws are defined by applicable province, territory or other jurisdictions.

Next Up: Probate Process

If required for your estate, the executor will need a document from the court to prove that the will that they are carrying around is authentic. More about probate in Chapter 8.

The executor will be assuming control over your finances/ assets, taking over your accounts and setting up a separate estate bank account from which to pay expenses, bills, debts and, eventually, distribute funds to the beneficiaries. They will also look for your creditors and pay your debts.

Another Big Job: Dealing with Your Taxes

This means taking care of your income tax for the year in which you die (called the *Terminal Return*) and dealing with any outstanding past tax returns you didn't file or were awaiting answers on. Before they can do all of that, they need to do what the estate industry calls *post-mortem tax planning* to plan for tax optimization and to determine which tax forms need to be filed. (I had to figure this out for my mother's estate, so I will share what I've learned in Chapter 8.) Incidentally, taxes don't stop when you die; they can carry on for each year the estate continues to run.

The executor may need the advice and services of estate professionals for any number of situations. For example, legal advisors for filing probate, real estate agents for appraisals or to help in the sale of property, tax advisors for dealing with tax filing requirements, appraisers if your assets needs to be appraised. The list can go on.

Executor Options: From Family or Friends to Hired Professionals

As I said above, the executor is expected to shut down your life's operations in an orderly fashion. Bear in mind that your choice for executor doesn't necessarily have to be a relative or someone who knows you well. There are professional options and hybrid options to consider. This topic on executors might be described or presented in number of different ways, so this is the picture I drew to understand some of the options:

Executor Options

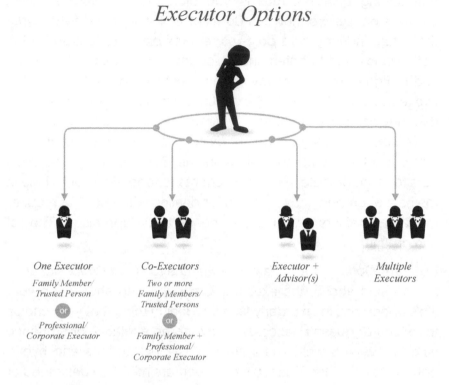

One Executor

*Family Member/
Trusted Person*

or

*Professional/
Corporate Executor*

Co-Executors

*Two or more
Family Members/
Trusted Persons*

or

*Family Member +
Professional/
Corporate Executor*

Executor +
Advisor(s)

Multiple
Executors

Executor Option 1: One Executor

Picking a Family Member or Trusted Person

Because conventional wisdom holds that the executor you choose is someone you trust, spouses/common-law partners, adult children, family members or close friends are often the first choices. They are selected because you believe they care, they are invested in you, have a stake in Your Death Project and are, therefore, more committed to it.

Regardless, the close family member or friend option for executor might only work if they have access to, and are willing to use, professional help to deal with complexities (and paperwork) of estate administration and income taxes, if required. You can save the executor considerable frustration by providing a list of contacts to work with.

There is an option that involves an agency relationship which is emerging in popularity. During estate planning, you might line up or recommend to the executor that they use a trust company or agency that provides professional or corporate executor services to do portions of the estate administration role. In doing so, the executor is still responsible for making all the decisions but some of the administrative tasks can be delegated to the trust company (as an agent) that does this for a living.

If the main reason you want to appoint a family member or close friend as the executor is to save on estate expenses, be aware that they, too, are entitled to executor fees. These fees are treated as taxable income to them; the executor would report this income in their annual T1 income tax returns. You are basically obligated to pay someone, because the law recognizes that winding down an estate takes time. Certainly, the executor can waive their fees, but that's their choice, not yours.[120]

Picking a Professional or Corporate Executor

Financial institutions, and their affiliated/subsidiary trust companies, and independent trust companies are moving into the executor business in a big way. In the context of a trust company, they might use the term *trust officer* or *trust administrator* to refer to the actual person(s) who gets assigned to your estate if you appoint them as the corporate executor. Some professionals, like legal advisors, also offer professional executor services. Not every professional advisor can be hired to be a professional executor – they may be restricted by their profession, by a policy within their company or a personal policy, so you need to ask.

If you decide to hire a professional or corporate executor and name them to act as an executor or co-executor, you'll be expected to sign a contract in the form of a compensation agreement, outlining fees, fee schedule and other terms upfront, and include specific words about the fee arrangement in your will. The compensation agreement is usually a set percentage on a specific portion and then a decreasing proportion thereafter. Depending on the size of your estate, there is nothing stopping you from shopping around and negotiating rates. You'll also want to do some homework on the legislated rates in your province/territory and be prepared to negotiate. The professional or corporate executor does this as a job and/or career, as opposed to leaving your estate to an inexperienced executor who is doing it for the first time. In that respect, they can be an impartial third party, and this puts them in a good position to deal with beneficiaries in a more formal way.

Executor Option 2: Co-Executors

Certainly you can select two or more family members or trusted persons to be the co-executors. The idea is that the responsibilities are shared by two or more people. If that is the case, you'll want to discuss with your legal advisor on how decisions should be made if there is a disagreement between the executors. Trustee law will require them to act together unanimously. If you name multiple executors you'll also want to consider the practical challenges of how they will need to work together, make decisions and sign documents, particularly if they are located in different cities. Something that also should be discussed with your legal advisor.

Another co-executor option is a family member or trusted person and a professional or corporate executor. The idea is that the professional or corporate executor has experience in estate administration and, as such, can effectively plan and navigate the processes/paperwork, and the various interactions when it comes time to deal with financial institutions, the government, pension funds, appraisers/evaluators, real estate agents, and such. This could be helpful if the executor is your spouse/common-law partner, son or daughter who will already be dealing with grief and may need the help.

Of course, the professional executor or co-executor option may be more than you need, especially if the estate is a simple one with everything going to a surviving spouse/common-law partner or only child, or if you have absolute faith in the ability of the executor to go it alone. Regardless, you can do them a huge favour and identify (or at least make them aware of) the professionals they might consider hiring for specific services versus hiring a professional executor. The legal advisor who drafted your will could be invaluable in guiding an inexperienced family member or friend through the entire process. You could also connect the executor with the professional advisor who does your taxes or the financial planner who handles your investment portfolio and make sure they know which funeral home to call and where the pre-planned funeral documents are. Giving you an appropriate send-off will likely be their first order of business.

Executor Option 3: Executor + Advisor(s) with Power(s)

This option is a hybrid of the above two options. It involves the appointment of an executor, but it also involves the naming of advisor(s) with specific power(s) to deal with a particular aspect of the estate administration. An example: The named advisor, such as a legal advisor, may be given the power to check in on things and oversee the activities of the executor or, in some circumstances, be given the power to remove the executor. Sometimes this role is referred as *protector* or *trust protector*.

Executor Option 4: Multiple Executors

In complex estate planning scenarios, depending on how many wills a person may need, they might consider having more than one executor (*i.e.*, one for each will). This is obviously a much more complex estate planning situation, but what is interesting is that, even in such a situation, a person has only *one* estate, which means the various executors will need to collaborate with each other and coordinate their activities, such as tax filing.

Preparing the Executor vs. Not Preparing the Executor

When I did an online search for executor checklists, I was fascinated with the terms and tenses of the words used to describe the tasks, many of them contemplate that the executor will be in discovery mode, trying to figure out what's involved with your life, what assets you own, and where they are. No matter how prepared you are, there will be surprises, and things that might have changed. However, if we put the project management hat on, wouldn't it be better if the executor was more prepared, and instead of discovering, searching and figuring out a plan from scratch, they were validating, updating and executing on a plan?

The Difference Between a Prepared & Unprepared Executor

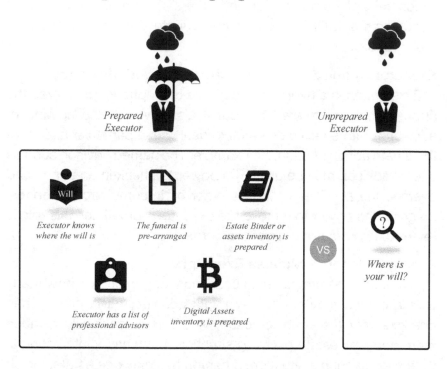

An Unprepared Executor's To-Do List:

- Look for your will.

- Figure out if they are the executor.

- Beg someone to provide keys to your home.

- Search for any important paperwork you may have left behind.

- Pore over calendars, journals and address books to figure out who to call.

- Call several funeral homes to see if pre-arrangements were made or the best option to proceed with. Hope that there is enough money to cover the costs.

- Find someone suitable to write your obituary.

- Try to figure out what assets you own.

- Hunt for a legal advisor and tax advisor to help.

- Build from scratch a plan for what needs to be done to close down your estate.

A Prepared Executor's To-Do List:

- Retrieve the will from where you told them to find it.

- Confirm that they are the executor.

- Review the additional information including any letters of wishes you left them in a pre-arranged location (along with a set of all the important keys they will need).

- Call family and friends from the pre-arranged list of names.

- Execute your pre-planned or pre-discussed funeral arrangements.

- Secure your assets.

- Update the draft obituary, tribute or memorial service biography.

- Validate your list of assets.

- Contact the pre-arranged executor support team (*e.g.*, legal advisor, tax advisor, trust company).

- Create an estate administration plan based on pre-planning left in your estate binder.

Your Digital Undertaker:
Project Management Checklist Applied to Chapter 5

1. Scope: *Why are you doing this?*

Selecting the right person to be the executor of your will is critical. They will be legally charged to represent you after you die and have a fiduciary duty to follow the directions outlined in your will and adhere to the applicable laws, including estate and trust laws.

2. Options & Trade-Offs: *What are the pros and cons?*

As outlined above, you have plenty of options and trade-offs to consider. If your estate is small and distributing it among beneficiaries will be relatively straightforward, the executor (a family member or trusted friend) may very well be up for the job. The hybrid option of engaging a professional or corporate executor as executor or co-executor can bring professionals to the table who do this for a living.

3. Preferences & Costs: *What do you need and what's it going to cost?*

At the most generic level, estate administration costs include the executor fees, and the cost and expenses associated with administrating your estate. For example, if the executor needs to hire a real estate agent and real estate legal advisor to sell your house, those costs are paid by your estate, and do not come out of the executor fees.

4. Procurement of Professional Services: *Your body can't bury itself!*

There is a lesser known option for executor, which is naming a government public guardian as the executor, and there are some situations where the courts might name them as executor (*i.e.*, where your named executor is not able or willing to do so). In British Columbia, the office is called the Public Guardian and Trustee ("PGT") of British Columbia;[121] and in Ontario, there are two such entitles – one is called the Office of the Public Guardian and Trustee ("OPGT")[122] and the other is the Office of the Children's Lawyer.[123] This is not free; they too charge fees and you will want to speak to them in advance of putting their name in your will. Search on your provincial/territorial website for information on naming these public guardians as the executor (*e.g.*, in British Columbia, search for "Naming the PGT as your Executor"[124]).

5. Risks: *What are the risks? What are the backup plans?*

Believe it or not, the executor can say no – not only should the executor be up to the task, they should fully understand what they are taking on and be completely agreeable to it, otherwise they may decide to turn it down after you die when they suddenly realize the volume of work involved. Even if they are totally aware of the work they will be taking on, their personal situation may change. Which is why naming a backup or alternate executor in your will is a smart move. Of note: an executor can only turn down the job, by renouncing the appointment, if they haven't started acting. Otherwise, they will have to resign by applying to the provincial/ territorial court to be relieved of their responsibility. That's why an executor who doesn't want to take on the role should engage a legal advisor before they start doing anything – so that they don't inadvertently accept the role through their actions.[125] The executor's job can be big and/or complex depending on your estate, so don't be surprised if they seek out *executor insurance*.

6. Communication: *It is on a need-to-know basis and someone needs to know!*

Picture this: Your boss assigns you a major project and heads out on vacation or doesn't stick around to answer any of your questions. You start this new project but quickly become unsure of exactly what needs to be done and feel like you are wasting time and resources. You grumble to your co-workers over coffee and when you go home at the end of several frustrating weeks, you tell your loved ones you are going to look for a new job. Naming someone an executor without preparing them for the role is doing exactly what that inept boss has done.

Will Your Executor

In Passing

One way to determine if you've made the right choice for executor: talk to them about taking on the role.

Chapter 6
The Science and Technology of Advance Care Planning

Before you dismiss this chapter as having nothing to do with anything digital, don't run off so soon. Advance care planning affects every type and age of technology user, from the casual beginner, the average day-to-day user, the super user who loves to try all the new gadgets, to the ultra-technical nomad who lives with no fixed address and can only be found on the digital grid. Suppose you are young and healthy, but one day you are, unfortunately, in a car accident and become incapacitated. Without pre-planning, including preparing legal documents that cover who has the right to act on your behalf, for both financial and healthcare decisions, your digital life might just end up in a muck, or worse – disappearing.

This could mean that your e-mail, your software, all your prized digital assets and even your cryptocurrency could all go into limbo for a while, until someone applies to the court and gets appointed, or a government public guardian steps in and deals with them. During that delay, things will start to automatically disappear with date/time-defined expirations, or your digital assets will become more susceptible to hacking because you are not around to monitor your security or, worse, you are too injured or ill to remember any of your passwords. Then, who knows what will happen to your digital possessions? (I'll get into that in Chapter 7).

One spoiler alert for the ultra-technical nomad: if something happens to you, your digital assets might be the least of everyone's concerns. They'll likely give up on that early on, without instructions or passwords. Your parents or your spouse/common-law partner might spend all your money on a slew of lawyers in multiple locations trying to determine where you are actually considered to have lived (*domiciled/resident*) and where your assets are located (*situs*), because there will be a debate about which jurisdictions' laws apply in decisions about your healthcare, your personal care, your finances, and if you die, about your estate.

This chapter is about how to legally leave someone in charge, and how to prepare for a day that most of us hope will never come. The two most important documents regarding incapacity planning are the *Power of Attorney (for financial affairs)* and the *legal document(s) for healthcare decisions*.

As with estate law, the provinces/territories/jurisdictions have their own regulations and terminologies for dealing with legal capacity and advance care planning. It can get confusing because different terms – *powers of attorney, representation agreements, living wills, healthcare directives, advance care directives, assisted decision making, supported decision making, representative decision making, substitute decision-making arrangements and proxy directives* – get thrown around freely. Further, there are numerous other healthcare, medical treatment and personal care documents, all based on provincial/territorial rules and many of them with different titles. These additional documents and their associated processes all have a valid reason for use in certain circumstances. To start simply, I'll focus on the two most important documents (Power of Attorney and legal document for healthcare decisions).

According to Speak Up, a campaign overseen by the National Advance Care Planning Task Group:

> *Advance care planning is a process of reflection and communication, a time for you to reflect on your values and wishes, and to let others know your future health and personal care preferences in the event that you become incapable of consenting to or refusing treatment or other care.*[126]

A definition provided by SeniorsFirstBC punches right to the heart of the matter on what could happen if you don't pre-plan:

If an injury or illness renders you incapable and you have not set up appropriate arrangements in advance, normally a 'committee' (legal guardian) will need to be appointed by the court to look after your affairs. The court process is time-consuming and expensive, and there is no guarantee that the court will appoint the person you would have wished to look after your affairs or grant the powers desired.[127]

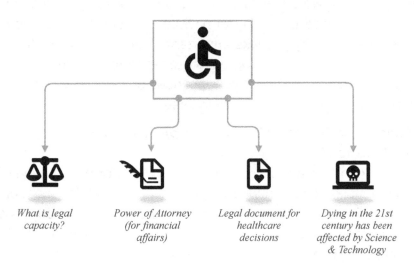

Advanced Care Planning

Planning for Incapacity

What is legal capacity?	*Power of Attorney (for financial affairs)*	*Legal document for healthcare decisions*	*Dying in the 21st century has been affected by Science & Technology*

What Is Legal Capacity?

Legal capacity is the ability to make decisions and understand the consequences of those decisions. Incapacity can be brought about by physical or mental illness that impairs your ability to function and make decisions. Legal capacity is not a medical test – it is a legal test, although in some cases the legal test might include an element requiring a medical evaluation. It becomes legally relevant when you can't communicate your wishes and/or need someone else to make decisions for you. How legal capacity is determined by laws in each province/territory depends on what kind of decision you are making or instruction you are giving. Regardless, when you lose legal capacity, you lose the ability to do certain things under the law, such as create a will, buy or sell real estate, enter into contracts, make financial decisions, or decisions about your healthcare.[128] For that reason alone, you should consider preparing legal documents in which you outline your wishes and appoint someone with the right or authority to make decisions for you and act on your behalf when you can't.

Why Should You Care?

Without wanting to sound alarmist, there is some urgency here because we are all just one banana peel away from a coma. Anyone can lose the ability to navigate through life. Anyone can lose legal capacity to make important choices. So, while the day may never come when you need someone to step in and make important decisions about your finances or medical well-being, it is prudent to prepare for it, just in case.

What's Your Default? What Could Happen If You Have Not Prepared?

The idea that we won't be in good health, or worse, won't be able to make decisions for ourselves, is not something most of us care to dwell on, especially if we take pride in our independence, but accidents and critical illnesses happen. Let us take a look at a scenario called What's Your Default, where you might lose your capacity to speak for yourself.

What's Your Default?

What could happen if you have not prepared.

What happens at the hospital?	*What happens with the rest of my life?*	*When it gets ugly and really costly?*	*When things are really complicated?*
Your Healthcare, Who Can Speak for You?	*Your Financial Life*	*Court Ordered Appointment*	There is a safety valve in the system - any member of the public or hospital can raise a concern about a vulnerable person to the Government Public Guardian.
Without a legal document for healthcare decisions, the hospital or care facility will use a default list of roles that has been outlined by the legislation in the province or territory where you live.	Who will look after your family, who can pay your bills, who can manage your assets and take care of your pets? Without a POA or a court order, there is no one who can legally act on your behalf.	Your family or loved ones will have to make an application to the court in your province or territory. You might not be happy with who makes the court application or with the results of the court order.	Depending on the situation, they have legislative powers to investigate or act as a statutory guardian. They can also make an application to the court to deal with your situation.

* *Roles, titles, terms, rules and laws are defined by applicable province, territory or other jurisdictions.*

The Default in Terms of Your Health and Medical Decisions

Generally, in non-emergency situations, doctors must get consent from a patient for medical treatment. The doctor would first look to get consent from you as the patient, but if you are incapacitated, they would need consent from someone else. Without a legal document for healthcare decisions or court ordered appointment, the hospital or care facility will follow an order of ranking that has been outlined by legislation in the province/territory/jurisdiction where you live. For example, in British Columbia, this is called the *Temporary Substitute Decision Maker*, and is covered under the *Healthcare (Consent) and Care Facility (Admission) Act*.[129] It outlines the order of ranking of those who will be asked to make healthcare decisions on your behalf. There are lots of rules about what they can and can't do, and the powers are limited; for example, a temporary substitute decision maker can't consent to experimental healthcare nor make decisions about where you live.[130] In an urgent or emergency situation, healthcare professionals can act without consent; again, this is covered by legislation in your province/territory.[131]

The Default in Terms of Your Money and Your Property

As outlined above, if you are incapacitated, without a Power of Attorney (for financial affairs), someone may have to apply to the courts to be appointed to handle your property and financial decisions. It might not be someone you want. For example, in British Columbia, the person appointed by the court is called a *committee* and all the rules are covered under the *Patients Property Act*.[132] Likewise, it could be the provincial public trustee[133] or the office of the public guardian (or equivalent in your province/territory)[134] which has a mandate to protect the interests of those who can't do so for themselves. Do you really want a government public guardian making financial decisions for you?

Notwithstanding, this is not a decision to be rushed. Think long and hard about who you would trust with the appointment to act as the Attorney in the Power of Attorney (for financial affairs), because you are handing over the financial keys to the kingdom, with the ability to access and control your money. If someone is pressuring you to appoint them, they might be the wrong person for the job. As a Powers of Attorney booklet from the Province of Ontario says: "There is always a risk that your attorney could misuse this power. If you have any doubts about the motives or ability of the person you are considering – or are under any pressure from your pro-posed attorney to pick him or her – do not appoint that person."[135] The Ontario Securities Commission GetSmarterAboutMoney website lists "Misuse of Power of Attorney" as number 7 on the list of 7 signs of financial elder abuse.[136] The Canadian Network for the Prevention of Elder Abuse ("CNPEA") also offers a resource called *Safe & Savvy: A Guide to Help Older People Avoid Abuse, Scams and Fraud*.[137]

There is no shortage of gold diggers, scammers and fraudsters out there ready to take advantage of you financially. Who hasn't received a phone call from someone pretending to be from the tax agency saying there is a warrant out for your arrest if you don't pay them immediately? That those calls are fakes might be obvious. But there are some that even I have to think twice about, like the phone call where a scammer is calling to say something is wrong with your computer. Then I realize, yes, I am home answering the phone, so am likely on my computer and hang up immediately, shaking my head and worrying that more vulnerable people might not see through the scams. Even worse, there is the most rampant issue online today – cybercrime, which includes being affected by computer viruses, malware or clicking on unscrupulous links in your e-mail. You might receive an e-mail from a friend that looks legitimate, saying they are in trouble, when in fact all that has hap-pened is that their e-mail has been hacked, and you hand over per-sonal or financial information because you think it is true. Always remember that government agencies will never call you asking for money, and legitimate financial institutions, companies or websites you deal with will never call or e-mail asking for your password.[138]

Unfortunately, gold diggers, scammers and fraudsters can also live close to home. Even a good, decent, kind person can misplace their moral GPS when given total power over another person's money. Perhaps they naively haven't made inquiries about the duties written in law about the fiduciary role they were appointed to, even if they are dealing with mom or dad. The reality is that the person you appoint in your Power of Attorney, by law, must always act in your best interests, not their own.

Understanding This Topic

It is relatively easy to get up to speed on this topic. If you want to start online, look for "advance care planning" in your province/ territory – specifically, start with the government website itself and then look for your specific health region or authorities. There are also a variety of charitable organizations or non-profit societies that are part of, or affiliated with, a health authority or region. They offer information sessions that are often hosted locally through seniors' centres, community centres or public libraries – check with them for the next session. One of the benefits of attending a session is that they will often provide a list of where you can get help or additional information.

Here are just a few examples of what information is available online at the provincial/territorial level. Keep in mind you'll want to find the one that is specific to your province/territory:

- Government of Manitoba – *A Legal Information Guide for Seniors (Wills and Estates, Power of Attorney, Health Care Directives)*;[139]

- Public Legal Information Association of Newfoundland and Labrador ("PLIAN") – *Seniors and the Law in Newfoundland and Labrador*;[140]

- Legal Information Society of Nova Scotia ("LISNS") – "Representative Decision-making for an Adult;[141]

- Ontario Ministry of the Attorney General – "Wills, Estates and Trusts" and "Powers of Attorney";[142]

- Prince Edward Island Community Legal Information Association of Prince Edward Island ("CLIA PEI") - *An Introduction to Putting Your Affairs in Order at any Age*;[143]

- Public Legal Education and Information Service of New Brunswick ("PLEIS-NB") –*When You Can't Manage Your Affairs...Who Will?*;[144]

- Government of Québec, Ministry of Justice – "Your Money and Your Possessions";[145]

- Centre for Public Legal Education Alberta – *Making a Power of Attorney in Alberta*.[146]

Power of Attorney (for Financial Affairs)

Just as a will appoints your estate representative when you are dead, the Power of Attorney (for financial affairs) names someone to act on your behalf while you are living. The exact title of this document varies by province or territory. The appointed person, called an *Attorney*, acts as your legal representative either because you have a specific purpose in mind or because you just want to be covered should you get hit by a bus and fall into a coma, or slip into dementia, as the latter might be far more likely. The Alzheimer Society of Canada predicts almost a million Canadians could have some form of dementia by 2032,[147] so preparing a Power of Attorney document just makes sense. *Attorney* doesn't mean that the person appointed must be a lawyer or legal advisor – it just means the person you have appointed.

Power of Attorney

Example for Financial Affairs - Two Provincial Examples

*Your voice on **property, financial decisions** and **legal affairs** when you need help or can't speak for yourself.*

Power of Attorney (POA)	POA (B.C.)	POA for Property (Ontario)
A legally recognized document for dealing with your financial affairs. Within this document you can appoint a person(s) who has the authority to act on your behalf for financial decisions and manage your assets. The fiduciary duties of that role are covered by legislation in your respective province/territory.	B.C. POA ends on when you become incapacitated. Enduring POA is required for incapacity situations. All POA's end upon death. Person appointed in B.C. is called an "Attorney".	Ontario POA for Property ends when you become incapacitated. Continuing POA for property is required for incapacity situations. All POA's end upon death. Person appointed in Ontario is called an "Attorney".

Roles, titles, terms, rules and laws are defined by applicable province, territory or other jurisdictions.

Power of Attorney (for financial affairs) – infographic examples[148]

Here are some of the provincial/territorial Power of Attorney examples:

- *In Ontario, it's called a Power of Attorney for Property and you appoint an Attorney.*[149]

- *In Québec, it's called a Mandate and you appoint a Mandatary.*[150]

- In Saskatchewan, it's called a *Power of Attorney* and you appoint an *Attorney*.[151]

A Power of Attorney needs to be *enduring*[152] or *continuing*[153] to be valid after incapacity, more on that later. For simplicity, I'll refer to this document as the *Power of Attorney*, and the person appointed as the *Attorney*. So we are all on the same definition page, I will use the British Columbia definition of *financial affairs* which "includes an adult's business and property, and the conduct of the adult's legal affairs."[154] See your specific province/territory for their exact definition.

Let's be clear on the different kinds of Power of Attorney (for financial affairs). You can appoint someone to act on your behalf for something specific, such as selling your cottage while you're out of the country, or running your affairs for you because they're good at it and you don't have much heart for it. That's a general Power of Attorney, also known as *immediate* or *non-continuing* Power of Attorney. For advance care planning purposes, however, I am talking about the kind that takes effect when you've lost competency – usually referred to as an *enduring* or *continuing* Power of Attorney. A general Power of Attorney ceases to be valid after you lose capacity. And, of course, any Power of Attorney ceases to be valid when you die. That's when the executor steps up to the plate with your will.

By the way, your spouse or common-law partner does not have automatic rights to handle your property or financial decisions if you lose legal capacity. This will be a surprise to a lot of people. They too, would need to have an enduring or continuing Power of Attorney in hand if they wanted to withdraw money from assets in your name, such as your bank account, cash in investments you own, to sell securities (*i.e.*, stocks) or give direction for your registered plans (*i.e.*, RRSP, RIF). In some circumstances, it can even apply to joint ownership – your spouse/common-law partner may not be able to sell the matrimonial home you jointly own. And it matters for mundane business as well. If the cable account is in your name, your spouse/common-law partner will not be able to make changes to it without a Power of Attorney.

A Few Things to Consider with Your Power of Attorney (for Financial Affairs)

You can tag team the Attorney. You don't need to limit yourself to one Attorney. You can assign two or more people and indicate whether they need to act in consensus or can make decisions separately. Requiring two or more people to work together could also build in a certain amount of oversight. Regardless, be sure to discuss the best way to implement oversight and reporting on their activities with your legal advisor, including what happens if they can't agree.

Financial Institutions are a world onto themselves. They may want you to sign their own forms to appoint someone as the Attorney at their particular financial institution. However, those financial institution's Power of Attorney forms are limited to that financial institution. A financial institution's form is often mistaken for all that is needed to handle all your other financial affairs, which it does not.

One more thing on Financial Institutions. When it comes time for the Attorney to act on your behalf, they will need to complete verification steps for each and every financial institution they will be dealing with. Just as the financial institution will want to know that a will is valid in the event of your death, they will want to know that a Power of Attorney is valid. For example, the Attorney can be expected to provide identification to verify who they are and provide a certified true copy of the Power of Attorney. How long the verification process can take depends on the financial institution. If appropriate for your situation, this is something you can initiate in advance and have your Power of Attorney registered with a specific financial institution.

Out of sight shouldn't be out of mind. If you have bank accounts and property in another jurisdiction – let's say you winter in Florida or Palms Springs – your Canadian Attorney could have difficulty acting on your behalf there. Check with your legal advisor to see if your provincial/territorial Power of Attorney is valid in the jurisdiction where your affairs/property will need managing, or if you need a separate Power of Attorney in the other jurisdiction.

The Legal Document for Healthcare Decisions

Different provinces/territories use significantly different terms to refer to the legal document for healthcare decisions where you capture your wishes/preferences and appoint someone to make healthcare decisions for you when you are incapable. You will also hear it referred to as a *living will*, although that term is more popular in the United States and tends to refer to preferences about end-of-life decisions. The *legal document for healthcare decisions* only deals with decisions regarding your healthcare, medical treatment, and your personal care when you are incapacitated. Regardless of what you call it or where you live, the legal document for healthcare decisions also appoints a legal representative who can make decisions about your healthcare, medical treatments and personal care when you are unable to do so for yourself. To contrast with the other important document, think of it as a power of attorney for your well-being (as opposed to your money and your property).

This document may also provide authority to make decisions about your personal care, such as diet, personal grooming, and where you will live if you become incapable of looking after yourself. So, it's very important to appoint someone you trust absolutely and who understands and shares your values. In some provinces/territories, the person appointed can only make healthcare decisions, not personal care decisions, so it is also important to understand the extent of the decision-making authority when completing the paperwork in your province/territory. This role is also sometimes referred to as the *substitute decision maker*.

Legal Document for Healthcare Decisions

Two Provincial Examples

Your voice on **healthcare decisions, medical treatments** and **personal care** when you can't speak for yourself.

Your Healthcare & Personal Care	*In B.C.*	*In Ontario*
The legal document for healthcare decisions documents your preferences for healthcare, medical treatment and personal care when you are incapacitated. Within this document, you appoint a person(s) who has the authority to act on your behalf for your health. The duties of that role are covered by legislation in your respective province/territory.	Representative Agreement #7 or #9 Person appointed in B.C. is called a "Representative".	Power of Attorney for Personal Care Person appointed in Ontario is called an "Attorney".

Roles, titles, terms, rules and laws are defined by applicable province, territory or other jurisdictions.

*Legal document for healthcare decisions – infographic examples[155]

Here are some examples of provincial/territorial legal documents for healthcare:

- In Ontario, the document is called a *Power of Attorney for Personal Care* in which you appoint a legal representative called an *Attorney*.[156] See how confusing the terminology can get? Ontario also uses the same name for the person named in the POA (for financial affairs).

- In Alberta, it is called a *Personal Directive* and you appoint an *Agent*.[157]

- In British Columbia, it is called a *Representation Agreement* in which you appoint a *Representative*.[158] It will be also referred to as *Representation Agreement (Section 7)* or *Representation Agreement (Section 9)* - *Rep 7* or *Rep 9* for short. If you are curious about the numbers 7 and 9 in the title, these are sections of the B.C. *Representation Agreement Act*,[159] which cover the differing scope of each type of agreement. There is another separate document in B.C. called an *Advance Care Directive*, which captures only instructions and there is no person that is appointed. The best explanation I heard for the B.C. Advance Care Directive is that, although it can be used at any time, it can be helpful when you have been diagnosed with a specific condition or terminal illness. That way, the directive deals with your specific wishes and instructions on treatments for that specific condition or diagnosis.

For simplicity, I'll refer to this document as the *legal document for healthcare decisions*, and the person appointed as your *healthcare representative*.

Often people choose their spouse/common-law partner or their adult children for this job, but you don't have to – especially if you think it might put too much pressure or stress on them, or if they could be put into a highly emotional state, as could occur if something happens to you. End-of-life medical care is complicated, with many difficult decisions to be made and processes to navigate. You want someone who has the strength of character to advocate for you as a patient, and the resolve to follow through on your expressed wishes. The question to ask is this: Who is the right person (or persons) to ask the questions, push for answers and make sure your wishes are met during a medical crisis or as your death nears?

Make Your Healthcare Wishes Very Clear

When drafting the legal document for healthcare decisions, be sure it includes guidance for your healthcare representative on how you'd like to live out your life. The idea here is that you should consider these difficult decisions now while you're competent, and share them with the person or persons who you appoint in your legal document for healthcare decisions. Spell out for them as clearly as possible how you want things to go and what quality of life means to you at the end of life or in a medical crisis. This is also a conversation to have with your doctor or the other healthcare professionals in your life. There are helpful online resources, like the *Speak Up Advance Care Planning Interactive Workbook*,[160] that can guide you through a series of questions and scenarios to help you outline your wishes on healthcare decisions. What you end up with could help frame your wishes for inclusion in your legal document for healthcare decisions or a conversation with your family and healthcare representative.

Dying with Dignity Canada, a non-profit organization, also offers advance care planning kits listed by province/territory.[161] One interesting part of their kits is that they include a set of questions about specific scenarios and the medical treatments that you and your healthcare representative can answer separately. You can then compare answers to make sure that your wishes are clear and will be acted upon when the time comes. It's a practical approach to checking to see if you and your healthcare representative are on the same page.

Dying in the 21st Century Has Been Affected by Science and Technology

The conversation about dying in the 21st century is changing. The experts in thanatology, the field of scientific study of death and dying, can certainly give you a deep view of the historical, cultural, religious, and social aspects of this complex topic. A fascinating topic, when you consider how the death culture has evolved – how the age we live in affects not only how we live, but how we die, how we choose to deal with death, and the rituals we embrace or pass down. David Kessler, in his book *The Needs of the Dying*, made the rather interesting observation that "society and the medical system have removed us from the process of death."[162] He goes on to describe how, since the 1940s, death has found a new home in the hospital. Barbara Okun and Joseph Nowinski, in their book *Saying Goodbye – How Families Can Find Renewal through Loss*, describe how grieving processes have changed.[163] With medical advances, death is no longer sudden, as it once was historically; death is now protracted, as the patient's life is extended. They introduce the idea of "the new grief" and offer an approach for how families can deal with it.

If we look at the innovations over the last 100 years, we now have access to incredible advances in medical research, scientific discovery, technology, pharmaceuticals, clinical care and public health. This has not only prolonged our life expectancy, but we are now more likely to die in a hospital or healthcare facility after extraordinary efforts have potentially been made to preserve or prolong our lives. According to Statistics Canada, in 2016, 60.7% of people died in a hospital, as opposed to 39.3% who died elsewhere.[164] This can mean that we, or those who speak for us when we can't, become so focused on fighting the good fight, we forget to take control of our end of life, and decide how we want to die.

Medical advances and legislative changes mean we now have more choices about when, where and how we die. But just like making a will, or making decisions about funeral arrangements, this is a subject best considered before we become gravely ill, and while we can calmly make decisions based on our values, beliefs and desires. We can then communicate those wishes to our loved ones directly and/or through the documents that are available to define them. This is important because we all want/hope to spend the last days of our lives fully in the manner we choose.

How we die is one of the last experiences our loved ones may have with us. Without clear directives, families can be torn apart over the kind of care and medical interventions a loved one should receive. One adult child may want to make use of every medical intervention possible to prolong your life, while another may favour letting you go gently. The differences of opinion, in the absence of communicated wishes from you, can lead to irreparable hard feelings and may make the grieving process that much more difficult for your family. Your healthcare representative not only speaks for you – he or she is your advocate. They can stand up for you and defend your rights to have treatments or decline treatments when you can't.

End-of-life planning is a specific plan encompassing an individual's decisions on care – their wishes regarding quality of life, values and beliefs about what they would like to happen at the end of their life.[165] In addition to the palliative and hospice movement, there is a new role emerging in end of life planning: the end-of-life doula or death doula.[166] Like a birth doula who works with an expectant mom, the end-of-life doula helps the dying person create and navigate through their own end-of-life plan, to support quality of life as the end draws near. As an independent non-medical practitioner, an end-of-life doula can work with the dying person and their family to help navigate the difficult conversations, weigh different end of life choices and options, identify priorities and wishes, understand therapies, and provide companionship and support. This role is currently unregulated in Canada.

To round things out, here are a couple more terms about end-of-life care you should be familiar with

The Government of Canada website called Options and Decision-Making at End of Life describes these options as including: "palliative care, do not resuscitate orders, refusal or withdrawal of treatment, refusal of food and drink, palliative sedation to ensure comfort and medical assistance in dying."[167] The Government of Canada has a convenient webpage with the contact information for end-of-life care services in each province/territory.[168]

- *Palliative Care* – In the situation of a terminal illness or life-threatening condition, palliative care is oriented towards easing pain, providing comfort care and reducing the stresses of a terminal illness.[169] Palliative care in some hospital settings can also include medical treatment to address the terminal illness. It can also include psychological support, bereavement support and family support. Palliative care can be provided at home, in the hospital, long-term care facilities or hospices.

- *Hospice Care* – Hospices are relatively new, and do not exist in all provinces/territories. Basically, hospices are separate entities that offer palliative care. How they are funded differs by hospice and province/territory. According to the Canadian Hospice Palliative Care Association ("CHPCA"), "hospice palliative care is aimed at relieving suffering and improving the quality of life for persons who are living with, or dying from, advanced illness or are bereaved."[170] Additional information can be found online through the health authority or health region in your province/territory, at the CHPCA,[171] or the Canadian Virtual Hospice (one of the CHPCA links).[172]

- *Medical Assistance in Dying ("MAID")* – In 2016, Medical Assistance in Dying was made legal in Canada through *An Act to amend the Criminal Code and to make related amendments to other Acts (medical assistance in dying)* (formerly Bill C-14).[173] While it is covered by federal statute, it's administered at the provincial/territorial level, where healthcare is managed and delivered. To be eligible, a person must have "a grievous and irremediable medical condition"[174] and voluntarily request medical help in dying with no outside pressure or influence. They must be at least 18 years old, mentally competent and must give informed consent.

- *Expected or Planned Home Death Documentation* – If you want to die in the comfort of your own home with your loved ones around you, there are processes and information for that. In British Columbia, it's called the *Joint Protocol for Expected/Planned Home Deaths*.[175] In Ontario, it's the *Expected Death in the Home Protocol*.[176] Such documents, filled in by you and your doctor, set the stage for death at home. The protocol covers what forms are required and who to call.

A Few Words about Grief

Everyone deals with loss and grief differently, and the phases of grief vary from person to person. The duration can be days, weeks, months or years, and will have a profound impact on those left behind. Some who have experienced grief will talk about the year of firsts – the first Christmas without dad, the first mother's day without mom, the first summer without Uncle Merv up at the camp and first New Years' without Aunt Mary and her home-made perogies.

How you prepare your loved ones to deal with grief is a major consideration in end-of-life planning. You can help them in advance by encouraging your loved ones to surround themselves with support after you're gone. This can be done by referrals to resources affiliated with the community or religious group you are connected to, social workers, grief support groups, grief counsellors, or psychologists. Some of these services can be included as part of funeral home packages – something to consider if you are pre-planning and/or pre-paying for your funeral arrangements.

Your Digital Undertaker:
Project Management Checklist Applied to Chapter 6

1. Scope: *Why are you doing this?*

Advance care planning is an important part of planning for any adult, at any age. It is also important for retirement planning and estate planning, for many reasons, one of which is that it can certainly affect how much of your estate is left. These legal documents, while vital, are relatively simple. As I've previously explained, most provincial/territorial resources provide guidance on how to create a Power of Attorney (for financial affairs) and the legal document for healthcare decisions.

2. Options & Trade-Offs: *What are the pros and cons?*

Just as it is an option for the executor role in a will, you could take the professional route and appoint the Attorney role for the Power of Attorney (for property and for financial decisions) to a trust company, a legal advisor or other professional fiduciary. Similar to the professional or corporate executor route for a will, you will be expected to sign a compensation agreement and include those arrangements in the Power of Attorney (for financial affairs). A corporate or professional option is not normally available for appointing a healthcare representative for your healthcare decisions – you're going to need someone else for that.

3. Preferences & Costs: *What do you need and what's it going to cost?*

The one area that I didn't cover was the terminology and choices with respect to caring for seniors when additional personal care is required.[177] This is another area where the terminology differs by province/territory and providers (government or organizations) offering these services. This is an important area to explore as it also deals with the cost and support available for your preferences. This can matter for retirement planning, because of the impact on your retirement plan. You will be making those healthcare and personal care decisions yourself while you have capacity. When you communicate your preferences to your healthcare representative, you will want them to implement these choices if you become incapacitated. For example: Do you want to stay in your own home or not? What support is available? What is covered by your province/territory? What costs are you prepared to pay?

4. Procurement of Professional Services: *Your body can't bury itself!*

From a risk management perspective, the Power of Attorney (for financial affairs) deserves the same level of rigor and legal advice as will drafting. An efficient option would be to have a legal advisor draw it up for you when they are drafting up your will. If finances are an issue, similar to the recommendation in Chapter 4 for wills, see if there are legal clinics or *pro bono* services available in your area.

There seems to be a more relaxed attitude about a DIY kit for the legal document for healthcare decisions, provided you are using the correct province/territory templates. Depending on how healthcare and medical services are organized where you live, your healthcare region or healthcare authority will most likely have further information. In addition, there seems to be help out there from various province/territory-based charitable organizations and non-profit societies for completing it.[178]

And remember that, just like with a will, you can change your mind down the road as life unfolds, family circumstances change, and/or your wishes or preferences change.

5. Risks: *What are the risks? What are the backup plans?*

The Power of Attorney (for financial affairs) is an extremely effective legal document in protecting you, but they can be a dangerous tool in the wrong hands. Choose wisely when you hand over the keys to your financial kingdom. Discuss with your legal advisor the best way to implement oversight of the attorney's activities. Describe what would make you more comfortable in terms of controls, safeguards and reporting. You might not be able to watch them, so who will? If the Attorney makes a mistake, depending on what was done, you could be liable as they are acting on your behalf. If you are the appointed Attorney, I'd highly recommend that you ask lots of questions before you sign up, as many of the legal expectations discussed in Chapter 5 for the executor, such as the fiduciary responsibility, are also expected in this role.

6. Communication: *It is on a need-to-know basis and someone needs to know!*

It's essential that you spend time with the people you appoint for the two roles, the Attorney and your healthcare representative. Sit down with both together, if you've named them separately, to make sure your expectations are understood. They need to work together, so it is helpful to ensure they both hear what you have to say – for example, if you want to be placed in a specific facility, have access to a specific type of care, or if the situation arises where you need additional care, as your healthcare representative will likely be signing off on the placement, and your Power of Attorney will likely be approving and paying the expenses. It's pretty critical that they hear what your preferences are. As with the executor, the Attorney for the Power of Attorney (for financial affairs) will also need other information, such as an overview of your assets, how you expect the Attorney to manage them, and which professional advisors they should consult and potentially engage.

Where should you put your Power of Attorney (for financial affairs) and the legal document for healthcare decisions? Keep them secure, but easily accessible. A health region in British Columbia recommends putting your legal document for healthcare decisions in a green magnetic plastic folder and attaching it to your refrigerator door. Another suggestion I heard was putting a card in your wallet indicating who the Attorney and your healthcare representative are. I guess, for now, that might also mean a note in your cellphone wallet cover.

The Power of Attorney (for financial affairs) also needs to be accessible when required, but it does need to be treated with greater care given that, as I said earlier, it gives the holder the keys to your financial kingdom. A discussion with your legal advisor on where to keep the Power of Attorney would be appropriate.

One other thing to consider: If you move between provinces/territories, it is a really good time to draft up new documents for your new home province/territory.

In Passing

Science and technology are not the only things that are changing the conversation about death – it is society that is changing the conversation. In the ether space, in addition to the traditional conversations that are based on religious and cultural beliefs, I did run across some interesting people trying to open up the dialogue about death. For example, Caitlin Doughty, a mortician, founded an organization in 2011 called the Order of the Good Death,[179] a group of deathcare industry professionals looking to be part of the conversation about how society handles death. Death Cafe[180] website, based on a model developed by Jon Underwood and Sue Barsky Reid, provides a platform where informal gatherings for sharing and talking about death and dying, can be posted.

Chapter 7
Death with a Side of Digital

I used to think that the worst thing someone could do was leave a vast collection of possessions in their home, basement, attic, crawl space and/or garage for their poor executor to clean up. I have experienced phone calls asking for help in clearing out a house or an apartment, and spent endless days separating the recyclables from the keepsakes. However, accumulating a large amount of stuff is not, from an estate planning perspective, the worst thing you could do. (Unless, of course, it's a major fire hazard. Then maybe it is.)

When you have gone to the great beyond, the easiest thing that the executor might do – compared to filing probate, preparing taxes, managing beneficiaries, and navigating through the instructions in your will, and the law – will be sorting through your physical possessions. All that's involved is pulling together some help, locating the items mentioned in the will, then sorting and tossing out or donating what no one wants. There may even be a sense of satisfaction in getting it done. With the proliferation of companies in the junk trade and the emerging death cleaning business,[181] it will be reasonably easy for the executor to hire help and/or order one of those oversized commercial grade steel garbage bins to be delivered to the front your home.

By the way, I don't mean to be flippant. There are two sides in the argument over how to deal with the mass of personal possessions. One side holds that you should get your house in order now by passing things along and reducing clutter. This is no different than what you might do if you wanted to downsize your home or if you decided to move. The thinking is that it is good for you and good for the executor, beneficiaries and survivors. The opposing view is that sorting through your treasures helps survivors get closure – that it is cathartic to revisit the past and reflect on your life. As these are your belongings, it's your call.

Either way, you should be aware that the generations coming up behind you are increasingly disinclined to receive all that silverware and fine china you've been storing for years.[182] Tastes have changed. While there are certainly still collectibles that have value, the list is shrinking. Few people would say no to inheriting a coin collection or valuable artwork, or even a sentimental item, such as the perfectly seasoned cast iron frying pan that reminds you of family gatherings with your grandmother's cooking. Most people just don't have the space to keep all those other space-eating hand-me-downs that they will never use.

No, there are worse things you can do than leave a junk pile. The most frustrating, of course, is not leaving a will (see Chapter 4) or leaving a will that no one can find. Among the list might also be not creating an inventory of your assets, or a list of the institutions associated with those assets. This will leave the executor in the role of a forensic scientist trying to figure out what your estate includes. Professional trustees and corporate executors could give you a litany of other examples, given they do the estate administration job for a living. The next worst thing is leaving the executor and beneficiaries in the dark about your digital life and digital assets.

The Digital Age

We now live in the digital age, where technology has transformed how we communicate and engage socially – even how we die. In any given year, more people are killed in accidents while taking selfies than from shark attacks.[183] The term *selfie*, representative of the social media age, has even made it into the dictionary. Almost all of us have digital lives, even if it's just a subscription to the online edition of your favourite newspaper or magazine, or keeping up with friends via social media. And if you keep photos on your smartphone or save points on your loyalty card, you own digital assets. We are only beginning to realize the potential of technological innovations, like autonomous driving, blockchain, virtual reality, augmented reality, robotics, drones, artificial intelligence, quantum computing, and are still coming to terms with the impact those inventions might have on our lives.

The Digital Age Has Affected Estate Planning and Estate Administration

The digital world, as such, has become very relevant in your estate planning context for two simple reasons. First, you might have wishes and/or preferences about what you want done with your digital life. Those considerations are exactly the same as your physical property. Second, you'll definitely need to leave some information behind for the executor on where to find your digital possessions and what you expect them to do. The big difference here with your digital possessions is that they are just a little trickier to find if you don't leave a list of what you have, and can be next to impossible to do anything with them if you don't leave the executor the digital access information (*e.g.*, passwords, additional vendor or software provider authentication/verification information, private keys) in a separate and secure location.

Technically speaking, without a password, all of the cyber security and privacy preventative measures put in place to protect yourself from identify theft, hacking, and cyber theft of your accounts, will act as barriers imposed on the executor. Even if the executor has the legal right to access your accounts in your jurisdiction, there is a very real practical aspect to this. In addition, passwords can get written down incorrectly, or expire. Further, as it stands today in terms of technology, process and the functionality of today's software, it may still be difficult in some cases for the executor to gain access, even with a password. You may also want to consider other pre-planning activities in addition to leaving passwords.

The topic of digital assets became important to the Society of Trust and Estate Practitioners ("STEP"), a global society of estate professionals, with a Canadian Chapter. STEP, in addition to several other relevant special interest groups on estate topics, launched a digital assets working group in 2013, then formed a special interest group ("SIG") in 2017.[184] Practitioners in the estate planning and estate administration field are welcome to join this special interest group – you don't need to be a STEP member.

The STEP Digital Assets SIG has created several guidance documents that estate practitioners can use with their clients in estate planning discussions to deal with digital assets. One of the guides is called the *Digital Assets Inventory*, which aids practitioners in having conversations with their clients and encouraging them to document the digital assets in their lives. Of note: This inventory also recommends that the digital access information (*e.g.*, passwords) is not stored as part of the inventory, but stored separately in a secure location. They also have information and a *Digital Assets Public Guide*, which includes information that will help you answer pre-planning questions, such as "What are my digital assets?" and "Why are my digital assets important?"[185]

To illustrate how your digital life has already affected your estate planning, consider your home office or study today, versus what it looked like back in the 1980s.

An executor walks into the home office of a deceased person in the 1980s. What would the executor have likely found? If they were lucky, the executor in the 1980s would have found an estate binder or even a file folder with an inventory of all the estate assets and other supporting information, such as pensions, insurance policies and funeral pre-arrangements. While we had information technology back then, most people likely kept hard copy records and left a paper trail that would have been relatively easy to follow. The rolodex or address book would have been helpful in providing names and contact information of key people in their life, such as family, beneficiaries, and friends to call to attend the funeral, or who they have dealt with professionally, such as their tax advisor. While it might not have been all that neat and tidy, the executor at least had a fighting chance of collecting the necessary paperwork about the estate, beyond what's in the will.

What Would Your Executor Find in Your Home Office?

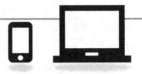

1980	Today
Typewriter	Smart phone
Fountain pen	Laptop
Personal letters	Tablet
Landline telephone	Smart watch
Bank statements	Home digital assistant
File folders with labels	Wireless router
Rolodex or Address book	Paper shredder
Safety deposit box key	Recycle bin
Tax statements	Printer/scanner/copier
Fax machine	Digital picture frame
Ashtray	Memory stick or Flash drive
Camera and rolls of film	Backup hard drives

Today's executor will walk into your home office and likely mutter under his/her breath: "please, please, please, let there be an estate binder or at least a printed copy of some statements that are not shredded." And to their surprise, a disembodied voice responds from the ceiling speakers connected to a home digital assistant:

> *Hey you, executor. I am the digital assistant and no, sorry Ms. Privacy didn't create an estate binder. She'd been meaning to, but used the time to set me up instead – she told me it was just more fun than collecting paperwork. Oh, and good luck finding any passwords that will give you access to all her laptops and electronic devices – they were written on a small note taped under the desk, but it fell to the floor and someone got it stuck under their shoe and walked off with it several months ago.*

Even paper shredders have gotten more technologically advanced. The executor might have been able to rescue the long strips of paper from older shredders, from the recycling bin and taped them together like you see in the movies. But no, now we all buy paper shredders with a cross cut like we're concerned that a SWAT team is going to appear at any moment. Kidding aside, there are certainly privacy, security and confidentiality reasons to shredding documents with personal information when recycling.

If they are lucky, today's executor will find an estate binder with an inventory of your estate assets and other supporting information, such as pensions, insurance policies and funeral pre-arrangements. However, if you have gone paperless and everything is on digital files somewhere, they could be in big trouble. Without passwords, they will not be able to turn on your computer or tablet and go through your digital or online files, or even peruse the contact list on your smartphone. And if you've been avidly shredding your financial statements and other documents to keep paper from proliferating, or for security concerns, they could be in a predicament.

While financial institutions in Canada have made it easier for an executor with the right paperwork to obtain information, the executor needs to know which financial institutions to go to, regardless of whether it's a traditional brick-and-mortar bank, an online only operation, a global bank, or a grocery store that became a bank. That doesn't even begin to cover all the possibilities for insurance companies, wealth management firms and the other endless financial management possibilities. If the executor does not know what institutions you deal with, it's not unreasonable that they could be faced with making dozens or hundreds of cold calls to figure out where you hold accounts or assets.

The push to go paperless doesn't stop there; utilities (i.e., water, power, gas), telephone and wireless companies, internet and cable television providers, retailers and more, are also driving their customers online, either directly or via their bank. It makes sense. It saves paper and postage. However, this digital trail doesn't necessarily leave many clues for the executor to follow. With no paper trail, it may be more difficult for the executor to find your assets so that they can begin shutting down services you will no longer be using.

This can add to the estate administration costs and, worst case scenario, result in assets that languish, unclaimed and unused, in cyberspace. Want proof? Go online to the Bank of Canada Unclaimed Balances Registry site.[186] At the end of 2017, there was a staggering $742 million in unclaimed accounts. For fun, try going to the unclaimed registry and type in your name.

It doesn't stop there. Some jurisdictions have unclaimed property laws or guidelines to hold on to uncollected assets for years – things like unclaimed wages or commissions or dormant accounts. Some have searchable databases, like the one operated by the British Columbia Unclaimed Property Society.[187] I encountered this entity when one of my university colleagues reached out to me asking me to look at a letter he had received from them. The letter stated that they were holding money for him from his time at university, 20 years ago, and asked him to provide some personal information to make a claim. Rightly so, in this day and age, he thought the letter was a fraud and called the university payroll department directly to determine if the letter was legitimate. It turned out to be true, and he collected enough money for a dinner out with his family. I applauded my friend for being skeptical and taking a couple of minutes to make a few extra phone calls to verify, independently, that the letter was valid.

While it may seem like a throwback to the pre-internet world, there is still a role in estate planning for a good old-fashioned binder with actual paper in it. Go ahead and also include a flash drive, a CD/DVD, memory stick, or other storage device, and leave it in the back of the binder; and, of course, it is not a bad way to back up the paper. However, as technology advances, there is nothing wrong with printing a hard copy of important documents, and it might be invaluable. Remember when floppy disks were the norm? Perhaps a flash drive might be extinct when you pass away. It could leave the executor on the hunt for a relic or old school device to review your information, only to find that the media doesn't work because it was too old or got corrupted.

You should be concerned with the confidentiality of all that information in an estate binder and take precautions. For example, lock it in a file cabinet, safety deposit box or ask your legal advisor for other recommended options for securing. Again, be sure to tell the executor how they can get at it when they need to. For financial-related information, a much more secure approach is to only list the name of the institutions you deal with, their phone numbers, addresses and perhaps a contact person. Leave off all the account numbers and any financial data entirely. Creating this simple list, without account or financial data, is light years ahead of what most people do, and it's all the executor needs. The executor could then go to the specific institutions and get the additional information when it's required. This list ideally would include your bills, debts and liabilities. It is helpful for bills, such as utility bills, and subscriptions to provide the address where the service is being provided (if different than the mailing or invoicing address) and name of the person on the account. If the account doesn't involve any financial holdings or data, including the account number can be helpful for the executor when calling in to pay the final bill and close it.

A Digital Asset by Any Other Name

Digital assets are those assets you own directly, or use (by holding a licence), that involve technology or are digitized. They could be stored electronically on your computer, laptop, tablet, smartphone, or online. There are several terms used to describe digital assets, such as *digital property*, *virtual assets*, *digital files*, *intangible assets*, *intangible personal property*, *technological assets*, *paperless assets*, *cyber assets*, *crypto assets*, *electronic records*, *electronically stored information*, or *electronic communication*.

The Canadian Uniform Law Conference's definition of a digital asset is nice and simple: "A digital asset may be defined as anything that is stored in a binary format or more simply an electronic record."[188]

When I'm asked to describe the characteristics of a digital asset, my answer is:

- it is something in a digital format;

- it likely needs some hardware and a power source to access;

- it can have some value or utility to you, just the way a physical asset can;

- it won't work well if it is not maintained, secured or backed up;

- the kids in your life probably know how to use it better than you; and

- good luck getting at it if you have lost your password and have not previously set up a recovery process.

Regardless of what they are called, and how they are categorized, what is relevant to estate planning, according to STEP, is that digital assets "may be of financial or sentimental value to you and your family. They can be as precious and important as physical assets that you can touch."[189] Digital Assets may also provide access to something "physical," such as a financial holding (known as an *underlying asset*, such as a bank account or stock account), or have privacy considerations (you might think of your privacy setting on your social media accounts, but this applies to all accounts), or could contain information about your identity that you'll want protected from identify theft.

In the technology space, there seems to be a variety of terms used to describe the business or company providing technology products or services, whether they are free or paid-for services (*e.g.*, technology provider, software business, software provider, service provider, social media platform provider, software vendor, business, hosting provider, hardware vendor, software platform provider, third-party technology provider). I'll refer to businesses or companies providing technology-related services or products as a *provider* (*e.g.*, technology provider, e-mail provider, software provider).

Characteristics of Digital Assets
That Can Affect Planning of your
Digital Wishes

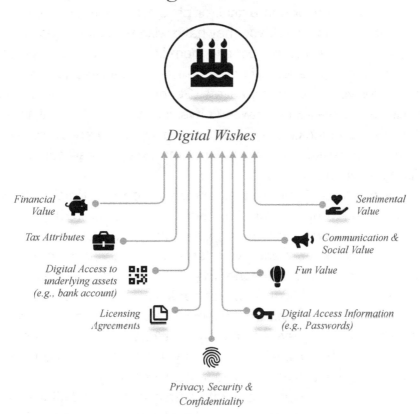

Digital Wishes

Financial Value

Sentimental Value

Tax Attributes

Communication & Social Value

Digital Access to underlying assets (e.g., bank account)

Fun Value

Licensing Agreements

Digital Access Information (e.g., Passwords)

Privacy, Security & Confidentiality

Digital assets often require access information, meaning you often need to provide some form of protected digital information to gain access – a user name, log-in information, an e-mail address, a digital key, a public key or user credentials, along with a password, a personal identification number, and/or private key. Digital access information can also include additional vendor or software provider authentication or verification information such as two-factor ("2FA"),[190] 2-step,[191] two-step,[192] multi-factor[193] or other authentication/verification method.[194] To simplify, I'll refer to the digital assets that require digital access as needing a password.

Why Are Your Digital Assets Important in Your Estate Planning?

Your digital assets are important in estate planning for all the reasons any of your non-digital, or physical, assets are important in estate planning. First, you may have wishes, preferences and/or intentions about what happens to them after your death, and those wishes need to be documented and communicated just as you would for your non-digital assets. Second, there are some similarities and differences between physical assets and digital assets that are worth looking at, as it can impact how you handle them in terms of estate planning, or what the executor can actually do during estate administration.

For example, if you want to leave your online music or movie collection to your children, you might not be able to. If you purchased and downloaded music or movies, you likely only have a licence to it, which means you can use it, but you might not be able to transfer it to someone. Check the licencing agreement or terms of service. This might be less of a concern if you skipped the downloading phase and went directly to a streaming service where you pay a monthly fee with no expectations that anything can be transferred. This example also gives you a relatively good idea of how quickly things are changing in the technology space.

The estate planning and estate administration of digital assets follows a similar process as non-digital assets. The key activities of estate planning such as documenting your wishes and plans are exactly the same for digital assets. This can include providing instructions for inclusion in your will. You might be familiar with some of these key activities that the executor will have to do in estate administration. These activities are exactly the same for digital assets, being:

- finding, securing and creating an inventory of assets;

- closing accounts, paying debts and paying expenses;

- assessing the value of assets, applying some post-mortem tax planning; and

- distributing according to the will.

Borrowing from the technology toolkit, when I've helped a client plan their technology project, I often found it useful to look at a client's processes and ask: what is the same and what is different? If we know what is the same, then perhaps we can use a similar approach to deal with digital assets as for any other assets in estate planning. Understanding the differences also allows you to deal with these characteristics directly in planning. Perhaps then you can figure out a new approach or engage new expertise to help you with the things that are different. The same principle will also apply to the executor when handling your digital assets, in that the characteristics of digital assets, in their similarities and differences to physical assets, will affect what they do.

Some of the Similarities Might Surprise You
- *Digital assets may have financial value.* You might have an e-book, generate advertising revenue from a social platform channel or blog, sell your art or photographs online, or run an online business. Cryptocurrencies or cryptoassets have certainly raised the awareness of the financial value of digital assets. As a further financial value example, some websites and domains can have value. Remember the tech boom of the early 2000s when you might have heard of the "million dollar URLs" (address of a website)? If you own a specific website (or domain), it could represent financial value if there is a buyer out there willing to buy it.

- *Digital assets may have sentimental value.* You don't often think of giving your technology a hug or that it will hug you back. The idea here is that, for now, digital assets may hold sentimental value, such as digital photographs, but wait for virtual reality, artificial intelligence and robotics to become mainstream in the home. What happens then?

- *Digital assets might have some of the same legal aspects of dealing with physical property*. Your e-book or digital photographs may be subject to laws such as intellectual property rights (*i.e.*, copyright) or have royalty attributes.

- *Digital assets have privacy, security and/or confidentiality considerations – i.e.*, who do you want reading your e-mail? Or perhaps you have preferences for what to do for your social media accounts (keep them going or shut them down).

- *Digital assets can have tax attributes*. If they have a financial value, there could be a tax liability.

- *The executor may need specialized or expert help* (*e.g.*, technical, legal, tax) to deal with digital assets in estate administration.

Some Key Differences

- *Some digital assets can be physically undetectable*. This could include your e-mail account, online subscriptions or social media accounts. An executor needs to know what you have, as these likely won't turn up in a physical search of your house.

- When passwords are required, and they typically are (no password often means no access), what then? I find it interesting that people are sometimes under the delusion that somehow the password will magically reappear or they'll get their password reset, but it just doesn't happen that easily anymore thanks to the preventative measures being put in place for cybercrime.

- *The value of digital assets can diminish over time*. This means the executor might not have a lot of time to extract the value of a digital asset before it devalues or expires.

- *Ownership rights is one of the biggies*. Many online accounts, software platforms or digital assets that you think you are buying are actually only licenced, and are governed by licencing agreements or contracts. Remember when you signed up for that account and there was a litany of information you had to read, scroll through and agree to before you could get access? That contract between you and the company (*i.e.*, provider, software vendor, business) is sometimes called a *licencing agreement, terms of use agreement or terms of service agreement ("TOSA").* They differ from one company to the next, but some don't allow you to give your digital access to anyone but yourself. The big surprise here is that you might not actually own the digital assets that you have signed up for, or you may be limited or prohibited from passing them along. For many digital assets, ownership or the licensing arrangement may end on death and/or transferring title may be restricted, or prohibited altogether.

- *Executors will need to confirm they have a legal right to access your digital assets* or online accounts in their jurisdiction (more on this later).

- Location of the digital asset (called *situs*) may be more challenging to determine than a physical asset because it's virtual.

- Privacy, confidentially and security is a concern for some physical assets, but it is paramount when dealing with digital assets.

In summary, understanding the similarities and differences aids us in understanding this new topic, relative to things we already comprehend. You don't need to get too concerned about whether a characteristic is different or not. What is truly important are the characteristics themselves and how to plan for them, and then how to help the executor administer them when the time comes.

The Practical Crux of the Digital Assets Matter

Now that we have become a little more comfortable with the characteristics of digital assets, let's explore the practical crux of the matter in dealing with them. I'll illustrate with this example: Say you have an apartment. You die, and no one seems to be able to find a set of keys to your apartment. The executor, named in your will, would likely first ask your family. Unfortunately, none of them have a key. Then, armed with the original will or proof of probate, the executor would ask the apartment manager to open the door. The apartment manager will see that the legal document gives the executor the authority and will comply by providing a set of keys. The executor is using the authority granted by law to gain access to that apartment.

Now, if the apartment manager was away, and it was urgent to gain access to the apartment, the executor could call a locksmith. The executor would show the proof of probate to the locksmith, and use the authority of the will to hire the locksmith. They might be able to gain access because they could use their magic drills and special tools. So, in the case of this physical asset, the law can help the executor to gain access by opening the door.

Turning to digital assets, let's talk about your computer. Let us say you left wishes that the photos on your computer were to be given to your children, but you forgot to leave instructions regarding where the executor could retrieve the password to your computer. This scenario assumes that you did not leave the executor any account operating system password, any other pre-set recovery drives with instructions, nor pre-set account reset codes. The executor would look around your office to see if you left any password-related information, and perhaps even ask your children if they knew.

The executor wastes time looking and has no luck, so he/she decides to go to a computer store for help. Their chances in gaining access to the data on your computer are really going to be, at best, a roll of the dice. There is the issue of whether or not you, as the deceased person, owned the computer. Did you leave the receipt, with the serial number, proving that it is yours? The executor, even with the proof of probate, will need to prove that this computer is yours. This situation is no different than your claims that you own any specific asset, such as a car. The executor can only deal with that asset if the title for the car is in your name.

The computer store, like the apartment manager, will recognize the authority of the proof of probate and try to help the executor. Unfortunately, they may not physically be able to get into that computer and access the data, especially if the hard drive was encrypted. Much of the technology we use today has been hardened to prevent access by hackers and cybercriminals, and to protect your privacy. Can executors use their authority under the law to open that laptop? Probably not, because it might be really locked down, with no magic drill or special tool that can get into some computers or encrypted data.

You might want to give the computer to someone, with the idea that they would load their own data on it, so they would own it and use it for themselves. Some computer hardware can be reset without a password. All the data and programs previously on it will be wiped out. For many people, the data on the computer, those digital assets such as photos and other artifacts, are what is really important.

Does technology have a back door? Some does and some doesn't. There is one additional challenge: Even if there's a back door, will the company that created it allow the executor access? There might be procedures and paperwork the executor will need to fill out. Even then, they might not gain access if the licencing agreement prevents them, or if the company does not comply for privacy reasons, jurisdictional law reasons or some other reason.

The law might not be enough to get into that computer, and that is the practical crux of the digital assets matter.

Estate Planning vs. No Estate Planning for Your Digital Assets: Examples

Online or Digital Photos

Estate planning related to digital photographs can be particularly emotional. Say you were the family photographer or family historian and have sentimental images of generations of weddings

143

and holidays that are captured and stored on your laptop. If you take pictures with your smartphone or a digital camera, you might store the photos on the device itself, your computer, or online (*i.e.*, in a cloud repository). Do you want someone in your family to get all of your photos when you die? Some of them? They might end up inaccessible, because the laptop is password protected and the password was never shared. The same holds true if you have scanned, or transferred, and digitized your photos, home movies or slides. Consider passing along those digital assets, long before it becomes an issue.

Another concern, for those items of sentimental value while you are living, is backing up your data. A smartphone, computer or hard drive can crash or fail. I've personally experienced computer crashes where I have lost all my data because in order to fix the machine, the technical help had to wipe out the devices' memory and data. Once it happened to me during a routine update of operating system software. Fortunately, I have been repeatedly saved by having two backups.

Additionally, it is always a good reminder for you to set aside a great picture you want to be remembered by. No one will want their mid-1970's or mid-1980's prom picture to be used in their obituary. It was just not a good time for fashion.

Planning can have other advantages too. Digital entrepreneurs are now offering other legacy opportunities, such as videotaping or recording yourself to leave messages to your loved ones. The creative possibilities in this space are just emerging, and I can't wait to see what virtual reality innovation will emerge for legacy or memorialization options.

E-Mail

With the exception of messaging apps, e-mail likely has become the key mode of communicating with people in your life. Do you want someone to have access to all your e-mails? Some of them? How many e-mail accounts do you have? What is their purpose? For work e-mail accounts, most people are not aware that the executor will not be able to gain access on death. How much information are we leaving in work e-mail or data stores that will become inaccessible? Are you using your work e-mail as your login for your personal accounts?

Passwords are critical for accessing most online accounts and, in a perfect world, you would create and maintain a digital asset inventory and a separate list of current passwords stored somewhere securely (available to the executor, of course). Unfortunately, this rarely happens and the issue is only going to get more complicated as biometrics, such as retinal scans and fingerprints, are used to authenticate access. The technology industry will need to consider these estate planning and estate administration requirements as they continue to tighten things to deal with identity theft and cyber security.

Digital Asset Planning

E-mail

Planned

Authorize your executor to access your e-mail accounts.

Don't forget information, including any 2-step verification and any other authentication protection.

Also consider other backups such as printing out important e-mails, backed up on a flash drive or in a cloud backup service.

Secure password information appropriately but ensure executor is aware of how to access it.

VS

Unplanned

Given e-mail is often used as access to other online accounts, executor may not be able to reset other accounts if they don't have your main email password.

Nevertheless, it's useful to know at this time that every e-mail provider has a different policy or approach to third-party access without a password. Specifically, if the executor contacts the e-mail provider to gain access to your e-mail, depending on the software or hosting provider, they will receive a different response. Some providers will provide the executor some, or all, of the contents of your e-mail, and in other cases, some providers won't provide any content and will only shut the account down.

Without a password, the noose has been getting tighter on what companies will release, if anything, and for good reason. Alive or deceased, e-mail contains valuable information that should be protected from unauthorized use, and for privacy considerations. In all cases, there will be a lot of paperwork and supporting documents required, and every provider the executor deals with may have different requirements, all adding to estate administration costs. If you are concerned, review the website for your e-mail provider for information about what an executor can do, and what, if any, pre-planning is available through that provider.

Time can be of the essence, as we know how long it can take to prepare and receive probate, depending on a person's situation. Unfortunately, many e-mail accounts have an expiry date, and might be deleted after a period of inactivity, which is generally a year. The issue isn't whether probate will take a year or not – the issue is that maybe you were sick before you died and stopped using e-mail at some point. Again, a lot of this can be mitigated with estate pre-planning.

Social Media Accounts or Community Platforms

If you connect with your family/friends, colleagues or communities of interest via different social media accounts or software platforms, do you want your accounts staying online for a specified period of time "in memory" of your passing? Or do you just want them shut down? What do you want done with your account information, including data (*e.g.*, recipes, photos, designs)? It could be double the trouble if your online name account is different than your legal name.

In contrast to automatically expiring e-mail accounts, some social media accounts or platforms can live on forever. It can be very distressing to have a business social media site cheerily recommend that you connect with a business colleague who died.

I've personally had this happen, and I just felt for the family who probably had no idea how to deal with this. The simple answer to dealing with this unfortunate situation is for the family to contact the software provider, by calling them or looking up the process on their website for requesting an account to be closed.

Today, very few accounts offer pre-planning in the form of appointing a "contact" and other legacy options. For grieving families, I am hoping that all social media and software platform providers will follow the lead of those who already provide this functionality.

Digital Asset Planning

Social Media Accounts

Planned

When the executor has memorialization access, the deceased person's social media account can be set up to "In Memory" status, allowing family and friends to leave their condolences.

Unplanned

The deceased person's business social media account sends out new networking requests (Algorithmically generated).

The family gets e-mail from business colleagues of the deceased about the problem.

A Few More Examples

Here are more examples of digital assets you may already have in your digital life, and some questions to consider from an estate planning perspective. Every software provider has terms and conditions; you'll want to check what it means for your digital assets and their use. You will also want to research if they provide user or technical guidance, cautions and directions for handling their specific digital asset.

- *Points or Loyalty Cards* – Perhaps you collected points over months or years and cash them in for products or services. Who do you want to receive your loyalty points, if they can be transferred? Check the licencing agreement or terms of use to see if transferring is possible.

- *Revenue Generators* – Maybe you wrote an e-book and get royalties on the sales. Perhaps you buy and sell things online, are a blogger/social media rock star with enough followers to generate advertising revenue, or you provide services through a crowdsourcing platform. Who do you want to receive the royalties of your digital e-book? Have you left the paperwork and documentation on your ownership and copyright? Are there things you can do in advance to facilitate the transfer to a new owner?

- *Books/Music/Movie/Software Licences* – Perhaps you purchased e-books, subscribed to streaming services, or procured software programs or licences for your computer or devices, such as word processing or photo editing/storing. You can check the licencing agreement or terms of use, but you will often find that you can't transfer the licence.

- *Electronic Games* – If you have credits on your gaming account, or you have an avatar in some strange world where you make instruments that you sell to other characters for exchangeable tokens, you can check the licencing agreement, or terms of use. You will want to know if your avatar can be sold or transferred, and if the credits can be traded or if their value could plummet after your death from lack of use.

- *Software as a Service (SaaS) and/or Subscription Model* – The concept is that you licence the use of software as a service over the internet, versus downloading or installing it. It may involve also licensing on a subscription basis (e.g., monthly, annually), versus buying it once. This is a shift, from the past, in licencing, distribution and pricing strategies by software providers. There are thousands of options here for every type of software for a multitude of uses (*e.g.*, writing documents or books, designing, graphic arts, collaboration software, illustrations, photography, and app or web development). Some of these software services also provide a cloud component where people store their work in progress or finished work (anything from a book draft to digital art work). Some options are emerging to allow you to transfer your finished items to another person – check your provider and their licencing agreements.

- *Cloud Services* – This is remote storage, or as I like to call it *the hard drive in the sky*, as opposed to the physical hard drive on your computer, laptop or smartphone. It is just as important to be able to access these digital accounts and assets, as your important documents might be stored there (*e.g.*, bills and receipts, if you use a device to scan them all in).

- *Smart Home Services* – You might have installed baby cams, security cameras, monitoring devices, and have your lights/locks/thermostat controlled by internet-accessible applications. What happens if you are no longer around to manage these systems? Who's your backup? Who has access to make changes when you can't? How is your attorney or executor going to get access into your house, condo or apartment if you have set up a remotely-monitored security system, locks or service?

- *Physical Assets Managed Digitally (Underlying Assets)* – Do you mostly access your financial accounts and credit cards online? This can be an extremely problematic area, and these types of accounts should not be accessed online by your attorney or executor, as it will often be a direct violation of the terms of use. They should be going to the financial institution and dealing with them directly as part of their fiduciary roles.

- *Cryptoassets or Blockchain-Based Applications* – You may hold cryptocurrency (also called *digital money, virtual currency or digital currency*). Do you want someone to receive your cryptocurrencies? Or do you want them cashed in? Have you left the executor the name of the cryptocurrency (given there are thousands) and the public and private keys to access them? In this currently speculative and unregulated space, there is no central authority or helpdesk for the executor to deal with. The Financial Consumer Agency of Canada has information about the use of, and the risks of using, digital currency.[195] As blockchain technology gets regulated or applied to other uses and applications, the need for executor access to public and private keys will only continue to grow.

Do You Need a Digital Executor?

The term *digital executor* is made up. In some respects, there is no such thing as a digital executor, any more than there is an art executor, house executor or a specific asset executor, other than the named executor(s) in the will, or the power(s) you give someone specifically in the will. Using the term digital executor to raise awareness is great. However, I think we need to be careful on the terminology, for a number of reasons I'll outline below.

Owning digital assets has become relevant in estate planning. The big difference with digital assets is that they are trickier to find if you don't leave a list, and difficult to manage if you don't plan ahead, provide passwords, have a backup plan or leverage any provider pre-planning functionality that is offered. So, the idea that your one and only executor might need some help, if they are not tech savvy, is relevant. Keep in mind, though, that not all digital assets need someone to be computer literate. For example, the online access to your bank account. The executor should be going to the bank or financial institution directly, and should not be using your credentials and logging into your online bank account.

Newsflash! Your digital and non-digital lives are very much intertwined. Suppose you have an online newspaper subscription and you want (or expect) that subscription to be cancelled after you die. Further suppose you consider two different people to be involved in your estate, namely, a digital executor and an executor. Which executor would you choose to deal with this online newspaper subscription? I would suggest that, just as you would have expected for a physical newspaper, you would want your executor to deal with that. If all your information about your physical assets (underlying assets) are managed online through digital assets (in an online account), then having someone called a digital executor is potentially giving away some, or all, of the executor's role. It could certainly cause confusion over who is responsible for dealing with what.

Perhaps keep it simple. One consideration is that the executor will have this extra job and should treat digital assets just like any other asset class. If the executor isn't computer literate, you might want to consider what additional information to leave behind to support the executor, and also encourage the executor to seek qualified technical help or qualified advisory support. This is the same way you might expect your executor to engage an art dealer or an art appraiser when dealing with your art collection, or engaging a real estate agent when dealing with selling your home. The executor will be expected to vet expert options, select the expertise they need, oversee their work and confirm that the work was done in the manner they expected.

Seeking legal advice and getting digital assets included within the scope of your will is really important. You can ask your legal advisor to draft language in your will to address your wishes and preferences for your digital assets, and the roles and responsibilities of the executor in dealing with them. In addition, you'll want legal advice and perhaps legal drafting, in a situation where you might have a specifically identified digital asset(s) of significance that you want handled in a specific way, with a specific person(s) (who is not the named executor).

From a practical perspective, if you decide you'd like to appoint someone called a digital executor or digital advisor to deal with all your digital assets and this person is different from your named executor, I would suggest you carefully consider identifying exactly which digital assets each one is responsible for, review the powers assigned, outline how conflicts will be dealt with when they arise, and seek legal advice. In some respects, it is no different than assigning someone powers to deal with a specifically identified physical asset, but the key is you'll want to be precise about which assets and the extent of the powers you're assigning. I've made the points earlier that our digital lives and our physical lives are very much integrated, the law is evolving and even the terminology within the technology industry varies on what's what.

From a project planning point of view, given where things stand today, a blanket statement that says a digital executor is to deal with digital assets, and the executor is to deal with everything else can seem a tidy way to do this. However, in my opinion, I believe these role assignments without pre-planning and contemplation of the impact of doing so could create confusion during estate administration. There could be lots of overlap. This is an area that is sure to evolve as executors navigate this and share their experiences, and you'll want to seek legal advice to help navigate this area. Here are some of the estate administration questions this scenario of two executors generates for me:

1. If a computer is a physical asset (in that it is not considered a digital asset because it is not an electronic record), but the files stored on it are, what then? Who does what?

2. Is the estate going to pay the digital executor? Certainly, shutting down an easy account might take minutes and a few mouse clicks, but what if you have lots of accounts that are more difficult?

3. What if the digital executor spends considerable time just trying to figure out what the digital assets are?

4. Regular assets can take time, in terms of getting an appraisal, finding a market, evaluating bids and contracting to make it happen. The same can apply to digital assets. For

example, if the estate needs to sell a web domain, whose job it is?

5. What if the digital executor makes a mistake that affects the rest of the estate?

6. What if the digital executor has expenses in conducting this role? For security and/or privacy reasons, they might require separate internet access or other technical tools to do the job.

7. What if the digital executor needs to hire professional help, incurring costs to the estate, because they need technical support or legal advice?

8. Who oversees the work of the digital executor?

9. Would the digital executor know they shouldn't access an underlying financial asset?

10. What if the digital executor is handling assets that have a financial value? Are they supposed to engage a tax advisor and complete the tax forms?

Having the Digital Assets Conversation with Your Executor

Certainly, completing a digital assets inventory will be a good first step. Leaving digital access information (*e.g.*, passwords, additional vendor or software provider authentication or verification information, private keys) in a separate, secure location in a manner that does not attract legal or criminal liability, reviewing any provider agreements, researching provider guidance, testing your access instructions and then advising the executor on how to get access, are all good planning activities, to name a few. You'll certainly want to revise the list and your approach as things change. However, similarly to your physical assets, you might want to go a little further in preparing the executor.

Giving someone a list of passwords without guidance is as dangerous as leaving your car keys in the ignition or dropping your wallet on the street. Worse, in fact, because passwords in the wrong hands or accidentally mishandled can cause a lot of damage – to your bottom line, to your identify and to your reputation. From a project management perspective, you can prepare the executor by reviewing with them what needs to be done, in a little more detail, for your various digital assets.

Before you have the conversation with the executor, you'll want to review the digital asset inventory and your wishes with your legal advisor, and inquire if a digital asset clause in your will is appropriate for your situation. You'll also want to ask your legal advisor if the executor has the legal right to access your digital assets after death, by inquiring about jurisdictional laws that cover their role, and any specific digital assets that might pose a challenge, given where they are located or because of licencing agreements. The answers to these questions will be important to review with the executor.

To assist in sorting out my own digital assets, I created a framework called *Your Digital Undertaker – Digital Life Triage Exercise*. This Digital Life Triage Exercise is based on pre-planning activities that can be applied to your digital usage in three groups (see the appendix to this chapter for a more detailed discussion):

1. It's a mouse click or phone call away. Easy pre-planning actions.

2. What were you thinking? Questions aimed at evaluating your digital usage in the context of maintainability, pre-planning and handover to your fiduciary.

3. The blue screen of death. Explores risks and areas that you might trip over in pre-planning.

The prevailing guidance today recommends creating a digital assets inventory as a starting point. This exercise attempts to provide an approach to taking the next step with your digital assets inventory in assessing your digital usage and identifying other pre-planning options specific to each item. This framework focuses on the user management options and pre-planning questions for an average digital user. Obviously, there will be other planning activities, including technical actions you'll want to consider based on the recommendations, guidance and cautions provided by the specific software business or provider. You can also use these questions with the executor, if it helps to frame the digital conversation into byte-size chunks.

Laws Will Need to Catch Up

As with most technological innovation, lawmakers often need to play catch-up, either by updating legislation or creating new laws, such as will be the case for digital assets. There will be a number of legal questions for the law to tackle with respect to digital assets, such as: What is digital property (as per a legal definition) versus other types of digital assets? What is and isn't digital property that you own?[196] How does one deal with a digital asset that has other laws involved (*e.g.*, intellectual property law, business law, other jurisdictional laws, conflict of laws)? Some technology providers have begun to allow a *contact* to be identified for pre-planning of digital assets – how does this role mesh with the fiduciary role of the executor and how will the law deal with conflict? Is the executor responsible for only digital property (*i.e.*, property owned by the deceased) or are they responsible for all digital assets? Is there a difference between the Attorney (in the Power of Attorney) and the executor role in handling digital assets?

One particularly grey area is the fiduciary role of the executor, in terms of what they can and can't do in handling digital assets in Canada. What the fiduciary is allowed to do is covered by jurisdictional laws of the place of either where the deceased or incapacitated person resides or the situs where the digital asset is located. The Uniform Law Conference of Canada has proposed the *Uniform Access to Digital Assets by Fiduciaries Act (2016)*,[197] for adoption by each of the provinces and territories in Canada. The proposed Act codifies the rights of the fiduciary to deal with digital assets, which currently is considered in existence for their role in dealing with other kinds of assets. As of writing this book, no jurisdiction in Canada had yet enacted fiduciary access laws on digital assets.

As described above, what an executor can do with the deceased person's passwords is covered by laws. The laws in every country are different and, in some cases, dramatically so. For example, with respect to the access by fiduciaries, the U.S. started with some of the similar objectives as the proposed Canadian Uniform Law Conference of Canada, but then the majority of the U.S. states enacted legislation that was the opposite of the proposed approach. As it stands, in the majority of U.S. states, the executor can't access the contents of a deceased person's accounts, unless the deceased person had given explicit approval while they were alive.[198] If you are interested in the status of this U.S. law, you can go the Uniform Law Commission site, where you can see which states adopted what.[199]

However, what the U.S. does legislatively just might affect us in some situations, because think about where some of the big technology companies are located. Suppose the executor has to go "knocking" on their U.S. door because they get themselves locked out of your account. If such a scenario occurred, based on a specific provider and a set of specific circumstances, that is a legal question (*e.g.*, conflict of law) for the legal advisors and far beyond the scope of this introductory topic. Let us leave it at this: Given how relatively new this subject matter is, any executor or Attorney, even a Canadian one, should be very cautious about using an incapacitated person's or the deceased person's passwords and should engage legal advice on how to approach this new digital territory before they begin.

Executors Should Proceed with Caution in Dealing with Digital Assets

As things stand, a prudent executor should be cautious in dealing with the digital assets of the deceased person. He/she should be encouraged to begin by creating a proposed digital assets estate administration plan for dealing with them. This plan could include the following activities:

- creating a list of the digital assets they find;

- evaluating how to secure them;

- reviewing the will;

- reviewing any other supporting documents;

- reviewing the licencing agreements;

- researching digital assets providers for guidance or cautions;

- determining which digital assets provide digital access to an underlying asset (*e.g.*, bank) – those that should not be accessed online by the executor;

- determining if assessing the value is required;

- determining if other expertise is required;

- finding any tax information; and

- detailing any proposed actions for accessing, securing, transferring or disposing of assets.

I would then recommend they seek legal advice on their proposed plans to access, secure, transfer or dispose of the digital assets. Then, while in the throes of estate administration, if an executor runs into challenges while dealing with a particularly difficult digital asset, they should re-engage a legal advisor. Similar to other assets, if it gets really complicated, they can also apply to the court for direction. For example, they may have questions about their ability to access a specific asset or how the law would interpret the deceased person's ownership rights of that asset.

A Comment about Dealing with Digital Assets for Businesses Supporting the Estate Industry

Technology is the new player at the client's estate planning table. As the laws catch up, businesses supporting the estate industry (such as law firms, trust companies, financial institutions) will also need to update their policies, practices and processes to deal with digital assets. For a professional fiduciary, such as a trust company, this will be a new world, with updates needed to their technology management policies, practices and tools to include handling of a client's digital assets. For example, for security reasons, most firms won't allow any outside computer (such as the one owned by the deceased) to be plugged into their network, nor do they allow the use of the internet for logging in by anyone other than their own employees for business-related online use. As such, dealing with a client's digital assets is everything that a firm's information technology department wouldn't want you to do on a work network. Separate protected environments may need to be set up or outsourced to third-party technology providers to deal with digital assets.

The technology industry has also yet to catch up to some of the requirements of the estate planning and estate administration fields in dealing with digital assets. Few companies currently have processes in place to allow users to select preferences for closing or transferring their accounts after they are deceased. We have read the heartbreaking stories of families dealing with tragic deaths having to go to court to petition for access to the online accounts of their loved ones. The future is going to get even trickier: How do you leave behind your biometric passwords, such as retinal scans or fingerprints? At some point, the market (meaning you as shareholders, clients and consumers) will pressure the technology industry to provide better options to allow people to securely leave their digital assets to their beneficiaries through an executor, and those options will need to be integrated with the law, as well.

Digital Assets and Taxes

Some digital assets have taxable attributes, so when assets are deemed disposed or the executor sells, transfers or disposes of them, there could be taxation implications. In essence, digital assets get treated exactly like regular assets. For example, if you own a valuable internet domain that can be sold, not only does the executor need to know about it, he/she will also need to know what you paid for it and the expenses associated with it, in order to calculate capital gains, if that is the tax treatment for that specific asset within your estate. Similarly, for other assets, you'll want to consider engaging tax advice for estate planning of digital assets of financial value.

As for cryptocurrencies, many people are wondering if they are taxable when sold. The short answer is yes, according to the Canada Revenue Agency website called "What You Should Know about Digital Currency."[200] How it is taxed, specifically, will depend on a number of factors. For example, there are some techies out there who receive cryptocurrencies because they are engaged in mining it (e.g., they receive cryptocurrency as income, revenue or business income). That tax treatment might be different than for someone who is buying/selling, someone using it to pay for products/services, an employee who receives it as remuneration or a speculative investor.[201] How it is treated for your particular set of facts can only be figured out with some advice from a tax advisor and/or a conversation with the Canada Revenue Agency. So, all that information you would have left for the executor about your other physical assets also applies to your financially valuable digital assets.

Obituaries in the Digital Age Need a Rethink

When someone died years ago, the executor or family would have posted an obituary in the print version of the local newspaper, likely in the city where the person died or back in their hometown. While that still happens, today when you have an obituary published in a newspaper, it is likely also available online and available to significantly more people than the paper copy. Here's my observation: if we guard our privacy and avoid identify theft throughout our lives, why do we give out so much personal information when we die? People think it's okay to put their full names (first, middle, last), nicknames, birth dates, the name of their spouses/partners, maiden names (if applicable), and the names of their children in an obituary that includes entire details about where they were born, lived and worked. We have all heard tales of thieves reading obituaries and targeting homes when everyone is at the funeral. If your obituary has been handed out globally, it may include personal information that could potentially be used for identity theft. In the digital age and with the proliferation of cybercrime, providing too much personal information is not necessarily a good thing. This certainly won't make the genealogy community happy at all.

Learn about the Impact of Privacy on Estate Planning from this Scenario about Mr. Privacy

Your usage of digital assets in regular life can undermine your estate planning objectives. Suppose you have a cousin, his name is Mr. Privacy. Every time you get together with him for a catch-up chat, your cousin's main concern always comes to a conversation about protecting his and his family's privacy, as he owns a small Canadian business where most of his family works. Mr. Privacy, through estate planning, decides, after discussing the various options with his estate advisors, to move his assets into a family trust for privacy reasons and succession planning. When you asked your cousin why he set up a family trust, his answer was that his primary motivation for the family trust was to protect his privacy – he does not want his family's net worth and his personal hold-ings to become public record. To do so, Mr. Privacy hired estate legal and tax advisors, spent considerable effort and time on the trust deed, and then spent the fees on the transactions required to constitute this trust relationship.

Mr. Privacy also spends considerable efforts to remain low key in his business dealings. In fact, although he is the owner of a Canadian small business, he enlisted a company spokesperson to deal with all the public-facing aspects of this business. Mr. Privacy is not very tech savvy, and his marketing director has been urging him to get a business social media profile, which he has ignored.

Let's check in to what is happening in Mr. Privacy's personal life

Mr. Privacy, at some point, had been introduced to social media by his grandson, who set him up. He now loves keeping up with family and friends on social media (who doesn't) once he got the hang of it, but what Mr. Privacy doesn't realize is that his privacy settings are open to the world.

For those who know a bit about social media, there are a variety of privacy and security options, depending on the provider, in addition to how much information you are filling out for your profile. To boil it down, consider these generic settings:

1. The first one is open to the world, very public.

- Meaning anyone with a computer, or a smartphone, and access to the internet can look up your name and look at your information, posts and photos.

- You ever wonder why news reports often include a social media picture of the person reported on? Well that's because the reporter or journalist went to various social media sites and downloaded that picture. You'll see it credited at the bottom of the photo in small print.

2. The next level of privacy setting is where you select specific people to see your profile and your content.

3. The third level lets you apply even further restrictions on who can see what aspects of your content within your social network.

So now let us examine what Mr. Privacy has already told the world with his social media account that was accessible by anyone (worldwide):

- He has photos of all his real property because he loves taking pictures of all his family events.

- His children and grandchildren post pictures of all the vacations they have been on, and photos of his pets and prized possessions.

- Mr. Privacy's friends congratulate him on his various company successes.

- His grandson follows him around lot, taking pictures of the inside of his place of business.

Let's just consider these digital photos for one moment. Because they are digital, the file contains additional embedded information, called *metadata* (*i.e.*, what kind of camera took the picture, the location where the photo was taken, the date the photo was taken). So now, potentially, someone will know exactly where those photos were taken, what he owns and where he lives. Depending on how long Mr. Privacy has been posting information, anyone, and I mean *anyone*, can create a pretty good picture of his life.

Your cousin, Mr. Privacy, has now undermined his primary objective of privacy and the expense in setting up the family trust to do so, simply by the way he failed to secure this one social media account.

Your Digital Undertaker:
Project Management Checklist Applied to Chapter 7

1. Scope: *Why are you doing this?*

How big are your digital shoes? Most people are surprised at the extent of their digital lives when they start to prepare a digital assets inventory, or start using a password manager (digital or paper) for the first time.

Can the executor fill your digital shoes digitally? The volume of your digital assets, along with some of the unique challenges of handling them, can become a time-consuming task for any executor, tech savvy or not. You'll want to encourage the executor to seek technical, legal and/or tax advice and any other professional advice in dealing with digital assets. In the same manner, they may need estate advice for your regular or physical assets.

However, there are also some digital shoes that the executor should not be stepping into, like your online banking information or your e-mail if you so decide that you don't want anyone to read it, or any other area where you have laid out specific wishes and preferences. In fact, as digital possessions are new and evolving, the best plan would be the one where you review your digital assets with the executor when you are reviewing your will and your estate plan.

2. Options & Trade-Offs: *What are the pros and cons?*

Estate planning for digital assets requires the same rigor you'd apply in dealing with your physical assets. To keep it simple, consider that there are five key steps:

Step 1. Understand what digital assets you have, using planning techniques similar to the consideration you might give your money or your physical assets in estate planning. (*i.e.*, create an inventory).

Step 2. Secure digital access information (*e.g.*, passwords) separately from the inventory. Digital access information should be left in a secure manner that considers security guidance from the online providers, avoids potential criminal liability, addresses privacy concerns or other actions that may contravene any terms of their licensing agreements. Test and re-test that the documented digital access information works.

Step 3. Consider your digital wishes and preferences in the context of the constraints imposed by the nature and characteristics of the assets themselves (*i.e.*, licensing agreements, legal property vs. what you don't own or have rights to, passwords and digital access).

Step 4. Work with your legal advisor to determine options to address your digital wishes and preferences. Document those choices and plans. Engage a tax advisor if your digital assets have a financial value or tax attribute.

Step 5. Review and determine how to give your executor and Attorney permissions and powers to deal with your digital assets (*i.e.*, ask a legal advisor about a *digital assets clause*, an insert that addresses digital assets specifically, the powers and indemnities given to the fiduciary dealing with their administration and distribution, software account pre-planning options, if available, and other options recommended by your legal advisor for your jurisdiction). This is important as well, as there are likely many digital assets you have that might not be considered something you own from a legal perspective. The basic role of fiduciary is for the property that you own or have rights to. If you expect your executor or Attorney to deal with all your digital assets regardless of definition, you'll want to review that you have given them permission within the context of applicable jurisdictional law(s). For this advice, you will want to consult a legal advisor on how to address your specific situation. By the way, this is not just a problem for digital assets. Physical assets have this issue as well in terms of what is considered property, and who owns specific property (*e.g.*, pets, genetic or reproductive material).

3. Preferences & Costs: *What do you need and what's it going to cost?*

Making a list may be inconvenient, but at least it isn't expensive. Remember, computers fail, hardware crashes, and technology becomes obsolete. Anyone who has had to recover data from a dead computer or a soggy smartphone, either curses themselves for not having a backup of their data, or kisses their backup hard drive (or sends digital thanks to their cloud backup). What's your backup plan for the executor to get your estate information? Even if you were super organized, left incredible digital instructions, because technology is technology, passwords can fail or expire, so you'll want to consider the backup plan for your digital assets.

4. Procurement of Professional Services: *Your body can't bury itself!*

The future is here. The digital age will impact your estate planning, from considering your wishes for your digital assets, engaging legal advice and preparing the executor, to potentially engaging specialized technical services. Clauses can be added to legal documents to address your digital assets. A digital assets inventory, or just a simple list of what you have, is good information to bring to your legal advisor when making or updating your will and POA.

But in some respects, it really is back to the future. Remember the Year 2000 (Y2K) bug? Other than the once in a lifetime New Year's party to welcome in the new millennium, you probably want to forget Y2K altogether because it was also the name of the technology project many working in business preceding the year

2000 were involved with. Y2K was basically a technology problem that goes back to the 1970s, when software designers decided to represent years using two digits (99 vs. 1999) in some computer systems. With the new millennium approaching, it was unknown whether a system could handle representing years with only two digits once the counter reset to 0 (*i.e.*, whether the system could distinguish between 2000 and 1900).

Not to dust off too much on memory lane for you on Y2K, but one observation I'd make is that most business or consulting firms approached it from a project management perspective because, at a minimum, they did create an inventory to figure out what technology and software applications they had and were often surprised in the process. The general approach underlying most Y2K project plans followed this basic methodology: the awareness phase, the inventory phase, the evaluation phase, the risk assessment phase, the remediation phase, the testing phase and the project closeout phase. Doesn't it look a little similar to what you might do in estate planning of your digital assets or what the executor has to do to deal with each asset, digital or not? Perhaps this chapter is just the awareness phase introducing that the idea that the digital age and digital assets era in estates is now well underway, raising your awareness, and hopefully encouraging you to complete an inventory and other estate planning steps, just as you would for your other regular or physical possessions.

5. Risks: *What are the risks? What are the backup plans?*

How you manage your digital assets while you are living will have a profound impact on your privacy and data security after you are gone (as I covered in the Mr. Privacy scenario). You'll want to pay attention to your digital assets while you are living, and give them the same care and attention in maintaining them.

Cybercrime and identity theft have become rampant; every other day, there seems to be a story of yet another company that got hacked. Not only do crooks prey upon those who are vulnerable or incapacitated, cyber thieves also readily target those that are fully capable, but lax in protecting their digital assets and guarding their online presence.

I would suggest you consider your home technology, your digital assets and digital access information as you would any of your other important home appliances or valuable assets. Exercise the same care and attention in terms of research when you purchase them, get qualified help in setting it up right, read the provider or company's advice on its use, review the operating manual, and spend the time and money required to maintain and secure it properly. This area, quite frankly, is just something all of us need to get better at understanding, protecting and maintaining, if we truly want to use technology sustainably in our lives for the long run. Technology, by its nature, can seem advanced, magical and maintenance free, but it is not.

The technology industry and digital asset providers offer guidance on how to protect your digital assets and protect your family in an online, connected world. The usual advice begins with:

- use advanced digital access practices (*e.g.*, strong passwords and additional authentication/verification methods, as recommended by vendor or software provider) for all accounts and devices;

- delete accounts, e-mails and content no longer required;

- regularly review the privacy/security settings on your accounts and devices;

- don't open documents or click on links in suspicious e-mails, or better yet, don't click on links at all – go to known websites directly;

- surf (visit) only reputable businesses or websites on the internet;

- keep up to date on software and hardware patches by staying current with the latest version;

- use virtual private networks ("VPN") to encrypt internet traffic;

- encrypt your data on all your devices;

- have at least two backups of important data;

- use virus/malware scanning software (if available and recommended for your operating system);

- double down on protective measures when teaching the young ones in your life about technology;

- engage accredited technical professionals from reputable companies to help you with your digital assets; and

- stay current on the technology you use with education and awareness.

Not keeping your software current and not using virus or malware protection is like driving with bald tires during a blizzard. Clicking on strange or suspicious links in e-mail is like drinking out of a stranger's glass – you never know what you're going to catch. Using public Wi-Fi without encryption (of a VPN) is like leaving the front and back door to your house open all night while you are away. Digital assets are worth protecting. Invest a little time in protecting them and it will go a long way to keeping you and your family's digital assets safe, and online lives private – and therefore, more secure for your estate.

Where can one get basic computer and technical information? There are lots of online resources, news sources, education, books, and magazines. Just ask your favourite techie on what sources of information would be good to get you going. Check with the vendor who sold you the equipment; some vendors offer training and orientation. I've also seen some good short articles in popular magazines, from time to time, on protecting yourself and your family online.[202] The Canadian government has a website providing some cyber security services and information, with topics such as "Protect Your Devices," "Protect Your Identity," "Protect Your Family," and "Cyber Security Risks."[203]

6. Communication: *It is on a need-to-know basis and someone needs to know!*

For all that is good and convenient about the digital age, it poses real challenges for your estate planning, and eventually for the executor. I've spent a lot of time in this chapter on considerations for pre-planning and what the executor might face in dealing with your digital assets. The same challenges apply to other fiduciary roles, like trustees or those who are the Attorney (for your Power of Attorney), should you become incapacitated. If you are no longer able to remember your password, it will present significant challenges for others who have to step in to manage your digital affairs. Perhaps when you review your digital assets inventory and wishes with the executor, consider including your Attorney in the conversation.

In Passing

A shout out to all those family members who perform user, technical and/or administrator support for their family and friends. You know who you are, because you endlessly rebuild computers and recycle equipment, so that friends and family can benefit from some of that cool technology. You've made house calls to friends when their machine went down or printers died. You've taught their children safe internet practices and you've tried your best to keep everyone educated about computing best practices. You've encouraged people to consider password managers, but have been happy that they just wrote down their strong passwords in a little black paper book that gets locked away when not used (because you believe low tech is sometimes the best tech). We've all relied on these techy wizards who patiently attended our techy needs, who smiled at us patiently when we complained about why one software program doesn't work like the other, assuming we are the general spokesperson for the entire technology industry. In fact, we really should have been paying for professional technology support long ago because our personal usage is far beyond recreational.

This message is for them, as well. They, too, need a documented and tested backup plan. What if you get sick? Or what if you are out of the country, for that matter? Who is authorized to do what you do? Do you have a backup for those domains you manage and the network router passwords? Heaven help us all if you go down and no one can get their e-mail.

Appendix to Chapter 7: Your Digital Undertaker – Digging 6 Feet under the Bits and Bytes

The following Digital Life Triage Exercise provides some additional questions for consideration in pre-planning your digital estate after you have completed a digital assets inventory. It can also help guide a conversation with the Attorney or the executor. This exercise is focused on pre-planning considerations applied to your digital usage (technology, digital assets or digital devices) in three groups, namely: *It's a mouse click or phone call away*, *What were you thinking?*, and *The blue screen of death*.

This triage assumes you are an average user, meaning that you are using digital assets in your day-to-day life (*e.g.*, e-mail, social media, and online accounts for memberships or utilities). The generic questions are focused on basic user account management options and pre-planning considerations. There will, obviously, be other planning activities, including technical actions you'll want to consider based on the specific recommendations, guidance and cautions provided by the specific software business or provider for each of your digital assets or devices. Even for the average user, there could be other legal, and tax, estate planning activities.

If you are a medium or super user, you will want to consider engaging specialized technical, legal and tax advisors for advice on how to deal with those digital assets in estate planning. (Medium or super users have digital assets of financial value, significant complexity, a large quantity of them, involve significant risks associated with confidentiality, privacy, or own them as part of a business.)

The Purpose of the Digital Life Triage Exercise

When I was in the Canadian Forces, in addition to our day-to-day operational roles, we spent a lot of time in exercises. The purpose of most of these operations was to test our capability and improve our ability to deal with any number of situations. We had a lot of different types of exercises, from the paper assignments (scenario-based discussions) to semi-live situations (simulation exercises), to the live exercises (involving real aircraft in a real situation that could be tested). They were challenging, but in the end, I was always impressed about how the scenarios would often identify details, risks or challenges that I might not have considered by just reviewing a manual. I found that you can still gain knowledge, even from a paper exercise. I've modelled this triage exercise after the simple idea that talking through a set of questions or scenarios can really help one understand a topic.

If you leverage this triage in a conversation with the fiduciaries (Attorney, executor), the onus is really on you to help them realize that there are limitations to having the list of passwords, that there are laws that apply to the digital assets themselves, and their role in handling them. Having the passwords may not be the final solution to estate administration of your digital assets. For this exercise, the intent is that you are not providing the executor with passwords during the discussion. Those passwords are yours, and should be kept secure. This triage assumes that the fiduciary will have the authority, by law, at the time they require it, to access your digital assets after you die.

Your Digital Undertaker
Digital Life Triage Exercise

Your Digital Life Triage Exercise

1. It's a Mouse Click or Phone Call Away. These actions are relatively easy to do. They include activities that you can do in advance, and provide guidance to the executor on how to handle some of the digital assets that may not need online access (*e.g.*, loyalty points). In some cases, the executor will need to understand your pre-planning efforts so they can communicate to, or remind, your beneficiaries how you have already handled specific digital assets, should they inquire. This grouping includes meeting with your legal advisor in the context of your will to discuss your wishes and preferences with respect to digital assets.

2. What Were You Thinking? This grouping starts by evaluating your digital usage and determining if how you are using it is aligned to what was intended, the practicality for consideration in estate planning and the ability of your fiduciary to access those digital assets. For example, if you use your work e-mail to log in to your personal accounts, or to store personal files, consider that, upon death or incapacity, your fiduciary will not be able to get access to your work e-mail. This grouping also considers how you manage your passwords (in general or as a system). Although some digital assets may not have financial value, there is privacy, security and confidentiality to be considered. This group also includes how to deal with digital devices (*e.g.*, tablets, computers, hardware, smartphones) that might hold digital assets. The executor may, or may not, need legal advice for digital assets in this group, depending on what they encounter. These pre-planning activities can require a little more effort, and the risk profile increases for the executor.

3. The Blue Screen of Death. This includes activities that involve the information, guidance and warnings that the executor needs to know for managing digital assets with financial value or data. The term *blue screen of death* is a throwback term used by some computer users to describe a situation where one is literally faced with a *solid blue screen* when starting up, or when one's machine had given up the *digital ghost*, in that it no longer works.

Included in this category is the e-mail account, which may or may not have financial value, but needs to be treated with extreme care. You'll also want to review with the executor which accounts they should not be accessing online (*e.g.*, bank accounts, underlying assets). You'll want to encourage them to seek legal advice in reviewing their access plans prior to accessing. They may also need tax advice for digital assets of financial value to determine if there are tax implications. These pre-planning activities will need significantly more thought and effort as the risk for the executor can be high.

Table 1: Your Digital Undertaker – Digital Life Triage Exercise				
It's a mouse click or phone call away	1.1 Create a digital assets inventory, and engage legal advice.	1.2 Pre-plan: Transfer, backup or shut down.	1.3 Pre-plan: Select appropriate online options and tools.	1.4 The good old-fashioned way by contacting the provider.
What were you thinking?	2.1 The practical utility of it all.	2.2 Secure and manage digital access, like passwords.	2.3 Secure digital devices.	2.4 Privacy, security and confidentiality.
The blue screen of death	3.1 E-mail may not just be e-mail.	3.2 Review digital assets that have financial value with estate advisors.	3.3 Underlying assets (e.g., bank account) that should not be accessed online by the fiduciary.	3.4 What the future may bring.

1. It's a Mouse Click or Phone Call Away

1.1 *Create a digital assets inventory, secure passwords separately and engage legal advice.*

Before you have the conversation with the executor, you'll want to review the digital assets inventory and your wishes with your legal advisor and inquire if a digital assets clause to be included in your will is appropriate for your situation. You'll also want to ask your legal advisor if the executor has the legal right to access your digital assets after death, by inquiring about jurisdictional laws that cover their role and any specific digital assets that might pose a challenge given where they are located, or because of licencing agreements. The answers to these questions will be important to review with the executor. Regardless of what type of digital assets you own, in light of the current state of the fiduciary law with respect to digital assets, you'll want to recommend to your fiduciaries that any digital assets or digital devices where the attorney or executor plans to use your passwords, should be itemized, the licencing agreements reviewed, and the plan to access and what the executor will do with these accounts should be reviewed by a legal advisor before logging in.

1.2 *Pre-Plan: Transfer to someone else, back up in another format, shut down accounts you no longer require.*

- **Transfer to someone else** – Figure out what information can be passed along now while you are living. One example is a genealogy account. If the functionality is available, share your genealogy data with another family member who already has an account on the same genealogy site. The very nature of these types of communities is that you share information to create or trace family trees. That way, the selected family member is allowed to see your information (that you have given them permission to) without using your password. They use their own account and password. Consider transferring digital assets or online accounts that you wish to outlive you (such as a blog) – engage a legal advisor on how to do this formally with all the right paper-work, especially if it is part of your business.

- **Back up in another format** – If the information or material (*e.g.*, photos and e-mail) is that important to you, back it up on a regular basis, print it out or prepare it in another digital format (memory stick, CD/DVD). For example, it is pretty simple to annually save or print all your favourite photos, or set up photo sharing so other family members can have access.

- **Shut down accounts you no longer require** – A great regular maintenance activity to do throughout your life to protect your online presence and personal information.

1.3 *Pre-Plan: Select appropriate pre-planning options and tools available from the software provider or digital assets company.*

If such a functionality exists and you consider it appropriate for your situation, select pre-planning options. For example, an online account setting where you appoint a contact person in advance – someone who can access your account after you have died. Consider adding the executor's name or the person you want to do this. Review what the contact person is able to do, and make further choices or selections as appropriate. For example, the contact person might also be able to change your account status to an "in memory"[204] status or close the account.

- Be aware that different technology providers have different names and terms for what they call this contact person and the process associated with setting them up. For example, they may be referred to as *trusted contact,*[205] *legacy contact*[206] or just *contact*.

- I hope the technology industry collaborates with the estate industry in creating some consistent terminology on this front, and that existing providers that don't provide this functionality add the capability. Perhaps they should start by picking a consistent name instead of the various terms to describe the pre-planned contact; how about *digital executor* instead?

- Use pre-existing recovery planning tools. Some providers provide options for you to set a recovery or emergency e-mail or cellphone number associated with your account. It might be part of the privacy and security settings to protect your account, yet it can provide an ability for you to recover your account. You could add the executor's e-mail and cellphone number as one of your recovery choices. The risk of doing so is that you might be giving them immediate access to your account. This is also something to discuss with your legal advisor, if this approach is advisable or not for your situation. Obviously, it is preferable to use functionality specifically designed for digital assets pre-planning, but there are still too few providers that offer this to date.

1.4 *The good old-fashioned way by contacting the company or provider.*

There are digital assets that do not require the executor to use your password. They can follow the company website directions on how to make a request or call. There is no consistent naming convention, but I recommend searching for words along the lines of "what to do when someone dies" or "how to transfer [miles, points, rewards] on behalf of another person."

- On the upside, some loyalty points and reward card providers do allow the points or rewards to be transferred upon death, with proper documentation. The executor is going to have to read through the applicable service agreements to figure out what can and can't be transferred, and what documentation is required. If you hold a specific account where you have significant points or rewards, you'll want to check with that provider to determine if the executor can transfer them after your death.

- If you are looking for information on what happens to your specific digital accounts after death, you can go to the provider directly and determine what they offer.

2. What Were You Thinking?

2.1 *The practical utility of it all.*

This grouping refers to all online accounts associated with managing your household (*i.e.*, utility bills, insurance, municipal taxes, security systems). Prior to the full-on digital age, most, if not all of these bills would have arrived monthly, quarterly or annually in our physical mailboxes. I highlight this grouping as being very relevant, potentially first to the Attorney (as named in your Power of Attorney), as they will likely need to keep things going until other decisions are made concerning your residence.

- It might be handy to have a listing of household related providers and account numbers, so your attorney or the executor can contact these companies and make other arrangements for payments to continue or discontinue service.

- If you own secondary property, such as a cottage, don't forget to put it on the list, as well.

- In many respects, this is just the information you might consider as additional documentation in your estate binder, but as many have gone online, it might be overlooked.

2.2 *The management of digital access (passwords).*

This applies to all the digital assets you have that require digital access information (*e.g.*, passwords) to access. This is about stepping back and figuring out exactly what information is required to log in to your various accounts, what payment methods have been provided, what pre-planning steps are worth exploring and what you need to communicate to the executor.

- Are you using your work e-mail address as your login for any of your personal accounts? This is something you'll want to consider cleaning up now, and shift to your personal e-mail or other access. If you quit, get laid off, go on leave, retire, become incapacitated or die, you, the Attorney (as named in your Power of Attorney) and the executor will not likely be able to access these accounts.

- Do you have several e-mail accounts, and use these different e-mail accounts to log into unique accounts?

- What methods of additional vendor or software provider authentication or verification information have you put in place, such as two-step or multi-factor authentication? For example, is your cell phone number or some other authenticator that generates code(s) required to log in? Is the executor going to be able to use those additional pieces of information at the critical time when they are using your main password? Here is a simple example: Suppose you set up additional verification or authentication for your account. When you log in, you get a text message with a code that is required for login, in addition to your password. Suppose you don't leave the password for your cell phone. How is the executor going to be able to get that additional piece of information?

- What billing and payments require renewing to prevent digital assets from expiring or disappearing?

- If you use biometrics, is there still a backup method for logging in that does not require biometrics?

- Consider the challenges that have now been introduced as the software industry moves to the monthly licencing model (*i.e.*, you may be paying for access to your data on a monthly basis). If you use your credit card or other payment method, and that is shut down after you die, will the account get automatically shut down? This is definitely an area you'll want to investigate. There will be accounts you'll want the executor to continue to pay for from your estate bank account, so that the digital assets are available to transfer later.

How do you manage all of your digital access (e.g., passwords)? If you have several online accounts, you have likely started to develop some sort of personal system to manage the associated passwords. It probably started with just your memory, and then most of us migrated to other choices, like paper-based lists or non-paper-based lists/software.

- Just as you may have a toolbox, a file cabinet or a key rack for physical items, password management is not that much different. You might have labeled or catalogued the files or organized the tool box in a particular way to make it easier to find the files or the tools. If you use a paper-based system, you'll want to consider securing it somewhere safe, such as in a safety deposit box or a locked file cabinet. Password management software, or password managers, are now available to help with this task. There are multiple options on how to use the various packages, and how security is managed around them.

- The counter argument for password managers is that you are consolidating all your passwords in one location, which could pose a risk. That is a risk assessment you'll have to do for yourself. As with all technology, you'll want to do your due diligence in selecting a password manager. Many of the popular technology magazines provide a comparison from time to time, as they do for other types of software.[207] If the solution for managing passwords is to save them in a simple text file on your computer or save them as an e-mail draft, this is not a particularly safe option either, as you could be hacked or your computer stolen.

- Shifting gears to thinking about sharing passwords, as would be required if you intend to leave them for your Attorney or executor. As with many software providers, this area of sharing passwords safely is an emerging field. Some password managers have various options to a degree, from selecting an emergency contact,[208] emergency access,[209] family sharing/family legacy[210] and functions which allow you to share passwords and segregate access to specific accounts or "vaults."[211]

- Again, similar to your digital assets inventory, or a separate list of your digital assets passwords, if you plan to use a password manager as part of your estate pre-planning, you'll want to review the licencing agreements with that software provider for allowing others access. In addition, given the multitude of options on password manager software, and the options on where you store the secured data file, you'll want to let the executor know how you have set it up. I expect this area to evolve as digital usage grows.

2.3 *Secure digital devices – they may be the gatekeeper to digital assets.*

Digital devices, such as computers, laptops, smartphones and tablets make up this grouping. They may or may not have financial value (or remaining value). The key planning concern, considering the crux of the matter I discussed earlier, is that without a password, getting access to these devices to retrieve data might be time-consuming, costly or impossible.

- Your digital device is an asset and typically contains digital asset(s) you might care about, and, as such, estate planning considerations need to be addressed. For example, it might contain an unpublished book manuscript, repository of photos, or an archive of user created information or documents. Now, if I had something of value like an unpublished book manuscript, I would certainly consider keeping backup copies in places other than just on the digital device itself.

- Is a digital device a digital asset or not? That's currently up for definitional debate. To some it is and to some it is not, depending on how deep you want to get into a definitional battle or legal debate. Whether it is or not, the executor will need to secure these devices in any case, because it is still an asset (call it a physical asset), and it may hold the digital assets (electronic records) they will need to protect or transfer your digital assets. In some ways, it is just a new spin on the old chicken and the egg debate. Having said that, in this case, your digital asset(s) "eggs" (*e.g.*, photos) might need that digital device "chicken," if that is the only place you stored those photos.

- You'll want to alert the executor about what digital devices you have, and where you have securely stored the passwords for your digital devices. Now, technology changes and it changes fast, so arguably who knows what specific digital device you will have at the time? The most important consideration is this: if you want the digital assets on the device to be accessible, you'll need to let the executor know where the passwords are kept for whatever device you have at the time, and update that list when your devices change. The practice of keeping an inventory, and keeping passwords updated and secure, is just a really good habit to get into, not only for the executor, but also for yourself. With cybercrime prevention the way it is, good luck getting access back yourself if you lose the password and haven't pre-planned.

2.4 *Privacy, security and confidentiality considerations.*

These are important considerations for dealing with digital assets, whether or not they have financial value. There are privacy, security and confidentiality considerations in managing them that you'll want to alert the executor to.

- Consider this highly recommended maintenance item: for digital assets, regularly review the privacy and security settings of every online account you use. In addition, consider how much of your personal and confidential information you are providing when you sign up for accounts. Certainly, there is some required information, depending on the account type, but in this day and age of cybercrime, considering what not to provide is just as important as what you provide.

- Confidentiality is an important discussion with the executor. Suppose you use an online account to write a book, write a personal diary, or store personal/confidential information in your e-mail. What do you want done with the personal or confidential information contained in your digital assets or online accounts?

- Social media, blogs – for those accounts that do not have pre-planning functionality to select a contact in advance, you'll want to document in your inventory and share with the executor what you would like done with the accounts: shut down, left running, and, if left running, for how long and how do they pay for them, if that is a requirement.

- This item would likely be covered by estate administration, but worth mentioning as it deals with cybercrime. To assist in mitigating identity theft, you might want to alert the executor to the fact that they should contact the applicable credit monitoring agencies upon your death, at the same time they are reaching out to the financial institutions.

3. The Blue Screen of Death

3.1 *E-mail may not just be e-mail – it may contain significant personal information and could have financial value.*

- Are you using e-mail for something else? As part of this pre-planning exercise, you'll want to consider how you use e-mail. Many people use e-mail for what it was intended for – sending and receiving communication. However, some people use e-mail for what it was *not intended*, such as keeping drafts of documents, storing documents, keeping track of passwords, creating chronologies or using it to write a book. This is, obviously, not recommended. Have a look at how you are using e-mail and consider moving your "non-e-mail activities" to more appropriate or secure software or storage.

- E-mail can have financial and/or sentimental value. Consider the news article of historical figures and what their physical letters sold for many years after they passed away. Consider the correspondence within your own e-mail account, the trips you've been on, the correspondence with family members and friends – perhaps some of them serve in the military and have been on missions, and e-mail has replaced physical letters from the front. You probably don't want to be leaving important communication, historical information or treasures trapped in an e-mail account.

- One's e-mail account now represents the account login for lots of other digital assets. For example, if you want to reset your password on another account, the new password is sent to your e-mail. It's pretty difficult to reset other passwords if the main e-mail account is inaccessible.

- A more relevant concern today about e-mail isn't just the executor getting access, it is getting hacked while you are living. The question you should ask yourself regularly is what is stored in your e-mail. If you leave your entire life in there, it is a hacker's dream. A backup consideration would be to print, download/archive/file or delete e-mails that you no longer need; use any secondary verification or authentication guidance offered by the account provider and a very secure password.

3.2 *Digital assets that have financial value should be reviewed with appropriate estate advisors (e.g., legal, tax, financial, insurance).*

This type of digital asset is one that has intrinsic value in itself (*e.g.*, web domain, cryptocurrency), which is also likely to have complicated access (password) components.

- If you have a digital asset of significant value, you'll want to ensure you have adequately provided access information and instructions. You'll want to test, test and retest the instructions you have left, and perhaps even walk the executor through the process.

- For example, cryptocurrencies are currently unregulated and unrecoverable if the private and public key combo is lost.

- There is no simple user account management formula for accessing digital assets, and certainly not for assets of financial value. This means that I can't give you a formula for coaching an executor through a generic access process. You'll want to itemize the steps, test them, and potentially, using a separate test account that has nominal or no value, walk the executor through the steps.

- You'll want to recommend to the executor that any accounts in this grouping, where the executor plans to use your passwords, should be reviewed by a legal advisor before logging in with the password.

- In addition, you'll want to encourage the executor to review their plan with a legal and tax advisor. You'll want to provide the executor with backup documentation you've collected to support the cost-base (or buying price) if the asset is subject to taxation.

- Given the implication for probate and tax, you'll want to inform the executor that they may need to engage a qualified technical appraiser to help with any assessment of the value of the digital asset.

3.3 *Digital assets that provide digital access to underlying assets (e.g., bank account) that should not be accessed online by the fiduciary.*

Digital assets that access some underlying assets should not be accessed online by the fiduciary, in particular financial institutions and other accounts where the law or licencing agreement identifies as such. The executor or Attorney should contact the underlying asset institution (*i.e.,* the branch of the financial institution that holds your bank account).

- Itemize the online accounts that access an underlying asset. The best examples are bank accounts or stock brokerage accounts. They should not be accessed online with your password by the Attorney or executor. There are other rules that govern the bank account as an underlying asset. You should tell the executor that, for these types of accounts, they should go directly to the institution that holds them.

- *Warn* your executor and Attorney about not using your passwords for these type of accounts, as this will likely be a direct violation of the agreement with your financial institution or other monetary holding institution.

3.4 *What the future may bring (e.g., drones, blockchain, virtual reality, robots, artificial intelligence, and robots with artificial intelligence).*

I did say this triage exercise was for the average user and this area sounds pretty advanced. At one point in the past, you might have dismissed the brick-sized cell phone when it first came out, because it was too expensive and too awkward, but now you have one that you can't live without. Things will evolve, and who knows what will end up in this category? If one day you have a robot walking around your home and it records everything you do and say, you might have an estate planning preference about whether all that data is retained or not upon your death. Just saying.

Now, you might have dismissed the whole cryptocurrency thing as just a fad. How real could digital money be? Well, not so fast. Just like a lot of things, economic theory tells us that if a market says something has value and someone is willing to buy it, then it could have value, even briefly. It will be interesting to see where cryptocurrencies go and how governments deal with it. If I could predict where it will all land, just as we all wish we could predict which stock will grow the fastest, I wouldn't be writing this book.

What I will say is this: in my opinion, the technology underpinning cryptocurrencies (like the blockchain invention) will be transformative. Every industry is looking at it in terms of how it can be applied. In the simplest of terms, blockchain is a much more secure ledger, database or spreadsheet. Every business needs a ledger, database, spreadsheet, or tracking system of some sort to run their business. So for both the private and public sectors, they are all looking to determine if the application of the blockchain technology can decrease technology costs, improve speed and solve problems that were too expensive to solve in the past. Businesses spend a lot of money building, maintaining and protecting ledgers and databases. The blockchain technology option offers an alternative ledger or database architecture to many of today's existing systems. This also means that there might be opportunities for applying blockchain to business problems or industry needs that were previously considered unfeasible.

We Use a Lot of Technology Today, and Don't Often Ask How It Works under the Covers

When the internet started, no one asked me how the World Wide Web worked. Perhaps because we all took to it like ducks to water. It was visual and it made sense. As pervasive as our day-to-day use of technology has become, it is never too late to ask a lot more questions about how something works under the covers. It can help one's understanding of how the technology is applied, and can aid in determining the best way to apply it to your situation. They say knowledge is power and, certainly, being more versed about how technology works will help all of us become better, and more informed, consumers.

Digital money is difficult to "see" and in the early days of cryptocurrencies, it was not an average user's game, as one did need some technical skills to navigate that world. Now, if you are just a smidge bit curious about how a cryptocurrency works, I'll digress and share with you what I have been sharing with audiences when I get asked how it works. I use this analogy:

> *If you have ever used a gift card you already know the basics of how cryptocurrency or blockchain works in practice. Let's say someone gave you a coffee gift card for your birthday. You might say to a friend: let me buy you a coffee, I've got $25 loaded*

on my card. We all know that the $25 is not actually on the card, even though we say it is.

If you turn over a coffee card, or most gift cards for that matter, you'll see it has an account number and a PIN number. These two pieces of information work together, like a key, to access your account balance associated with a particular store. As soon as you place your coffee order and pull out your gift card, the cashier scans it on their point of sale system. A message is sent from the store to a computer at the store's headquarters. It verifies you have enough of a balance associated with that account number on their ledger and then deducts your current purchase from that account. It then sends a message back to the store that the transaction was completed.

*Consider the physical plastic coffee card as a **hard wallet**, because it has two numbers imprinted on it. A photocopy of the back of a card in some sense is a **cold wallet** because it contains the same information on a piece of paper. If you use the store's app on your smartphone, instead of the physical plastic gift card, the store's app on your smartphone is like a **soft wallet**, because it has a copy of the same account number and PIN number.*

How does this compare to cryptocurrencies? Everyone who uses a specific cryptocurrency has a separate public key and a private key that they hold in a wallet, similar to a coffee store app. It is often called the public and private key pair or combo. You'll also need a separate wallet for each type of cryptocurrency you have. Consider all the digital assets in your life, like an e-mail account. Most digital accounts have two parts to getting access;

namely, the account number or e-mail address on one hand, and a password or PIN on the other. A cryptocurrency is no different, with the public key and the private key. They work together as a pair. You give out your public key for conducting trans-actions, but you should never give out your private key, just like a PIN, as it gives someone access to your cryptocurrency "holdings."

To give someone cryptocurrency, or to pay a mer-chant with it, you need their public key (in that you need their account number or address). This is the opposite from a credit card, where you hand over to the merchant all the important information on your credit card when making a transaction. To complete a transaction, you send them an amount of cryptocurrency from your wallet to their wallet. It's much like sending a money e-transfer from your online back account – the receiver never gets your account information or password. You never give out your private key, ever!

If you have ever lost a gift card, you now know exactly what will happen to your digital currency if you lose the public and private key pair. You'll be out of luck. This assumes you didn't register the gift card on an app, or take a photocopy of the back of the gift card.

You many never own cryptocurrency, but down the road when blockchain is implemented, say to track art, real estate or some other transactions, you'll need these two pieces of information – the public key and the private key pair for whatever blockchain you are trying to access, and of course the name of the blockchain that it is on.

In all cases and groupings in this Digital Life Triage Exercise, your wishes, intentions for all your digital assets and the underlying agreement of the digital assets should be reviewed with your legal advisor, and then the executor. Privacy, security and confidentially will be a concern in dealing with all digital assets. You should encourage the executor to seek professional technical advice, legal advice and tax advice, if they need guidance or help regarding digital assets.

Chapter 8
Death and Taxes – They Get You Coming and Going

Now that we've explored the fun topic of your digital life and digital assets, here come the taxes. One of the most interesting questions I've received a lot lately in the digital assets world is: Are cryptocurrencies subject to tax? Do I have to pay tax when I sell my digital currency? My answer, as an IT management professional, is simply this: The short answer is yes,[212] and I would be happy to refer you to a tax advisor who can help you out if you'd like to explore what that means for your situation.

Let's assume for a moment that virtual or digital currencies are not subject to taxation. If so, then we've just undermined the entire global monetary system. Who would use government-issued money (*fiat currency*), when one could buy, sell and use a digital currency that grows in value with no tax implications. With most things of value, value exchanges or transactions are subject to taxation. For example, believe it or not, bartering[213] is subject to tax, as are gains on the sale of personal-use property greater than $1,000.[214]

The use of digital assets to drive value has been around for a while, in that people make money from social media platforms/channels, online ads, websites, selling e-books, vacation rental/lodging apps and ridesharing apps – and they have all been required to report and pay taxes.[215] How a cryptocurrency is taxed is covered by jurisdictional tax laws and rules. Yes, there is also a global debate about whether or not cryptocurrencies are a currency, a security, a commodity, payment system or some hybrid; we'll leave it to the individual jurisdictional regulators and legislators to decide what they are and how they are taxed.[216] According to the Financial Consumer Agency of Canada, "Digital currencies are not a legal tender... Digital currencies are considered a commodity and are subject to the barter rules of the Income Tax Act."[217]

As I shared in my story in Chapter 1, I spent more time dealing with taxes than any other subject area in dealing with my mother's estate. As the executor, I was responsible, by law, for making all the decisions about her estate. Many of these decisions were tax related. For example: Should I file for the Goods and Services Tax/Harmonized Sales Tax ("GST/HST") rebate? Was that worth the expense of hiring an accountant? In order to make these decisions and effectively deal with my mother's estate, I felt I really needed to understand the subject matter. This is what I learned about some of the basics and key features of the death tax landscape in Canada.

I was extremely fortunate to find an estate and trust accountant professional who was very patient in answering all of my questions when my zealousness for researching the Canada Revenue Agency website would send me down one rabbit hole or another. He would chuckle when I showed him the various flow charts I created to understand the death-related tax processes. Nonetheless, he enthusiastically shared his knowledge, because how often do people get jazzed about taxes?

Your estate planning situation, or what the executor will encounter in administering your estate, will be unique to your situation. My mother didn't have any registered plans, nor did she own a business and as such, her circumstances will perhaps be different from yours. Being a resident of Canada is complicated enough tax-wise, so this awareness chapter on death taxes assumes you are resident and domiciled in Canada. If you are resident and/or domiciled somewhere else, or live in two places, there are more complexities at play. The point in sharing my own experience with estate taxes is to give you a sense of what the executor will need to learn, the significant amount of time that may be required to collect information, and some of the decisions they might need to make. Hopefully, this encourages you to consider taxes within your estate planning process, and prompts you to encourage the executor to engage estate tax advisory help when the time comes.

If after reading this chapter you feel you can handle a little more research on your own specific situation, and feel a little more comfortable about engaging tax advisors, I will have succeeded in sharing what I have learned. To that end, here are the five key things I discovered about taxation of a deceased person's estate:

1. *Death triggers taxes* – There are, potentially, several tax bills (*e.g.*, probate, and federal, provincial or territorial taxes).

2. *The big death tax bills* – In fact, because your life assets are deemed to be "cashed in" on the day you die, there likely will be several large tax bills driven from capital gains, registered plans, and the ongoing estate itself.

3. *Post-mortem tax planning: the "gottas" & some "breaks"* – Part of the executor's job is to determine what tax forms need to be filed and to make a plan to optimize the amount of taxes that the estate will pay. In addition, there are some special considerations and rules available as a result of your death.

4. *Tax filing surprises* – The volume of information to be collected, the forms to be filed and how long it takes to settle the estate tax-wise can be daunting for the executor. As such, there are some steps you can take in advance to reduce the burden.

5. *Asset location can trigger other taxes* – Where your assets reside (called *situs*) can attract additional taxes and fees even if you are a Canadian resident (*i.e.*, if you own out of country property).

Canadian Tax Concepts
Upon Death

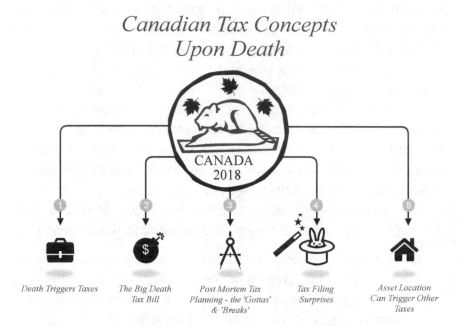

1	2	3	4	5
Death Triggers Taxes	*The Big Death Tax Bill*	*Post Mortem Tax Planning - the 'Gottas' & 'Breaks'*	*Tax Filing Surprises*	*Asset Location Can Trigger Other Taxes*

One thing I can't emphasize enough: Engaging a qualified estate tax advisor is a very good idea for both upfront tax planning and, potentially, to assist the executor. This could be a legal advisor or accountant with expertise in taxation and estate planning. A legal advisor who understands the tax rules may also handle the transactions you might want in your estate plan, such as setting up a trust. After death, a tax advisor, such as an accountant, can help the executor make sure all the right forms get filled out and provide optimization recommendations on how to minimize taxes owed. Why do I recommend getting professional help? Because Canadian tax law is complex. It includes statutes (both federal and provincial/territorial), published regulations and case law (judge-made law). The current Canadian federal *Income Tax Act*[218] alone is more than 3,000 pages long.[219]

Given the complexity, you may wonder what the point is in understanding or planning for taxes on death. You won't be around, so why not leave it to the executor to sort out? One single reason: With no tax planning, your estate will almost certainly pay more in taxes, which will leave less for your loved ones. Furthermore, the executor will curse your name for the tax nightmare you left them. Worse yet, they could find the job too onerous and bail.

Here is a short scenario to illustrate why good record keeping is important to saving money on taxes. Suppose the executor finds a collection of gold coins in your safety deposit box. You left no information about when you bought them or what you paid. You instruct in your will that they should be sold and the proceeds distributed to your beneficiaries. The executor needs to know the price you paid for each of the gold coins in order to calculate the amount of taxable capital gains.[220] Capital gains is the difference between what you paid for them and what he/she can sell them for, less expenses.[221] Without proof of what you paid for the gold coins, the executor will likely spend time and money to try forensically determine the original price, or pay a professional to do it for them. If they can't figure it out, it could significantly increase the taxes owed, because without proof, it will be assumed you paid nothing for it. This illustrates just one of the reasons why people end up paying too much tax – they don't keep good records of their assets. You can't blame the Canada Revenue Agency for that.

1. Death Triggers Taxes: *There are, potentially, several tax bills (e.g., probate, and federal, provincial or territorial taxes).* Technically, Canada does not have an estate tax, nor an inheritance tax, but there are taxes and fees that kick in when you die, and they can be significant, with or without tax planning. There are three main types of individual taxes/fees for Canadian residents:

1. probate taxes or fees (governed by jurisdiction);

2. federal and provincial/territorial taxes administered by Canada Revenue Agency (except for Québec, which manages its own provincial taxes); and

3. other taxes or fees based on the jurisdiction of an asset (if an asset is located in another jurisdiction or country).

What Is Probate?

Probate is the legal process through which your provincial or territorial court formally recognizes your will and the executor. The courts will record this validation process in a stamped document called a *Grant of Probate*,[222] *Estate Certificate*[223] or *Letters Probate*,[224] or something similar, depending on where you die, because probate processes and the associated taxes/fees are governed by jurisdictional law. The jurisdiction's probate process also sets the rules on what assets within your estate are considered to be subject to probate in order to assess probate tax. I'll refer to this as the *proof of probate*.

This, in some cases, can be a daunting task. For example, in Ontario, one of the steps requires a Ministry of Finance Estate Information Return[225] to be submitted. It is a detailed form and requires considerably more than a best guess on the values of the assets itemized. The time it takes to prepare a probate application will be dependent on the number of assets you hold, the complexity of those assets, the time needed to collect and process the information required for the application steps, and the way that you have structured your will(s) and estate. The time it takes to make its way through the court process depends on how complex your situation is and the court scheduling itself. Note: If the estate is small and simple, it may not require probate – see the rules in your jurisdiction.

Government agencies, financial institutions and third-party institutions will want to see the proof of probate from the court when dealing with the executor, and with good reason. Consider this: The executor goes into your bank branch with your will in hand and asks that they transfer the funds from your account into an estate account so he/she can eventually distribute money to your beneficiaries. Without the proof of probate from the court, the bank can't be sure that the will they're looking at is the original and the valid last version. They will want proof before they start moving money around. The proof of probate from the court provides that. Having said that, financial institutions can release some money before probate to deal with things like funeral costs or the probate tax itself (in accordance with their institution's processes). For the big ticket transactions like transferring funds and distributing assets, they will need to have that proof of probate.

The probate process also protects the executor from liability should another will be found later. It also starts the clock ticking by imposing time limits on claims against the estate. Without probate, your estate could be open to some challenges forever, which could be a huge problem for the executor if he/she has distributed all the money. Should a court challenge be successful, the executor could be held liable.

The downside to the probate process, of course, is that it costs the estate money, usually a percentage of the estate, in taxes often called *fees*. However, look up what the probate taxes are in your jurisdiction; they are not all the same. While some province/territories have set taxes for probate, most jurisdictions base these taxes on the value of the list of the estate assets. The rates, and the estate's dollar value level at which they kick in, vary greatly from jurisdiction to jurisdiction. While specific rules differ by jurisdiction, probate fees apply because of the type, ownership or location of an asset.

Table 2: Illustration of Jurisdictional Probate Differences (assuming estate is worth $200,000)

Alberta[226]	$200,000 would be: $400 (flat fee, the maximum is $525 for any sized estate)
British Columbia[227]	$200,000 would be: $2,250
Manitoba[228]	$200,000 would be: $1,400
Nova Scotia[229]	$200,000 would be: $2,698
Ontario[230]	$200,000 would be: $2,500
Québec[231]	$200,000 would be: $0 (if the will is a Notarial will)

NOTES:

This is illustrative only, so you will need to look up the current formula rates for your jurisdiction for various dollar values and for other fees.

The Ontario Ministry of the Attorney General has a convenient Estate Administration Tax Calculator on their website.[232]

If you search online for "probate fee calculator," there are informational calculators often found on law firm websites or estate-related services within a jurisdiction.

For the executor, the probate process usually involves finding assets, collecting a list of assets, determining the value of those assets and submitting information, such as:

- your original will;

- your death certificate;

- a list of your assets that are subject to probate, such as your bank accounts, house and anything of financial value (those defined by the jurisdiction as being subject to probate); and

- names and address of the beneficiaries in your will.[233]

It can take weeks or months for the executor to gather the required information and complete the probate process steps required by the jurisdiction. Just getting a list of assets subject to probate and assessing their value (their fair market value at the date of death) can eat up a lot of time, especially if you haven't prepared a list of assets for the executor.

Also, in some jurisdictions (*e.g.*, British Columbia), the executor may also need to send each potential beneficiary[234] – those who aren't named in your will, but would have likely been a beneficiary in an intestate situation (without a will) under jurisdictional estate law (in British Columbia, during the probate process, these people are called *Heirs-at-Law/Persons Served*[235]) – a copy of your will and obtain confirmation they got it, which can also eat up a lot of time and effort tracking people down.

There are also useful publications on provincial and territorial websites, law firms' websites, and Self Counsel Press[236] to help you understand what's involved. While there are do-it-yourself forms that the executor can use and submit as probate documents, some jurisdictions require a legal advisor to make a submission on your estate's behalf. Therefore, it's wise to set the executor up with a legal advisor to help prepare and submit probate documents. This could be the legal advisor who drafted your will and knows your estate, but not necessarily so.

For probate planning purposes, some people put assets in joint ownership with the right of survivorship. While it seems convenient to put assets in joint ownership with a person, it can lead to misuse and abuse, according to several Globe and Mail articles, one called "Ten Reasons Why Joint Ownership May Be Problematic,"[237] and another called "In Estate Planning, Know the Hazards of Joint Ownership."[238] Generally, a good rule of thumb on joint ownership is this: If someone is trying to convince you to put your asset in joint ownership with them, a red flag should pop up. Go get legal and tax advice.

Canadian Generic
Probate Process
(If required for your particular estate situation)

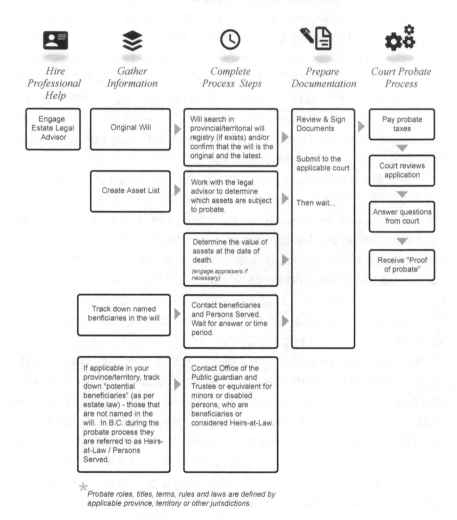

Hire Professional Help	*Gather Information*	*Complete Process Steps*	*Prepare Documentation*	*Court Probate Process*
Engage Estate Legal Advisor	Original Will	Will search in provincial/territorial will registry (if exists) and/or confirm that the will is the original and the latest.	Review & Sign Documents	Pay probate taxes
	Create Asset List	Work with the legal advisor to determine which assets are subject to probate.	Submit to the applicable court	Court reviews application
		Determine the value of assets at the date of death. *(engage appraisers if necessary)*	Then wait...	Answer questions from court
	Track down named benficiaries in the will	Contact beneficiaries and Persons Served. Wait for answer or time period.		Receive "Proof of probate"
	If applicable in your province/territory, track down "potential beneficiaries" (as per estate law) - those that are not named in the will. In B.C. during the probate process they are referred to as Heirs-at-Law / Persons Served.	Contact Office of the Public guardian and Trustee or equivalent for minors or disabled persons, who are beneficiaries or considered Heirs-at-Law.		

Probate roles, titles, terms, rules and laws are defined by applicable province, territory or other jurisdictions.

2. The Big Death Tax Bills: *The cost of cashing in.*

Where do the big death tax bills come from? Simply put, every asset you own is deemed to have been disposed of on the day you die (deemed disposed). In other words, all your assets are deemed to have been "cashed in" and will be taxed as if you sold them on the day you stopped breathing. The government will tax you as if everything you have – every house, stock, gold bar, everything of financial value – has been sold. While, obviously, those items aren't really sold (as the ownership of all your assets remains in your estate until it is disposed of or passed along to someone else), you will have to pay all the tax on the deemed "sale" or the deemed "withdrawal."[239]

What is capital property versus an income account? It depends on the asset you hold and why you hold it. There's a distinction between *deemed disposed* as it applies to capital property and an income account. Think of real estate, like your house or cottage, as capital property, and think of income from investments or your registered plans (RRSPs, RSPs, RIFs) as an income account. Stocks are often treated as capital property, but they are also, in some cases, considered an income account; it is not clear cut. In the case of someone who regularly buys land or real estate on speculation and flips it, that real estate might be treated as income property, not capital property. A day trader might be viewed as owning stocks as business income. The distinction is important because capital property has historically been taxed more favour-ably than an income account. To determine whether your assets are income assets or capital assets requires investigation, advice from a tax advisor or a call to the Canada Revenue Agency.[240]

As with all matters related to tax, there are rules, more rules and changing rules. The point is this: The treatment of your assets could be completely different than that of someone else in a similar situation with similar assets. So, if you hear someone describe the tax treatment of their particular assets, it may or may not apply to your situation. Only some research on your part, or a discussion with a tax advisor or the Canada Revenue Agency, will determine what it means for you.

The Big Death Tax Bills: The Cost of Cashing in the Form of Capital Gains on Assets

As I've explained, a capital gain is the dollar value difference between what you bought an asset for (cost of asset) and when you sold it (proceeds of sale) or it is deemed disposed when you die (assuming the asset goes up in value – otherwise, it's a capital loss). Capital gains is one of the basic constructs that determines how much tax you may need to pay on disposing of, transferring or selling your capital assets. According to the Canada Revenue Agency, you have a capital gain when you sell, or are considered to have sold (as in death), an asset or property for more than the total of its adjusted cost base and the outlays and expenses incurred to sell it.[241] Common types of capital property include land, buildings, shares, bonds and mutual funds.[242]

Here are a few examples of what can happen. If you think an example with stocks is boring, just substitute in your own cryptocurrency example.

Selling stock (securities) while you are living. Suppose you buy 100 shares of a stock that cost $85 per share, worth $8,500 when you bought them, and later sell them at $95 each, or $9,500:

1. If these shares are considered capital property, in Canada, 50% of your $1,000 gain is subject to taxation in the year of the sale, assuming there are no expenses associated with the sale.

2. $1000 is the capital gain, $500 is the taxable capital gain due to the 50% inclusion rate.

3. If you are in a 25% combined tax bracket (federal and province/territory), you will pay 25% on the $500, which equals $125 in taxes.

4. You're done!

Dealing with your stocks after you died. Here's what happens if you die with the same 100 shares of a stock purchased for $8,500:

1. You die on January 10th, and the stocks are deemed disposed (cashed in) that day.

2. The January 10th market price is $95 per share, or $9,500.

3. The executor lists the stocks as valued at $9,500 and files your T1 Individual Tax Return (Terminal Return), noting a capital gain of the deemed disposed stock as being $1,000. Assuming you're in a 25% combined tax bracket, your estate will pay 25%, on the $500 which equals $125 in taxes.

4. Just to be clear: Your estate will owe $125 in taxes and the stocks have not yet actually been sold. Also, don't be surprised if you are no longer in the 25% tax bracket, when the value of your RRSP/RIF or other capital assets get added to the total income amount.

5. *You may not be done paying, there could be another tax bill!* The $9,500 becomes the new cost base for your estate, the starting point for a future capital gains calculation when the stocks are really sold, or transferred.

6. If the executor sells the stock a year later, by which time it has gone up to $120 per share, for a total value of $12,000, your estate may need to pay more tax on the additional capital gain of $2,500 ($12,000 minus $9,500).

7. With the inclusion rate of 50% of the capital gains being taxable, the estate would pay a further tax on the $1,250 at a rate determined by the estate's tax bracket.

Home sweet home: dealing with your house after you have died.

1. You die on January 10th, and your house is deemed disposed (cashed in) that day. This scenario assumes that the house is in your name only, that it is not a joint asset, and that your will gives instructions to sell it upon your death.

2. When you die, the house passes to your estate.

3. If you bought the house for $250,000 and the market value is $400,000 on the day you die, there will be capital gains of $150,000.

4. If it was your principle residence, as recognized by the Canada Revenue Agency,[243] your estate might be exempt from paying tax on the capital gains.

5. *The house is tax free from capital gains to this point (T1 Terminal Return).* To be eligible for this capital gains deduction, the executor will still need to file and claim the Principal Residence Exemption ("PRE") on your Terminal Return (T1).

6. The $400,000 then becomes the new cost base in your estate for capital gains purposes.

7. *What happens next is a surprise to most executors and beneficiaries.* The executor will put your house on the market weeks, months or years after you die, because it will likely be impossible to sell it on the exact day you die.

8. Suppose they sell it for $500,000. The $100,000 increase in market value is subject to capital gains, with the inclusion rate of 50%, or $50,000, being the taxable capital gain to your estate. Your estate doesn't qualify for the PRE for the increased value at this point.

9. *Another tax bill on the house when it is finally sold (T3 Trust Return).* The additional $50,000 taxable capital gains will be included in the T3 for the estate as taxable income.

Your cottage at the lake: dealing with your cottage after you have died (two tax bills).

1. Suppose you bought a cottage (or cabin) for $100,000 several years ago, which you use for family weekends and summer vacations. This property is in addition to the house above. This scenario assumes that the cottage is in your name only, that it is not a joint asset, that your will gives

instructions to sell it upon your death, and that the executor has already claimed the PRE on your house.

2. When you die, the cottage passes to your estate.

3. If you bought the cottage for $100,000 and the market value is $300,000 on the day you die, there will be capital gains of $200,000.

4. The executor files your Terminal Return (T1), with the capital gains of $200,000 subject to being taxed, assuming the cottage has not been claimed as your principal residence.

5. *The tax bill for the cottage on death (T1 Terminal Return)*: Your estate would pay tax on 50% (inclusion rate) of the gain, being $100,000 (50% of $200,000).

6. The market value of $300,000 becomes the new cost base for the cottage, the starting point for the next capital gains calculation when it is actually sold.

7. The executor will put your cottage on the market weeks, months or years after you die.

8. Suppose the executor sells it for $350,000. The $50,000 ($350,000-$300,000) increase in market value is subject to capital gains, with the inclusion rate of 50%, or $25,000, being the taxable capital gains.

9. *The second tax bill for the cottage when sold (T3 Terminal Return)*: The additional $25,000 will be included in the T3 for the estate and taxed at the tax bracket of the estate.

One last word on the PRE. The PRE is claimed upon sale, deemed disposition (as in death), or transfer of property, on a year-by-year basis. There is a form you complete with a year-by-year declaration. If you own several properties where you live (*e.g.*, house and cottage), a tax advisor can help determine if they both meet Canada Revenue Agency rules for the PRE. Although you can only claim one residence in a particular year, you could alternate which residence is claimed as the PRE in a particular year to reduce the capital gains.[244]

Speaking of the cottage (cabin or camp), estate and tax planning for these family retreats in Canada have received more focus and coverage in the last several years due to the estate planning challenges and tax treatment considerations, as the example above illustrates. Among a number of articles by multiple media outlets, the 2018 early summer edition of *Cottage Life* had an article called "Have You Had the Talk? – some smart strategies for handing down the cottage to your kids," with 8 pages dedicated to the topic of dealing with taxes and cottage succession.[245]

When you sell a cottage, you can reduce the amount of taxable capital gains by claiming eligible costs for specific upgrades and enhancements, such as hiring a contractor to put on an addition. Be prepared to back those claims up with detailed receipts and explanations. The same applies after you've died, so make sure the executor will have access to the receipts for the work done so they can be added as adjusted cost base additions, thus reducing the total gain. Again, this points to the need for keeping good records and reviewing them with the executor.

Note: At the time this book was being written, the capital gains inclusion rate was 50%. Furthermore, I haven't included any discussion about owning a business, but it is worthwhile to note that there are other capital gains exemptions that can be claimed for qualified farm property, fishing property and small business corporations in Canada. The Canada Revenue Agency has information on what qualifies and how to claim, and you'll want to seek tax planning advice if it might apply to you.[246]

The Big Death Tax Bills: Income Surprises Can Drive Up Taxes

Remember the happy dance you did when you contributed to your RRSP and got a tax refund? Every dollar put into a RRSP was a dollar off your annual taxable income for that year, and was sheltered as such. The point of a RRSP is that when you withdraw the funds down the road, normally after you have retired, it will be taxed at a lower rate, as you expect your overall taxable income to be lower in retirement.[247]

The balances remaining in your RRSP and/or RIF when you die is taxed as if you cashed in (withdrew) the entire amount minutes before you died. This means the entire value of the plan(s) at your date of death is included as a lump sum into the taxable income of your Terminal Return (T1). So, if you have a significant amount left in your RRSP and/or RIF, it will drive up the amount of income in the Terminal Return (T1) – likely subjecting you to higher rates of tax.

There is a tax deferral rollover opportunity to your spouse or common-law partner, but only if you designate them as your beneficiary (in your RRSP[248]) or your beneficiary/successor annuitant (in your RIF[249]) or your will. The future tax liability is now in the hands of the new registered plan owner. It's worth noting that there are also some exceptions for naming financially dependent minors and financially dependent disabled children as beneficiaries. You'll need to work with a tax advisor to understand who is eligible and how these rules work. Note that beneficiary designations work differently in Québec, so check with your province/territory.

Registered Plans Are Not All the Same

Don't get fooled into thinking one registered plan works like another, or that the terms are the same. There are even differences between an RRSP[250] and an RIF[251] in definitions, terms, tax reporting, and how your spouse/common-law partner can take over a plan (*i.e.*, beneficiary vs. successor annuitant). This also applies to the lesser known Registered Disability Saving Plan ("RDSP").[252] When it comes to Registered Education Saving Plans ("RESP"),[253] if you are the original subscriber and not a joint owner, or haven't named a *successor subscriber*, then the plan collapses when you die. The government gets its contribution back and the remaining amount is included in your estate and distributed as per your will. You need to ask questions about how the plan works for your situation on your death.

3. Post-Mortem Tax Planning: *The "gottas" & some "breaks."*

Part of the executor's job is to develop a plan to comply with tax filing forms/requirements, tax payment deadlines, and a plan to optimize the amount of taxes that the estate will pay. The planning activity is referred to by the estate industry as *post-mortem tax planning* or *post-mortem planning*. If you thought the executor had to file only one final tax return after you die, surprise! There are many forms to be filed and several things that need to be done.

The Canada Revenue Agency gives you a "break" on a few tax rules when you die, which is one more reason why the executor should consider getting a tax advisor who understands estates, in order to optimize the tax bill, if at all possible.[254] As one example, if you have *net capital loss carry forwards* (which are unused losses on capital from prior years), or losses in the year of death, and are not able to apply it against capital gains, they can be used to offset any income in the year of death, and 1 year prior. For all your living years, you can only use capital losses against capital gains. In addition, as you'll read in Chapter 9, there is favorable treatment of charitable donations.

Also, the Canada Revenue Agency gives special consideration to whether you have designated your spouse/common-law partner as your beneficiary for a specific asset, such as your home or a RRSP account, or named them in your will.[255] In general, when you die, your estate can roll over your assets tax free to your beneficiary spouse/common-law partner. However, you can't afford to be sloppy about the paperwork – if you get married, separate, divorce, re-marry or become common-law, update the applicable paperwork to reflect your new situation. Your bank or registered plan holder won't know that your marital situation has changed, unless you tell them.[256] Think about the nightmare for your second spouse/common-law partner if you leave your first spouse/common-law partner as the beneficiary on your life insurance policy or your registered plan. The second spouse/common-law partner is not likely to get the asset without going to court. Even then, who knows what the outcome will be?[257]

With joint ownership, things get complicated and your estate could get a tax bill. Jointly owned assets or property can get messy when it comes to your tax bill at death, as I found out dealing with my mother's rental property. What happens tax-wise, depends on several factors, including:

- the type of joint ownership you have (*i.e.*, tenancy in common versus joint tenancy, rights of survivorship);

- the relationship you have with the surviving owner (are they your spouse/common-law partner, or not);

- whether it qualifies as a principal residence;

- who paid what for the property;

- what is documented about the ownership;

- what your will says;

- post-mortem tax planning decisions; and

- the laws in the jurisdiction where your property is located.

Unfortunately, there is no nice clean formula here – only something a legal advisor and tax advisor can help you sort out for your specific situation. Furthermore, if you live in, or have property in Québec, you'll also need a Québec legal advisor because rights of survivorship of joint property ownership and beneficiary designations are not recognized in Québec like in other common law jurisdictions.[258]

4. Tax Filing Surprises

Completing all the necessary tax forms can be a lot of work for the executor.[259] The most daunting part is that everything you own at death needs some form of assessment or examination, valuation and calculation, something you likely have never done all at once for everything you own. For example, the executor will need to determine how much an entire stock investment portfolio is worth at the date of death, and its entire adjusted cost base. This can be a considerable reconciliation exercise for the executor. Having some or a partial list of your assets, and any supporting documentation, will most certainly take away some of the burden.[260]

They won't send flowers, but the Canada Revenue Agency wants to know you've died. That will be one of the first forms that the executor will need to file. The executor will need to inform the Canada Revenue Agency that you have died, and that they are acting as your legal representative.[261] There is basic information the Canada Revenue Agency will want copies of, such as copies of your will, your death certificate and the probate document (if applicable).[262]

Sometimes the surprise for the executor starts with the work required to ascertain all your assets and figure out what you own, before they get on with assessing. If you are dealing with a deceased person in Québec, in addition to the federal tax forms, there is another whole set of tax forms to be completed as well. Provincial taxation in Québec is not managed by the Canada Revenue Agency, as it is in the other common law jurisdictions.[263]

The executor will need to confirm that you are up to date on tax filings and payments. If not, he/she will have to file tax returns for any years that you didn't file, and pay any taxes due (with interest) from your estate. This is more common than you might think. If a person's health fails them in the years before their death, taxes could go unfiled, leaving executors to catch up on prior years' returns. There can be advantages, however. For example, even if someone didn't cross the taxable income threshold, an executor could file for possible GST/HST rebates (by filing prior return) for up to 10 years before death. He/she would have to decide whether to make the trade-off in terms of the effort and the cost to file non-required prior years' tax returns, of course. Regardless, the executor will still need to confirm with the Canada Revenue Agency what previous tax returns, if any, are required.

T1 Individual Tax Return (the Terminal Return or Final Return)

As I indicated previously, the form that the executor needs to fill out is the T1 Individual Tax Return, which is referred to as your *Terminal Return* or *Final Return*. It's essentially the same form you file as an individual every year, except that the assessment period is from January 1st to the date of your death. For example, if you die on March 1st, a T1 will be required for the period from January 1st to March 1st. This tax return is due within a specific time period after you die. Consult the Canada Revenue Agency website for specifics on filing requirements and deadlines.[264]

As there won't likely be neat statements that line up with that period, the executor will have to make inquiries and perform calculations on your financial/taxable situation during that abbreviated year.

There are other optional tax returns to cover different types of situations that arise because of death. One return is referred to as the *Return for Rights or Things*. It catches situations that should have been on the Terminal Return (T1), but didn't make it in for specific circumstances allowable by the Canada Revenue Agency.[265]

T3 Statement of Trust Income Allocations and Designations Tax Return(s)

There are more tax forms to be filled out after the executor files the Terminal Return (T1). Anything that happens after your date of death is considered part of your estate. For tax purposes, your estate is considered a trust by the Canada Revenue Agency, with the executor as the trustee who looks after it (as opposed to a separate trust you might set up in your will, called a *testamentary trust*).[266] Every estate must file a *T3 Statement of Trust Income Allocations and Designations* to account for any money or income the estate earns, from the date of death until all the assets are sold or transferred and the estate is wound up.[267]

A T3 is required every year until the estate is wound up. How long can an estate possibly last? I heard of an executor whose father had re-married and made a provision in his will for his second wife to live in the house for as long as she wanted or until her death, at which time it was to be sold and the proceeds split among the executor and his siblings. The second wife lived for another 25 years. Because the father had not put the house in a separate testamentary trust to be handled by a separate trustee, it was left to the executor to take care of as part of the will and estate – a two-and-a-half-decade estate headache.

T3 Statement of Trust Income Allocations and Designations Tax Return(s) – the Graduated Rate Estate

Again, your estate is considered a trust by the Canada Revenue Agency, with a unique set of rules that apply. Provided it meets Canada Revenue Agency requirements, an estate is called and recognized as a Graduated Rate Estate ("GRE"),[268] meaning that the taxes owed in a year are levied as graduated (sometime called *marginal*) rates, similar to how an individual is taxed. It's an upward sliding scale. The more money the estate is worth, the higher the tax rates. However, the graduated rates apply only for the first 36 months after death. However, after 3 years, the estate is taxed at the highest rate, which means the executor will be under time pressure to sell any assets and property within the 3 years after your death, or face a higher tax bill for the estate.

Clearance Certificate

Your estate is finished when all your taxes and bills are paid, all your assets are disposed of, and all your beneficiaries are given what they are entitled to, as outlined in the probated will. However, before the executor can distribute cheques to the beneficiaries, he/she must obtain a *Clearance Certificate*[269] from the Canada Revenue Agency (assuming the beneficiaries are Canadian residents; if they are not, there is another set of rules to follow). The executor will be responsible for any taxes owing if they distributed the proceeds from your estate without first getting a Clearance Certificate. Further to this, getting a Clearance Certificate does not preclude the Canada Revenue Agency from re-assessing your estate down the road and going after your beneficiaries if further tax is owed.[270]

Canadian Generic
Tax Filing Process

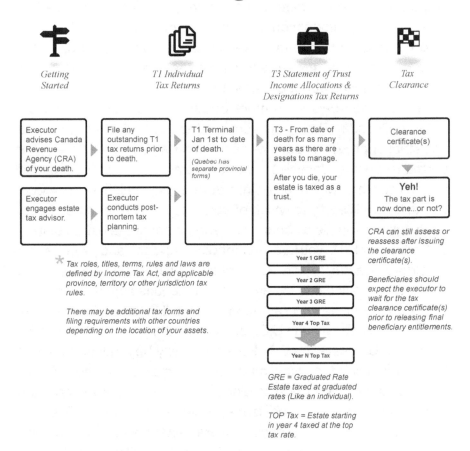

| Getting Started | T1 Individual Tax Returns | T3 Statement of Trust Income Allocations & Designations Tax Returns | Tax Clearance |

Canada Revenue Agency has a convenient one stop webpage resource for executors called "Individuals – Executors," where they list all the applicable guides, forms and other publications.[271]

5. Asset Location Can Trigger Other Taxes: *Where your assets reside (called situs) can attract additional taxes and fees even if you are a Canadian resident.*

Legally important is the physical location of where your assets are considered to be. It is called *situs*, a Latin word for site. If you live and die in one province/territory and have an asset, such as a cottage or cabin, in another province/territory, you should inquire on what laws apply and what extra estate planning options and steps should be considered. In addition, you'll likely want to know what additional information or processes the executor will need to follow, and any probate taxes/fees that may occur (if applicable). Who your beneficiaries are and where they live also matters, and we are just talking about Canada here.

The situation gets even more complicated if you have assets outside Canada. There are some rather complicated laws and rules that apply upon death, depending on what is considered your permanent home (domicile), your temporary home (residence) and your citizenship, which factor into determining which jurisdictional estate laws will apply to which of your assets. Furthermore, it gets even uglier if you die without a will and an adequate estate plan.

For example: If you are a Canadian resident and own assets outside of Canada, such as stocks or real estate, they may be subject to additional taxes and fees in the jurisdiction where they reside upon your death, in addition to Canadian taxes. For example, if you own property in the U.S., on your death, your estate could be subject to U.S. estate tax. The executor may be required to file an U.S. estate tax return. How much tax you may pay in the U.S. will depend on your worldwide holdings, because there are exemption levels. Consult with a tax advisor knowledgeable about U.S. estate tax requirements, as part of your overall estate planning. The good news is that Canada has tax treaties with specific countries that often have negotiated credits and exemptions that might allow taxes you paid to another country to be recognized back home in Canada (so that it can be claimed on your Canadian tax return).[272]

This is just the tax view. For assets that are located outside Canada, you'll need to understand what other official documentation and legal processes the executor may be required to deal with when he/she goes to sell or transfer that property upon your death. This is something only a qualified professional advisor with cross-border legal and tax advisory expertise can help you with.

The same applies to any relationship you have with any other country. Don't assume another country's estate and tax rules are the same as Canada's. In fact, *assume they are different* and plan for it.

Your Digital Undertaker:
Project Management Checklist Applied to Chapter 8

1. Scope: *Why are you doing this?*

Estate planning to optimize and minimize taxes is complicated, but to boil it down to the basics, you need to do three things. First, prepare a list of your assets, confirm the ownership, document the price you paid for it (adjusted cost base), review beneficiary designations and keep really good records and receipts as things change. Second, work with an estate tax advisor to work out an overall estate tax plan. Third, bring the executor into the loop.

2. Options & Trade-Offs: *What are the pros and cons?*

How detailed your tax plans need to be depends on how complicated your personal relationships are. People with second or third marriages and/or common-law relationships, children from any marriage and stepchildren, may have more thinking to do than those married to their first spouse/common-law partner. Of course, how extensive your assets are and where they are located will have an impact on how comprehensive your tax and estate planning needs to be.

3. Preferences & Costs: *What do you need and what's it going to cost?*

There really is no simple way to reduce or defer taxes to be paid at death. There are many books dedicated to optimizing taxes and even more editions that attempt to keep up with changing tax laws, but they are not light reading for most of us. Tax planning, as part of estate planning, requires a holistic and informed process with qualified tax advisors with estate expertise.

4. Procurement of Professional Services: *Your body can't bury itself!*

As I said previously, engaging a qualified estate tax advisor – a legal advisor or tax advisor with experience in estate taxation and estate planning/administration – is a very good idea. It will cost your estate money in professional fees, but could save much more in reduced taxes or it can help you avoid estate litigation.

5. Risks: *What are the risks? What are the backup plans?*

Tax rules change yearly, so even the best laid tax plans for your estate will have to be updated. Once you die, they may need to be adapted by the executor as they complete post-mortem tax planning.

6. Communication: *It is on a need-to-know basis and someone needs to know!*

The easiest way to avoid paying more taxes than necessary is to make sure the executor has the information they need. Just as they need access to your will, they also need access to your previously filed taxes and documentation on your assets. This includes information about how to deal with assets held in another jurisdiction or another country. You should make sure the executor is aware that you hold assets that are eligible for the capital gains exemption, or if you have capital losses from prior years that can be applied.

In Passing

When you use a tax advisor to do your taxes, you fill in a form to tell the Canada Revenue Agency that the advisor is acting on your behalf. When you die, this form is no longer valid. The executor will need to sign another form to engage your tax advisor, or whoever they engage, to submit forms and deal with the Canada Revenue Agency on your estate's behalf.[273]

Chapter 9
Don't Forget Me When I'm Gone

Do you want to leave a little something behind so you're not forgotten? Is there a cause or charity that you feel strongly enough about to provide it with some of the proceeds of your lifetime assets? Maybe you were the beneficiary of someone else's generosity at some point in your life and would like to pay it forward. Also, donating time or money is a good way to demonstrate to the next generation that there is much more to life.

As it turns out, Canadians are very giving. According to Statistics Canada, "82% of Canadians 15 years and older made donations to a charitable or non-profit organization."[274] Collectively, it all makes a big difference and donation contributions rose 23% in the 9 years between surveys to a total of $12.8 billion in 2013:

> When asked about the reasons for donating, the vast majority (91%) of donors said they felt compassion towards people in need. The other reasons often cited include the idea of helping a cause in which they personally believed (88%) and wanting to make a contribution to their community (82%).[275]

Tax benefits

Something you're passionate about

Why Give? Why Leave a Legacy?

Support your favourite charity

Pass down family history/genealogy

Inspiring your family and future generations

Support your favourite non-profit organization

Carry on a family tradition

The (Tax) Advantages of Altruism

Beyond altruism, there are tax benefits to consider. If you leave a registered charity – as in registered with the Canada Revenue Agency – a donation in your will by specifying them as a beneficiary, your estate gets the donation tax receipt when the gift is made.[276] And there are very favourable rules for that donation in terms of the percentage allowed and there is greater flexibility, in that the donation can be carried back and carried forward in addition to your Terminal Return (T1) – see Canada Revenue Agency for the specific rules.[277] This can matter for estates in which real estate or other assets don't get sold for several years.

Like everything else in taxation, there are rules that must be followed, so it is important to review the current options and the tax implications with your tax advisor. The Canada Revenue Agency also recognizes securities and capital property for gifting purposes.[278] Your estate plan should include details of any contemplated tax treatment instructions so the executor has a roadmap to follow.

Coming to Terms with the Terms

Planned giving is also known as charitable planning, gift planning, philanthropic planning, gifting through will and estate planning, or legacy giving. This means your goals are documented, planned and communicated in a gift plan, to be executed during your lifetime, after you pass, or both. It involves defining your charitable or philanthropic wishes, evaluating the options, selecting a charitable organization or non-profit organization to make it happen, and choosing a method of donation, such as a direct contribution or via a donor advised fund (which I will explain shortly).

The words *charity* and *philanthropy* are often used interchangeably. One of the best definitions I heard is that philanthropy is *something you do of value outside the circle of yourself, your family and the people you love*.

There are two kinds of entities that Canadians recognize in charitable giving and philanthropy, according to Canada Revenue Agency's website: *registered charities*[279] and *non-profit organizations*,[280] but there are differences:

- By law, a charity must do one or more of the following four things:[281] relieve poverty, advance education, advance religion or benefit a community, and in doing so, it must also meet the public benefit test – it must be registered with the Canada Revenue Agency and issue donation receipts for income tax purposes. A charity can be a private foundation, a public foundation or a charitable organization.

- Non-profit organizations (or non-profits) are associations, clubs or societies "organized and operated exclusively for social welfare, civic improvement, pleasure, recreation, or any other purpose except profit" and non-profit organizations may do equally important societal work as a charity, but can't issue donation receipts for income tax purposes.[282]

There is no shortage of either – there are over 170,000 charities and non-profits in Canada, of which 86,000 are registered charities.[283]

Where to Begin Doing Good?

First, are you sure you have enough? This is likely the first question your estate advisor will ask. It is important to stop and assess your capability to leave something behind. Work with your various estate advisors (*i.e.*, legal, tax, insurance, financial advisors) to determine whether you're in a position to give.

Next, if you are going to give your hard-earned money away to a charity or non-profit, make sure it will be going to an organization or cause that you believe in and feel good about. I consistently heard from those I talked to about how important it is to take the time to decide what it is you value, what is important to you, and what impact you want to make. If you are starting from scratch, volunteering is a good way to check out an organization to see if what they are doing aligns with your values.

Additionally, volunteerism extends into many other roles that could benefit from your skills or working life experience. In addition to the traditional volunteer roles, these organizations may have leadership or board roles open. They may also need to fill positions in a variety of other business-like roles, such as skilled tradespeople, office support, data entry and IT skills. If you are open to searching for roles, obviously going directly to a charity or non-profit is the best starting point. As an example, the two online platforms I found for searching for roles were CharityVillage (click on "Volunteer")[284] or Volunteer Canada (click on "Volunteer Centre").[285] If you are interested in board education focused on charity or non-profit board roles, see the Canadian Board Diversity Council ("CBDC").[286] If you just want to dip your toe into what's going on in the charity space, check out Giving Tuesday, a national day of giving after Black Friday and Cyber Monday. Starting in the U.S., it has migrated to Canada.[287] Travelling to do volunteer work seems to be the new thing, and how about pet therapy?[288]

The Canadian Association of Gift Planners ("CAGP"),[289] a national non-profit organization whose members are involved in gift planning, collaborated with the GIV3 Foundation,[290] a non-profit that encourages Canadians to donate, volunteer and inspire others, and Philanthropic Foundations Canada,[291] an association that includes private and public foundations, charities and corporations, to produce *A Guide for Professional Financial Advisors: The Philanthropic Conversation*.[292] While the target audience is professionals, it contains enlightening material for the rest of us. It is available online. The CAGP also has a campaign called *LEAVE A LEGACY*™.[293] You may have seen their special features in your local newspaper. Their inserts have a number of articles aimed at encouraging you to consider gift planning.

The Traditional Donor Pyramid: Where Do You Fit?

Some charities and non-profits use a form of the donor pyramid model for classifying donors and raising funds.[294] There are many different variants and terminology used to describe the donor pyramid model – generically, it starts with a bottom layer with the ad hoc, occasional or one-time donations, overlaid by the middle layer of annual or regular donations and/or larger donations. At the very top of the pyramid sits the legacy or planned gifts – those gifts left to them by estates. Charities spend a lot of time and energy in *stewardship*, in the charity vernacular, encouraging donors to move up the pyramid, trying to convince ad hoc or occasional givers to become regular ones, and regular ones to make larger donations. They are especially keen to turn supporters into planned givers who will leave a legacy gift (*i.e.*, large gifts now, or specified in their will).

Generic Donor Pyramid

● *Coveted Legacy Donor*
Considered the pinnacle of donations.

A significant gift

● *Regular Contribution*
You donate monthly or annually to a specific cause.

A donation given on a regular basis

● *Ad Hoc Donation*
You respond to a plea, attend a charity event or get hit up at a store cash register.

An impromptu donation

If you're already contributing to a charity or non-profit, and decide to make a gift through your will or estate plan, it might be a good idea to call them up to see if they have a professional gift planner you can talk to. Again, you'll want to review your gift plans with your estate advisors before committing to anything, because there are many options, pros, cons, risks and tax treatments to consider. Here are a few examples:

- If you plan to donate to charity and expect a receipt for income tax purposes, it could backfire if the charity isn't registered with the Canada Revenue Agency or if, sometime down the road, they lose their registration.

- If you made plans to donate to a charity that is no longer in existence – say it folds or is assumed by another organization – and you haven't left an alternate, it could lead to challenges that might require court intervention.

- Suppose you decide to leave one-quarter of your estate to a charity and the rest to your three adult children. You've just put that charity on equal footing with your kids (as a 25% stakeholder in your estate). When you leave a charity with a residual gift versus a fixed dollar gift, they will have the same beneficiary rights, which means they can ask the executor about how he/she is managing the estate, they will get to sign off on estate expenses, and if they are not happy, can ask the courts to get involved.

- If you commit funds to a charity, but are vague on the exact name of the charity, multiple charities could potentially fight over your donation at your estate's expense. You'll want to confirm the correct and exact spelling of the name of the charity, their address and, ideally, their registration number. As an experiment, I searched using the basic search function for "[Charity Name]" on Canada Revenue Agency's website and was amazed at how many charities have similar charity names but are actually different entities. Try it yourself, search for a word like *cancer*, *heart*, *church* or *animal* to see the list of different registered charities that have just that one word in their name.

Doing Some Homework on the Charity before You Donate

The CBC news article titled "Check Charity before You Give" encourages Canadians to research the charity before donating, as "some charities have more impact than others."[295] There are a couple of resources I discovered that can give you more information about a charity or non-profit if you are planning to do some research in advance:

- As you might with any other business, you can ask the charity or non-profit directly for financial information on how they are using the donations (gifts). In addition, you'll want to understand if their program and strategic direction are aligned with where you want to apply your gift.

- You can go directly to the Canada Revenue Agency's List of Charities[296] where you can not only see if a charity is registered and get its registration number, but also learn how it spends its money.

- *MoneySense,* an online magazine and website, publishes an annual Charity 100 list where they grade Canada's leading charities based on fundraising costs, charity efficiency, governance and cash reserves.[297]

- One interesting website I was referred to was Blumberg Segal LLP's website directory on Canadian charity statistics called CharityData.[298] Their website encourages you to go to the Canada Revenue Agency's List of Charities for current data, but they claim CharityData is much easier to use if you're looking for past data. When you enter the name of a Canadian charity, it provides summary data, such as revenue, total expenditures and detailed historical data (across a number of elements such as staff, fundraising, assets and programs).[299] I found staff statistics and top 10 highest paid employees to be the most interesting piece of information.

- Another interesting website was Charity Intelligence Canada Ci, which has charity data on their tool called CharityIntelligence.[300] When you enter the name of a Canadian charity, it provides a charity rating, grade and spending breakdown, amongst other analytics over the past several years.

- Canadian Donor's Guide to fundraising organizations in Canada is published online annually.[301] Their website features that their guide includes "data on charities collected by questionnaire as well as pertinent editorial content."[302]

When you start planning out your estate plan, whether it's with a bank, financial institution, a trust company or your financial planner, the subject of philanthropy is likely to come up. It just will. In my opinion, you ought to be prepared so that it isn't sprung on you, like at the grocery store counter where you're made to feel guilty for not contributing $2 to a cause (even though you might be a volunteer at said cause). The more you have thought about your charitable or philanthropic goals, the less likely you will be caught unprepared when professionals raise the conversation.

If nothing else, think of the executor. If you misspell the name of the charity, don't name a backup charity, or don't give the executor the power to name an alternative, it might very well lead to much frustration and wasted time which will likely run up bills (*e.g.*, legal fees, court costs) to be paid out of the estate.

How to Donate

| *Directly* | *Indirectly* |

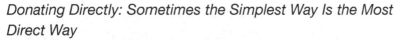

• *Registered Charitable Organization* Donate directly through will	• *Charitable Trust*
• *Non-Profit Organzation* Donate directly through will	• *Charitable Remainder Trust*
• *Insurance Policy* Name charity or non-profit as beneficiary	• *Set up your own Foundation*
• *Registered Plans* Name charity or non-profit as beneficiary	• *Donor Advised Funds (DAF)*

Donating Directly: Sometimes the Simplest Way Is the Most Direct Way

For any amount of money, from a small gift to a large gift, the simplest way to leave a gift is to donate it directly to the charity or non-profit. Your estate advisors will likely bring this up during estate planning, and you can ask them what the available options are, depending on what assets you have and the size of your estate.

Some examples:

1. *Donate directly to a registered charitable organization by naming them as a beneficiary in your will.* This can be eligible for an official donation receipt for income tax purpose. You'll have to confirm that they are registered with Canada Revenue Agency.

2. *Donate directly to a non-profit organization by naming them as a beneficiary in your will.* This won't be eligible for an official donation receipt for income tax purposes, but it might still be important enough to you.

3. *Donate directly by buying insurance.* Insurance offers options as part of a planned giving strategy. For example, you can name a charity as a beneficiary of an insurance policy, or you can sign over the ownership of the policy, and receive tax receipts for the annual premiums you pay. Again, check with your insurance advisor and tax advisor on the rules.

4. *Donate directly using your registered plan(s).* You can make a charity the beneficiary of your RRSP, RIF or tax-free savings account. Be aware, though, that like any planned giving, this can get tricky in terms of how to do it correctly in order to not have unintended legal or tax consequences. Get some estate tax advice.

Donating Indirectly: When Direct Doesn't Work – Donating through Intermediaries or Other Legal Structures or Organizations

There might be a variety of reasons when donating directly to a charitable organization or non-profit doesn't work for you. Some of those reasons may include that the gift is too large for the charity to handle all at once, that you would rather donate a gift over time (deferred), that you want to protect your privacy, or that you want others to make the gifting decisions along the way.

Beyond a straight, one-time donation to a charity, there are lots of ways – and some surprising ones – to give your money away.

And, as mentioned above, the planned gift doesn't necessarily need to be money – it can be securities or other things, like real estate or works of art.

Again, any choice involving planned giving, regardless of what it is, requires the same estate professionals that you would engage with other giving, such as a legal advisor, financial advisor, tax advisor, and in this case, a gift planner (depending on the charitable or non-profit organization you are dealing with).

Here are some other options available to give you a sense that there are a variety of choices:

- *Create a charitable trust.* You can set up a charitable trust while you are living or in your will as a testamentary trust. Just like many other trusts, you transfer assets irrevocably to the trustee and a trust deed outlines your charitable wishes. As with all trusts, there are lots of legal and tax rules involved.

- *Create a charitable remainder trust.* This is a trust in which you transfer property (asset), such as a house or an investment portfolio, to a trustee. The trust deed sets out that you are the life beneficiary, where you can live in the house or get the investment income while you are alive – upon your death, the asset goes to the specifically named charity. As with all trusts, there lots of legal and tax rules involved.

- *Start your own foundation.* If you feel strongly about a particular cause and you want to control how the money gets applied, then you could consider creating a foundation. This is not for everyone, as you'll need a minimum of $2 million to $3 million, depending on what you want that foundation to do and where the funds for the ongoing costs are going to come from. Setting up a foundation is not much different than setting up a business – there are many compliance requirements and it will require ongoing administration. However, many financial institutions and high net worth management companies have philanthropy consultants/advisors on staff, or on a referral basis, who can help you out on this.

- *Use a Donor Advised Fund ("DAF") mechanism through another foundation.* Donor advised funds are not new, but are relatively unknown. Basically, you make the donation to a foundation that distributes the money.

More Detail on the Donor Advised Fund Mechanism

Donor advised funds allow you to make a donation to a foundation that then distributes the money via bursaries, endowment funds or grants. Some gifting plans can have the flexibility to change who receives the donation in any year and can involve engaging your family in the decision making. The administration and overhead costs are managed by the foundation and there are fees associated with those activities. Such funds are a practical alternative to setting up your own foundation or charitable trust. Also, some people use donor advised funds because they don't want to deal with a single charity directly, or they want to protect their privacy or remain anonymous.

The "traditional" donor advised fund involves donating a capital asset that generates income. That income is what is distributed to the charity. The donation of capital generates an endowment fund that creates a lasting legacy, which makes it an ideal estate planning option, in that the capital can be real estate or an investment portfolio.

Here's an example: Suppose you are committed to animal welfare and have donated annually to a local animal shelter. You want to leave a legacy in your will so that money is donated every year to three different shelters. You don't have enough money to set up a foundation, nor do you see it as cost effective to set up a charitable trust. You could meet with an already existing foundation and develop a gifting plan. You review this plan with your legal advisor and your tax advisor. After your death, the executor will transfer the gift to the foundation, who will execute it according to your documented wishes, which could include guidance on how you expect the shelters to be selected. The foundation would continue to give money to three different shelters every year.

Another example: When you went to university, college, vocational or trade school you might have applied for and received a grant or bursary for that school. With donor advised funds, you can return the favour and set up an annual grant for a deserving student. You meet with the commercially-affiliated or community-based foundation, draw up a plan and decide on an annual grant. Of course, you can always go to the educational institution to determine if they have a donor program aligned with your wishes, in which you deal with the institution directly.

Donor advised funds are an interesting option if you don't have a specific charity in mind or if you have several charities that you want to provide donations to over a period of time. (However, if you know the charity or charities and want to give them a lump sum, you can still use a community-based foundation for this, too.)

There are also commercially-affiliated foundations, like the aforementioned community-based foundations. Some also offer options to facilitate gifts to other registered charities. Both the commercially-affiliated and community-based foundation will work with you to set up donor advised funds. The minimum starting point is usually in the range of $10,000 to $50,000, depending on the foundation and what you are trying to accomplish.

Some organizations that can offer Donor Advised Funds:

- *Donate to a community foundation.* If you don't have a specific charity in mind and want to donate to a specific cause in your community, you can approach a private or public foundation. One type of community foundation can be under the umbrella of The Community Foundations of Canada website,[303] which lists more than 190 community foundation members. Community Foundations of Canada members pride themselves in their understanding of the local community needs. Vancouver Foundation, as an example, is one of the largest foundations in the Community Foundations of Canada network.

- *Donate to a commercially-affiliated foundation.* Planned giving is now big business and many of the major banks, financial institutions and wealth management companies have either sponsored charitable foundations or forged relationships with existing ones as their philanthropic arm, or as part their charity ecosystem.

- *Donate through an online charitable platform or financial technology-based intermediary.* I'll refer this category as *charity tech* or *charity online.* These online accessible foundations basically let you donate cash (*i.e.*, you have $100 or $1,000 and you donate it). They also let you defer your charitable decision. For example, you know you want to donate $1,000 and get the tax receipt right away, but are not sure *where* you want to donate right away. You can donate through one of these standalone organizations (as a flow through), get the tax receipt and then make the decision on which charity down the road. Another example: if you have $1,000 and want to donate to more than one charity, it can be done easily online as well. Here are a few examples:

  ○ *Charitable Impact Foundation (CHIMP Technology Inc.)* – They allow an individual donor to sign up and donate on their online platform to Canadian charities.[304]

  ○ *CanadaHelps.org* – They offer one-stop shopping to donate online to Canadian charities on their platform. They have a function that allows the individual donor to donate securities and mutual funds.[305]

You might also be familiar with donating at your workplace through an intermediary, such as a workplace charitable program, that, for example, allows you to select one or more charities and deduct the amount from your paycheck.

The Beauty of Donating Securities, Dead or Alive

As I mentioned above, money isn't your only donation option. You can donate securities – stocks, bonds, mutual funds, exchange traded funds ("ETFs").[306] As part of the research on this topic, I tried and successfully donated stock. It took a website search to confirm that the charity I selected could accept stocks. Then I made a call to that charity to get their form and a quick overview of how the process worked. I also had to fill out another form from my online stockbroker account. Once the stock transferred, I received a donation tax receipt for the full value of the share price at the time of transfer. Then, at the end of the year, there was a special form in my Individual Tax Return (T1) from Canada Revenue Agency that I filled out so I didn't have to pay the capital gains.

What's the benefit of donating securities? You get a tax receipt for the market value of the security on the transfer-in-kind, and don't have to pay capital gains tax on the increase in value from the time you bought the security until the donation. If you want to do this as part of your estate plan as a contribution after death, it's important to document it so that the executor donates the securities to a qualified recipient – versus just cashing it all in and then donating – to get this favourable tax treatment for the estate. You'll want to review this with your legal advisor, financial advisor and tax advisor.

Donating securities directly to a charity, while living or through your will, is also known as *donating-in-kind*.[307] You can donate other things in-kind, such real estate, art, *etc.* The key is that the charity must be willing and able to accept these items in-kind. Even if they do, you'll have to do your homework to figure out the Canada Revenue Agency rules, if you want a donation tax receipt. Talk to the charity and your tax advisor. By the way, the Canada Revenue Agency also recognizes the gifts of ecologically sensitive land[308] and the donations of certified cultural property.[309]

Your Digital Undertaker:
Project Management Checklist Applied to Chapter 9

1. Scope: *Why are you doing this?*

While investigating this topic, time and again I heard from estate planning experts that people should consider charitable giving during their lives, in addition to, or instead of, providing their gift after they've gone. Certainly, there are annual tax benefits when you donate to a registered charitable organization. There is also another perspective: why let someone else get the credit after you die – why not see the impact of your donation while you are living?

2. Options & Trade-Offs: *What are the pros and cons?*

Whether you decide to do it before or after you die, there are a variety of philanthropic options depending on your goal, your budget, your level/degree of expected engagement and the degree of tax planning you would like to do.

3. Preferences & Costs: *What do you need and what's it going to cost?*

What your charitable/philanthropic efforts will require, and what it will cost, will depend entirely on how much you want to give and how you want to give it. Once you have confirmed that you have enough to meet your own needs, you can decide what it is you would like to do.

4. Procurement of Professional Services: *Your body can't bury itself!*

Regardless of what you decide to do and how you decide to do it, you'll want to review any planned giving with your legal advisor, financial advisor and tax advisor. Tax rules change yearly, so even the best laid tax plans for your gift planning will have to be updated as things change. And once you die, they may need to be adapted by the executor as they complete post-mortem tax planning.

5. Risks: *What are the risks? What are the backup plans?*

Giving money away isn't as easy as you'd think. A little bit of due diligence will go a long way to making sure your wishes are fulfilled and your estate is protected from disputes and protracted legal battles.

6. Communication: *It is on a need-to-know basis and someone needs to know!*

Be sure to talk over your charitable or philanthropic plans with your family and those closest to you. If you want to give all your money to a hospice for dogs, this should not come as a surprise to them later. The easiest way to ensure your estate gets the tax benefits of your charitable or philanthropic planning is to make sure the executor has all the information and documentation they will need.

In Passing

With the digital age making a range of social media available, there are new ways, like crowdfunding, for many people to contribute and make a major impact. There are a growing number of platforms to choose from. It is buyer beware and they may not issue official donation tax receipts. However, the simple fact that most people generally know what crowdfunding is, versus the relative obscurity of donor advised funds, says something about the impact social media is having on philanthropy.

The charitable and non-profit sector, along with every other sector, is realizing that the average donor wants to be reached in new and ever changing digital ways, and that the information about their organization and programs will need to be readily accessible on websites or apps. I expect the more tech savvy Millennial generation will want to see digitally how their individual donation is making a difference, and will want to use the same online platforms and apps they have come to appreciate for efficiency and ease of use in the retail space.

Another area of consideration in the legacy category is family history and genealogy. Nothing has been more transformative on this field than the internet and DNA testing.

Genealogy Files

As more and more people are becoming interested in their family genealogy and analyzing DNA for ancestry and health information, this presents a number of things that need to be identified and managed as part of your estate plan and will. You should consider documenting where you keep your genealogical files as part of your digital assets inventory. Who are the genealogists or history buffs in your family who would be grateful to have your files or be given access to your records? This is something to consider by passing this along sooner than later; leaving passwords (or forgetting to) is not the most reliable plan to passing down all your long hours of family history research. DNA genealogy doesn't stop at humans – it now also extends to pets!

Family Mementos and Memorabilia

If you are the proud possessor of the family Bible, grandma's photo collection or great-grandpa's military medals, it is an important consideration that these items are included in your estate plan, and you should identify who you'd like to have these important family mementos after your death. Ideally, you could pass these items over to the next generation while you are alive and use that as an opportunity to explain the importance of the memento to them, and confirm that they are actually interested in receiving them. Do you have a copy of your family stories, whether published or not? Do you want your published family history book to end up in the book donation bin? Do you have diaries that might provide a unique insight into a certain era or historical event?

As with planned giving, you can make arrangements in advance, and plan who the recipient(s) will be. Another consideration is to turn important historical materials over to an appropriate historical society in your city, jurisdiction (*e.g.*, Vancouver Historical Society[310]), local library (*e.g.*, Toronto Reference Library[311]), or genealogical society (*e.g.*, Ontario Genealogical Society[312]).

If you are downsizing, these are some of the items you might not have space for, but could offer the family history buff a source of valuable information (*i.e.*, source of names, historical events, buildings, location, birth and death dates) about your family history – letter and card collections, postcards, wedding invitations, memorial cards, birth, marriage, and death announcements, military or service documents or medals. Some of these can be of historical significance or value, if you want to sell or donate them.

Chapter 10
Getting Your Digital and Non-Digital Affairs In Order – Done!

Have you ever gone away on a trip and left someone at home in charge of your family, your household, and your pets? Or you simply asked a neighbour or friend to collect the mail and remove the flyers so it doesn't look like you are away. If you are the average person, you didn't just walk away without making some plans. At a minimum, you worried about how things were going at home – did the mail get picked up, did the garbage get put out on the right day, did someone mow the lawn, or shovel the driveway, or did the dog get enough exercise? To address your worries, you called to check in, nice and casual, possibly even to tell someone you missed them. Or at the other end of the spectrum, perhaps you left a note, a set of instructions on the kitchen table and felt it necessary to check the remote cameras and call in regularly. In all cases, perhaps you were reassured that if something did happen, that the family would call right away. Regardless of how you choose to check in, or not, on some level you might have prepared your loved ones for your time away.

Let's consider your ultimate trip from this earthly planet, the last time you permanently leave your loved ones. This last journey needs the same care and attention, in terms of your will and estate plan. For reasons that will seem endless, people do not get their will prepared because they can't cope with the topic of death, other priorities take over, and, of course, none of us knows when it is going to happen, so what's the rush?

Planning ahead, by documenting your wishes in a will and estate plan, can help get your affairs in order. Perhaps you can even go a little further and leave an estate binder – consider it those notes on the kitchen table you would have left for a shorter trip.

People often talk about the executor like some abstract person that miraculously shows up, who knows everything about you, figures out precisely everything you wanted and knows exactly what to do. That is just not possible, and next to impossible in the digital age. If I have done anything in this book, hopefully, I have convinced you that the executor is much more than that. The executor is a project manager with the big project of winding up your life. They will need some additional support, pre-planned guidance and mentoring from you to help them be successful in meeting your wishes.

And now technology has moved right into the personal realm; it is no longer just a toy we use for our entertainment. We use technology in every aspect of our day-to-day lives, from communicating through our family's online calendars or e-mail, managing our appliances, and maintaining our cars. We would all secretly have to admit it that if we lost our smartphones and all the data they contain, our lives would be completely out of control. Digital assets and digital devices now permeate our lives. Elements that were once only a factor in our workplace have now permanently crossed over into our personal lives. They need to be considered in the planning of your estate.

Our exploration together of death in the digital age is coming to an end. The premise I set at the beginning of our journey was that dealing with our digital lives is predicated on understanding how death works in the physical world for your non-digital assets. Doing so in an efficient way, in my opinion, requires that you apply some constructs from the project management profession and that you consider getting your affairs in order simply as a project. Hopefully, you have already been exposed to some of that project lingo in your work environment or seen it on TV. I also introduced you to *Your Digital Undertaker: Project Management Checklist* – questions that you can use in planning Your Death Project, whether that was digital or not. However, digital assets, too, need to be planned for so that your wishes and intentions for them can be documented and communicated, because they have sentimental value or financial value, just like all of your other assets.

In many respects, as you face the deathcare and estate industry, you are at the same disadvantage that many find themselves in dealing with the financial industry or other specialized professions or industries. The professionals in the deathcare and estate industry just know a whole lot more than you do, and you don't know what you don't know. Further, as with situations involving money, as your estate does, there will be lots of competing interests and agendas in selling you one option over another.

However, you know your life best. Your wishes are your own, and you may even have a really good gut sense if something makes sense or not about what you are being told and who is telling you. I am hoping that this book will arm you with a set of project management tools and questions to ask. Hopefully, you will then take the next big step – to embrace the estate planning process and confidently engage estate professionals to advise you on your planning journey. Further, you probably even have some of your own work experience that you can call upon as well – taking notes, following up, asking questions, bringing someone you trust as a second set of eyes and ears, and not making a decision without some due diligence. It might seem intimidating to meet with a legal advisor, go to a funeral home, deal with a tax advisor, or deal with your digital assets, but you can tackle this. There will likely be many options for any wish or requirement that you have, and the question is really about understanding the choices, the pros and the cons, making informed decisions based on the trade-offs, costs and risks you are prepared to accept.

In order to effectively describe using the project management tools within the environment of the estate industry, it was important to cover some of the basic concepts and terminology in the deathcare and estate industry. Keep in mind, I have only scratched the surface of this industry, and did so in a generic way to illustrate how things might work in general. In this great country of ours, laws like estate law and family law are different in every province, territory or jurisdiction, and they change over time.

Your Digital Undertaker: Project Management Checklist Recap

I trust that you have observed that a few themes emerged when using the project management tools as they were applied to the deathcare and the estate industry. They are probably worth summarizing:

1. Beginning with the Basics of Scope: *Why are you doing this?*

Among the reasons for getting a will and an estate plan might be to achieve the peace of mind that comes from knowing that when you die, your wishes will be met, your intentions achieved, and the people you love will be provided for. Understanding the scope of any project is the first step in project management. Having a compelling reason to do a project can help you get motivated to see it through. Perhaps your wishes to protect your family and loved ones can be that inspiration for you.

2. Considering Options & Trade-Offs: *What are the pros and cons?*

There is no right way to do anything; there are only options and associated pros and cons. Considerations such as cost, risk and convenience will influence decisions made on any project. Knowing about the options and trade-offs is very important. If you are only hearing about one option, then your homework is not done.

3. Advancing through Preferences & Costs: *What do you need and what's it going to cost?*

Once you have made a decision on which options you would like to pursue after considering the trade-offs, the logical next step is documenting the specific preferences (requirements) and calculating costs for the selected options.

At first, learning about the laws and how they affect your situation can be alarming and concerning, but that will pass. Understanding the options and how to deal with them will become more comfortable over time. The second thing worth mentioning is the iterative nature of the estate planning process. As you deal with any major item, wish or requirement in your life, whether that be an asset, beneficiary considerations, or your own specific wishes, you'll want to be patient. The first draft of your estate plan becomes a second or third draft as you cycle through estate considerations. Eventually that too will settle down, and you will be thankful that you did spend the time working through the iterations. One of the least understood options for estate and incapacity planning is the trust relationship, so I added a bit about that in Chapter 4 to encourage you to ask questions to see if this could apply to your situation.

4. Supporting through Procurement of Professional Services:
Your body can't bury itself!

Procurement management means managing whatever outside help you need to complete a project – the products and services you will purchase or hire. This means researching what you need, getting quotes and making decisions about what to buy and who to buy it from, and then making sure they follow through.

Getting accurate estate advice, unfortunately, is not as simple as surveying your friends and family at a social event. In general, project managers only hire qualified people whose references and experiences check out. The same thing applies here. When engaging professionals, it is more than reasonable to ask questions before the work begins. What is the hourly billing rate, retainer fees, or what is the estimate of the total costs up front? You should also expect to receive a written engagement letter on what scope of services you'll receive.

5. Assessing and Mitigating Risks: *What are the risks? What are the backup plans?*

At the start of a project, a good project manager will try to identify potential risks – essentially, things that could go wrong and derail the project – and think about possible backup plans to deal with them if the event occurs. The process of assessing risk for Your Death Project will be as individual as you, given each person has a unique set of life circumstances.

Further, understanding that the law system under which we are governed changes with society, public policy and other influencers, so writing a will and power of attorney once in your life might not do either. Your life situation will likely also change as time marches on, so it would make sense that some maintenance of the critical elements of your estate plan need to be revised.

6. Addressing Communication: *It is on a need-to-know basis and someone needs to know!*

Nothing can derail a project more quickly than poor and ineffective communication. If the people involved in the project don't know what each other is doing, it can lead to misunderstandings, hurt feelings and cost overruns (usually through duplication of effort or neglecting to do something important because you thought someone else was all over it).

All the best estate planning might be for naught if the executor can't find your documents, if they are not able to understand your wishes, or worse, if your beneficiaries or others challenge your will. So getting a will done, the job doesn't end there on Your Death Project; it means taking the project one step further and considering communication and risk management as part of your estate planning process.

Communicating your wishes to your loved ones and beneficiaries is critical, but there are some other important people to talk to – the executor, the Attorney for your Power of Attorney (for financial affairs), your healthcare representative for your legal document for healthcare decisions, your estate advisors, and any other fiduciary role you identify as part of your estate plan.

One More Project Management Tool to Leverage

I will leave you with a small question set that I created for myself called Your Digital Undertaker Question Matrix, that summarizes the key questions I covered earlier in each of the chapters (*see appendix to this chapter).

In Passing

When you tackle a topic such as death, it should not be a surprise that, even in social settings with my own colleagues, family and friends, I heard lots of stories about how families deal with death. Among the stories were the reflections of time spent with the dearly beloved, including the special memories of discovering letters, photos or mementos that told the tales of a life well lived. I also heard sad stories of what happens when there is no will, the long and painful role of the executor, and the astonishment at all that can go wrong when expectations are not managed, wishes not documented or a paper trail is not left behind.

In my own journey, the one surprising find was that estate professionals have some of the same stories as they dealt with death with their own families and loved ones. If anything, you can feel heartened that those tough and awkward conversations you are trying to have with your parents and loved ones are not something that comes easy for anyone. You're not alone!

The digital age has already impacted your estate because it has affected how you manage and access your assets and, moreover, how you communicate with institutions that hold your assets for you or those you do business with. Put yourself in the future shoes of the executor who is responsible for winding up your life. Their job just got more complex if you don't spend the time considering the impact of the digital age on estate planning. What was once considered optional, such as an inventory or estate binder with the necessary information left for the executor, is headed to a mandatory recommendation when you consider how digital your estate really has become.

My wish for you, as consumers of the deathcare and estate industry in Canada, is that your increased level of awareness of the project management tools and questions I've shared will drive you to have deeper and more meaningful conversations about death. Few industries have been untouched by the digital age, and perhaps you too can be part of the informed consumers that drive that transformation by asking more educated questions, using social media to share your experiences, and encouraging the estate industry to adopt technology that will make the estate planning and estate administration processes easier to interact with.

Here ends cracking the code to death and its digital afterlife!

Sincerely,

Your Digital Undertaker

Appendix to Chapter 10: Your Digital Undertaker Question Matrix

I will leave you with a project management based question set called Your Digital Undertaker Question Matrix, which summarizes the key questions I covered earlier in each of the chapters. If you want the background on how it was constructed, keep reading. Otherwise, if you want to get right to it for your personal use, jump to the question matrix on the last page of this appendix.

In industry or government, an organization might want to measure or benchmark their project management proficiency or competency to determine its effectiveness at driving business results, improving the bottom line and garnering client value and loyalty. The results of this "test" will help an organization assess where they need to improve their project management expertise, and also where they are driving results and should consider keeping those processes. There are tools, methods and models that do this kind of assessment. They are available commercially, or an organization might create their own in-house version, depending on the size of the organization. The Government of Canada calls their assessment tool the Organizational Project Management Capacity Assessment Tool, if you are looking for an example of one in practice.[313]

The basic structure of these project management assessment tools is that they measure a number of project management competency or process areas in terms of their levels or grade, typically on a scale of 1 to 5. The typical assessment uses questionnaires or other independent measures to determine the status or state of a specific project management competency area. Then, a grade or level is assigned based on the answer, and actions are identified to move from one level to the next in each process area. For example, you might get a level 1 if you use a documented process, a level 2 if you use technology to automate the process, a level 3 if you review and update the process regularly, a level 4 if you have a continuous improvement program in place with employee engagement and a level 5 if you have created an industry best in the class innovative approach.

In simplistic terms, the assessment tool is a matrix of *elements* versus *levels*, used to assess where you are against where you should be, need to be or want to be. It sounds like a test, but it doesn't need to be. The beauty of this assessment approach is that each element doesn't necessarily need to be a level 5. You might decide to be at a level 3 in some areas because the industry in general or your competitors might be at that level. In other areas, you might decide to spend the time and resources to get to a 4 or 5 because that is the specific area that contributes most significantly to the business outcomes or you want beat out your competition.

To create the Your Digital Undertaker Question Matrix, I created a basic matrix structure using the chapters/topics in this book as the elements, against Your Digital Undertaker: Project Management Checklist as the levels. Because there is no grade in this exercise and there is no incorrect answer, I inverted the matrix from the more traditional assessment tool. The elements you will see in the first column of the table are the topics from Chapter 3 (funeral) through to Chapter 10 (getting your digital and non-digital affairs in order). The levels in the first row across the top of the table are from the Your Digital Undertaker: Project Management Checklist (from Chapter 2 and applied against each subsequent chapter). Recall from Chapter 2, the project management questions that I selected were based on their natural ability to advance a conversation through the planning aspects of a topic. They were also designed in this manner to slot nicely into this matrix and show progression against a level.

The matrix cells are filled with questions generated by using each of the respective project management tools (from scope to the combined risk/communication) that are specifically applied to each chapter/topic. For example, for Chapter 3 (funerals), the first question in the row in the matrix is about scope: Do you want to be buried, cremated or donated? Similarly, the last question in the row is about risk and communication: Does the executor know about your pre-planned and pre-paid funeral arrangements?

There are certainly a lot more questions you'll need to come up with and answer for your own personal estate planning journey, based on your life situation, but I hope sharing my starter question matrix inspires you to start that next step. In addition, depending on where the estate planning journey takes you, estate profession-als in their respective specialized fields will have more in-depth questions for you, based on the services, products, options, legal and tax considerations of your estate planning elements.

Table 3: Your Digital Undertaker Question Matrix – Starter set of questions about death to consider in Canada		
Chapter	**Level 1** *(Scope)*	**Level 2** *(Options & Trade-Offs)*
Your Body Can't Bury Itself! (Ch.3)	Buried, cremated or donated? Wishes are communicated.	Final resting place considered. Organ donor card considered.
Your Digital Life Needs a Will, Too (Ch.4)	Understand the legal importance of a will. Default discovered – what happens if you do nothing?	Will/estate law in Canada is provincial/territorial. Other jurisdictional laws can also affect you.
Other Estate Planning Options	Trust(s) investigated as an option for estate & incapacity planning.	Insurance - reviewed your term, permanent & other needs.
Your Executor (Ch.5)	Executor was interviewed. Executor is willing. Backup executor named.	Executor is aware of fiduciary obligations under the law.
Advance Care Planning - POA (Ch.6)	Understand how a Power of Attorney (financial) works for incapacity.	Appointed person (called Attorney) is aware of fiduciary obligations.
Advance Care Planning - Health (Ch.6)	Understand how legal document(s) for healthcare decisions works.	Appointed person is aware of their obligations. Backup person named.
Death with a Side of Digital (Ch.7)	Living in the digital age still needs a paper trail. Expect technology & laws to change over time.	Reviewed what a digital asset is & that it requires a password or pre-planning for fiduciary access.
Death and taxes (Ch.8)	Understand how tax is triggered upon death & keeping records is critical.	Executor made aware of tax filing dates, obligations & tax rules (e.g. CRA).
Don't Forget Me (Ch.9)	Legacy beyond money is considered (e.g. volunteering).	Options for charitable & philanthropic wishes are explored.
Getting Your affairs in order - Done! (Ch.10)	Everyone's life is complicated. Planning & communication is critical.	Your loved ones may experience grief. Your pre-planning can help.

Table 3: Your Digital Undertaker Question Matrix – Starter set of questions about death to consider in Canada		
Level 3 (Preferences & Cost)	Level 4 (Professional Services)	Level 5 (Risks & Communication)
Celebration of Life preferences are documented.	Engaged pre-planning professionals.	Pre-planned & pre-paid. Executor has been briefed.
Reviewed your estate plan with estate professionals for risk, tax, law & complexity.	Engaged legal advisor (authorized by your province /territory) for advice and drafting.	Secured will in a safe place & told executor. Manage benefiary expectations.
Insurance - explored as an estate planning option.	Joint ownership & situs of property reviewed with legal advisor.	Reviewed beneficiary designations in context of jurisdictional laws.
Reviewed your will, estate plan & estate binder with executor.	Professional (e.g. trust company) considered for executor or agent.	Update executor when big things impact your will or estate plan.
Reviewed POA with Attorney. Considered oversight & backup.	Professional (e.g. trust company) considered for Attorney or agent.	POA is in a secure location where Attorney can access.
Considered senior care planning & end of life options.	Discussed wishes for care with family & healthcare (e.g. GP).	Document for health decisions is where your family can find it.
Created a digital assets inventory & identified wishes for your digital assets.	Reviewed digital assets inventory with legal & considered a digital assets clause.	Protect yourself & your family online with technology & user best practices.
Consider tax advisor (e.g. accountant) for tax filing while living.	Engaged estate tax planning advice & documented plans.	Understand tax law changes & revise estate tax plans.
Expected tax treatment of planned giving is documented.	Engaged estate professional advice & gift planners for plans.	Legacy wishes are included in your will & estate plan.
Understand that death can bring out the best & worst in people – mitigate the risks.	Engaged qualified estate professionals authorized in your province/territory.	Revisit will, estate plan, advance care plans as law & major events change your life.

Endnotes

1   Social Development Canada. "After a Death." Canada.ca. June 27,
    2018. Accessed September 07, 2018. https://www.canada.ca/en/
    employment-social-development/services/benefits/family/death.
    html.

2   Ministry of Health. "Wills and Estate Planning." Province of British
    Columbia. July 27, 2018. Accessed September 07, 2018. https://
    www2.gov.bc.ca/gov/content/family-social-supports/seniors/
    financial-legal-matters/wills-and-estate-planning

3   "What Happens When You Die Without a Will?" CBA British
    Columbia. Accessed September 07, 2018. https://www.cbabc.org/
    For-the-Public/Dial-A-Law/Scripts/Wills-and-Estates/177.

4   S.B.C. 2009, c. 13

5   "'It Doesn't Make Sense': Change to CPP to Provide Flat-Rate
    Death Benefit Isn't Actually Enough to Cover Funerals." National
    Post, December 16, 2017. Accessed September 7, 2018. https://
    nationalpost.com/news/canada/change-to-cpp-death-benefit-
    panned-as-insufficient-to-cover-funeral-costs.

6   Statistics Canada. *Table 19.5 Internet use, by activity and age
    group, 2010.* CANSIM table 358-0153 (database). October 7, 2015.
    Accessed September 8, 2018. https://www150.statcan.gc.ca/n1/
    pub/11-402-x/2012000/chap/information/tbl/tbl05-eng.htm

7   Department of Justice. "Canada's System of Justice." Government
    of Canada, Department of Justice, Electronic Communications.
    July 27, 2017. Accessed September 09, 2018. http://www.justice.
    gc.ca/eng/csj-sjc/; "Acts and Regulations." Canada.ca. October
    01, 2018. Accessed October 01, 2018. https://www.canada.ca/en/
    revenue-agency/programs/about-canada-revenue-agency-cra/
    acts-regulations.html; Canada. Library of Parliament. House of
    Commons. "How a Bill Becomes Law: The Legislative Process"
    in *Guide to the Canadian House of Commons*. Ottawa, ON:
    Library of Parliament, 2016. https://lop.parl.ca/About/Parliament/
    GuideToHoC/pdf/guide_canadian_house_of_commons-e.pdf;
    "Canada, a Country by Consent: The Canadian Government:

How Laws Are Made." Accessed October 01, 2018. http://www.canadahistoryproject.ca/can-govt-today/can-govt-today-14-how-laws-made.html.

8   "Topic 1: Judge-Made Law or Common Law." LawLessons.ca. Accessed October 01, 2018. http://www.lawlessons.ca/lesson-plans/1.2.judge-made-law-or-common-law.

9   Financial Consumer Agency of Canada. "Estate Planning, Wills and Dealing with Death." Canada.ca. June 14, 2018. Accessed October 01, 2018. https://www.canada.ca/en/financial-consumer-agency/services/estate-planning.html.

10 Financial Consumer Agency of Canada. "6.2.1 Life Insurance." Canada.ca. May 18, 2017. Accessed October 01, 2018. https://www.canada.ca/en/financial-consumer-agency/services/financial-toolkit/insurance/insurance-2/2.html.

11 Cauwenberghe, Christine Van. *Wealth Planning Strategies for Canadians*. Toronto: Thomson Carswell, 2011, 4-8.

12 Cauwenberghe, 7.

13 Cauwenberghe, 4.

14 "Project Management Institute." PMI. Accessed October 01, 2018. https://www.pmi.org/.

15 Treasury Board of Canada Secretariat. "Government of Canada Project Management." Canada.ca. October 01, 2015. Accessed October 01, 2018. https://www.canada.ca/en/treasury-board-secretariat/services/information-technology-project-management/project-management.html.

16 Financial Consumer Agency of Canada. "11.4.3 The Main Methods of Estate Planning." Canada.ca. August 09, 2018. Accessed October 01, 2018. https://www.canada.ca/en/financial-consumer-agency/services/financial-toolkit/financial-planning/financial-planning-4/4.html.

17 *Civil Code of Quebec*, C.Q.L.R., c. CCQ-1991.

18 R.S.C. 1985, c. 1 (5th Supp.).

19 "About the Profession." Canadian College of Funeral Service. Accessed October 01, 2018. http://ccfs.ca/Content/About_the_Profession/.

20 "The 'If Something Happens' Binder." CARP. Accessed October 01, 2018.

http://www.carp.ca/2012/01/27/the-if-something-happens-binder/.

21 "About CARP." CARP. Accessed October 01, 2018.

http://www.carp.ca/about/#about.

22 S.B.C. 2004, c. 2.

23 S.B.C. 2004, c. 35.

24 Eastwood, Joel. "The Traditional Funeral Is on Its Deathbed."
Thestar.com. May 26, 2014. Accessed October 01, 2018.
https://www.thestar.com/news/death_and_dying/2014/05/26/
the_traditional_funeral_is_on_its_deathbed.html; Payne, Jason.
"Cemetery Space Dwindling in Many B.C. Communities."
Vancouver Sun. October 29, 2017. Accessed October 01, 2018.
https://vancouversun.com/news/local-news/cemetery-space-
dwindling-in-many-b-c-communities.; "More Canadians Choose
Cremation over Caskets." CBCnews. June 06, 2013. Accessed
October 01, 2018. http://www.cbc.ca/news/canada/windsor/
more-canadians-choose-cremation-over-caskets-1.1305126.

25 "Columbariums: Finding One's Final Niche."
CBCnews. November 02, 2014. Accessed October 01,
2018. http://www.cbc.ca/news/canada/newfoundland-labrador/
columbariums-finding-one-s-final-niche-1.2819980;

Frequently Asked Questions." City of Courtenay. Accessed
October 01, 2018.

http://www.courtenay.ca/EN/main/city-hall/cemetery/colum-
barium/frequently-asked-questions.html.

26 "Mausoleum Space Running out as Popularity of Cremation
Grows in Prince George." CBCnews. October 31, 2017. Accessed
October 01, 2018. http://www.cbc.ca/news/canada/british-colum-
bia/mausoleum-space-running-out-as-popularity-of-cremation-
grows-in-prince-george-1.4379423.

27 "Arrange a Funeral, Burial, Cremation or Scattering." Ontario.
ca. Accessed October 01, 2018. http://www.ontario.ca/page/
arrange-funeral-burial-cremation-or-scattering.

28 Payne, Jason. "Cemetery Space Dwindling in Many B.C.
Communities." Vancouver Sun. October 29, 2017. Accessed
October 01, 2018. https://vancouversun.com/news/local-news/
cemetery-space-dwindling-in-many-b-c-communities.

29 "Whole Body Donation." Rates of Recidivism | Ministry of
Community Safety and Correctional Services. Accessed

October 01, 2018. https://www.mcscs.jus.gov.on.ca/english/
DeathInvestigations/WholeBodyDonation/DI_body_donation.html.

30   "Body Bequeathal Program." Pediatrics. Accessed October 01,
2018. https://med.uottawa.ca/department-innovation/division-
clinical-and-functional-anatomy/body-bequeathal-program;
"Body Program." Department of Cellular & Physiological Sciences.
Accessed October 01, 2018. http://cps.med.ubc.ca/bodyprogram/.

31   Tancock, Kat. "Organ Donation: What You Need
to Know." Canadian Living. September 18, 2009.
Accessed October 01, 2018. http://www.canadianliv-
ing.com/health/prevention-and-recovery/article/
organ-donation-what-you-need-to-know.

32   National Defence. "What Happens After a Canadian Armed Forces
Member Dies." Ombudsman | National Defence | Canadian Armed
Forces. March 26, 2018. Accessed October 01, 2018. http://www.
ombudsman.forces.gc.ca/en/ombudsman-questions-complaints-
helpful-information/what-happens-after-a-caf-member-dies.page.

33   "The National Military Cemetery."
Beechwood Cemetery. Accessed October 01,
2018. http://www.beechwoodottawa.ca/cemetery-burial-
options/sections-honouring-military-and-police-services/
the-national-military-cemetery-2/.

34   Veterans Affairs Canada. "Funeral and Burial Assistance." Health
and Well Being - Services - Veterans Affairs Canada. December
29, 2017. Accessed October 01, 2018. http://www.veterans.gc.ca/
eng/services/financial/funeral-burial; "The Funeral and Burial
Program." Last Post Fund. Accessed October 01, 2018. http://
www.lastpostfund.ca/EN/funeral.php.

35   Government of Canada. "Death Benefit." Canada.ca. December
21, 2017. Accessed October 01, 2018. https://www.canada.ca/en/
services/benefits/publicpensions/cpp/cpp-death-benefit.html.

36   "The Death Benefit." Retraite Québec. Accessed October 01,
2018. https://www.rrq.gouv.qc.ca/en/deces/deces_conjoint/
autres_rentes/Pages/prestation_deces.aspx.

37   Government of Canada. "When Death Occurs: Royal Canadian
Mounted Police Pension." Canada.ca. July 09, 2018. Accessed
October 01, 2018. http://rcmp-grc.pension.gc.ca/act/vie-life/dec-
dth-eng.html.

38   Ministry of Social Development and Social Innovation. "Funeral Costs." Province of British Columbia. August 16, 2018. Accessed October 01, 2018. https://www2.gov.bc.ca/gov/content/governments/policies-for-government/bcea-policy-and-procedure-manual/general-supplements-and-programs/funeral-costs.

39   "Preplanning a Funeral." B.C. Funeral Association. Accessed October 01, 2018. http://www.bcfunerals.com/public-funeral-planning/preplanning-funeral.

40   "Pre-arranged Funeral Contracts." Éducaloi. April 11, 2016. Accessed October 01, 2018. https://www.educaloi.qc.ca/en/capsules/pre-arranged-funeral-contracts.

41   "Preplanning a Funeral." B.C. Funeral Association. Accessed October 01, 2018. http://www.bcfunerals.com/public-funeral-planning/preplanning-funeral.

42   "Preplanning a Funeral (Pre-Payment)." B.C. Funeral Association. Accessed October 01, 2018. http://www.bcfunerals.com/public-funeral-planning/preplanning-funeral.

43   "Home." OFSA. Accessed October 01, 2018. http://ofsa.org/; "Homepage – OACFP." Ontario Association of Cemetery and Funeral Professionals. Accessed October 01, 2018. https://oacfp.com/.

44   "Home." Bereavement Authority of Ontario. Accessed October 01, 2018. https://thebao.ca/.

45   "B.C. Funeral Association." B.C. Funeral Association. Accessed October 01, 2018. http://www.bcfunerals.com/.

46   Fédération Des Coopératives Funéraires Du Québec. Accessed October 01, 2018. https://www.fcfq.coop/en/.

47   "For Consumers." Nova Scotia Board of Registration of Embalmers and Funeral Directors. Accessed October 01, 2018. http://www.nsbrefd.com/For-Consumers.html.

48   "Home." Funeral and Cremation Services Council of Saskatchewan. Accessed October 01, 2018. http://www.fcscs.ca/.

49   "Home." Funeral Services Association of CanadaHome. Accessed October 01, 2018. https://www.fsac.ca/.

50   "What to Do Following a Death." All Ontario. September 18, 2017. Accessed October 01, 2018. https://allontario.ca/what-to-do-following-a-death/.

51   "Home." Memorial Society of B.C. Accessed October 01, 2018. https://memorialsocietybc.org/.

52   Canada Revenue Agency. "Eligible Funeral Arrangements." Canada.ca. September 06, 2002. Accessed October 01, 2018. https://www.canada.ca/en/revenue-agency/services/forms-publications/publications/it531/archived-eligible-funeral-arrangements.html.

53   "Compassion for the Shipment of Human Remains." Air Canada Fleet. Accessed October 01, 2018. https://www.aircanada.com/cargo/en/shipping/shipping-solutions/ac-compassion/; "Human Remains." West Jet. Accessed October 01, 2018. https://www.westjet.com/en-ca/book-trip/westjet-cargo/shipping-information/human-remains.

54   Financial Consumer Agency of Canada. "Making a Will and Planning Your Estate." Canada.ca. June 22, 2018. Accessed October 01, 2018. https://www.canada.ca/en/financial-consumer-agency/services/estate-planning/will-estate-planning.html.

55   "Funerals" Canadian Consumer Handbook. Accessed October 02, 2018. http://www.consumerhandbook.ca/en/topics/products-and-services/funerals.

56   "Funeral, Burial, Cremation or Scattering: Your Rights." Ontario.ca. Accessed October 02, 2018. https://www.ontario.ca/page/funeral-burial-cremation-or-scattering-your-rights.

57   S.O. 2002, c. 33.

58   "Home." Bereavement Authority of Ontario. Accessed October 01, 2018. https://thebao.ca/.

59   "Preparing a Will." Canadian Bar Association Legal Health Check. Accessed October 01, 2018. https://www.cba.org/CBAMediaLibrary/cba_na/PDFs/CBA%20Legal%20Health%20Check/Inhouse/HealthCheckWills.pdf

60   British Columbia *Wills, Estates and Succession Act,* S.B.C. 2009, c. 13, s. 1

61   "Majority of Canadians Don't Have a Will: Poll." CTV News. January 24, 2018. Accessed October 02, 2018. https://www.ctvnews.ca/lifestyle/majority-of-canadians-don-t-have-a-will-poll-1.3772853; "CIBC Poll: Nearly One Third of Baby Boomers Don't Have a Will." Cision. Accessed October 02, 2018. https://www.newswire.ca/news-releases/cibc-poll-nearly-one-third-of-baby-boomers-dont-have-a-will-510205181.html; Golombek,

Jamie. "Your Estate Matters! Common Traps and How to Avoid Them." CIBC. February 2017. Accessed October 2, 2018. https://www.cibc.com/content/dam/personal_banking/advice_centre/protect-whats-important/estate-planning-cibc-en.pdf.

62   Financial Consumer Agency of Canada. "Making a Will and Planning Your Estate." Canada.ca. June 22, 2018. Accessed October 02, 2018. https://www.canada.ca/en/financial-consumer-agency/services/estate-planning/will-estate-planning.html.

63   *Wills, Estates and Succession Act,* S.B.C. 2009, c. 13, Division 1.

64   R.S.O. 1990, c. S.26

65   R.S.N.B. 1973, c. D-9.

66   *Escheats Act*, R.S.C., 1985, c. E-13, s. 2.

67   "What Happens When You Die Without a Will?" CBA British Columbia. Accessed October 02, 2018. https://www.cbabc.org/For-the-Public/Dial-A-Law/Scripts/Wills-and-Estates/177.

68   "Estate and Personal Trust Services *Frequently Asked Questions*." Public Guardian and Trustee of British Columbia. Accessed October 02, 2018. http://www.trustee.bc.ca/faq/Pages/estate-and-personal-trust-services-faq.aspx#faq4.

69   New Brunswick *Wills Act*, R.S.N.B. 1973, c. W-9.

70   Nova Scotia *Wills Act*, R.S.N.S. 1989, c. 505.

71   Yukon *Wills Act*, R.S.Y. 2002, c. 230.

72   Ministry of Health. "Wills Registry." Province of British Columbia. July 18, 2018. Accessed October 02, 2018. https://www2.gov.bc.ca/gov/content/life-events/death/wills-registry.

73   R.S.O. 1990, c. E.21.

74   R.S.O. 1990, c. E.21, s. 2.

75   "Wills. What Is a Notarial Will?" Éducaloi. May 25, 2018. Accessed October 02, 2018. https://www.educaloi.qc.ca/en/capsules/wills.

76   "Home." Chambre Des Notaires Du Québec. Accessed October 02, 2018. http://www.cnq.org/.

77   *Indian Act*, R.S.C. 1985, c. I-5, ss. 45-46; "Wills and Estates on Reserve." Aboriginal Legal Aid in B.C. Accessed October 02, 2018. https://aboriginal.legalaid.bc.ca/benefits/willsAndEstates.php.

78   "About Us." Self-Counsel Press. Accessed October 02, 2018. http://www.self-counsel.com/about-self-counsel-press; Justice Services Branch. "Make a Will Week." Province of British Columbia. August 29, 2018. Accessed October 02, 2018. https://www2.gov.bc.ca/gov/content/life-events/death/wills-estates/make-a-will-week.

79   "Lawyer and Paralegal Directory." The Law Society of Upper Canada. Accessed October 02, 2018. https://www2.lsuc.on.ca/LawyerParalegalDirectory/loadSearchPage.do.

80   "Law Society Referral Service." Law Society of Ontario. Accessed October 02, 2018. https://lso.ca/public-resources/finding-a-lawyer-or-paralegal/law-society-referral-service.

81   "Search Our Lawyer Directory." Nova Scotia Barristers' Society. Accessed October 02, 2018. http://nsbs.org/member-search.

82   "Find-A-Lawyer." The Canadian Bar Association. Accessed October 02, 2018. https://www.cba.org/For-The-Public/Find-A-Lawyer.aspx.

83   "Member Directory." STEP. Accessed October 02, 2018. https://www.step.org/member-directory.

84   "You Can Talk to a TEP." STEP: Advising Families. Accessed October 02, 2018. https://advisingfamilies.org/.

85   Canada Revenue Agency. "Income Tax Folio S5-F1-C1, Determining an Individual's Residence Status." Canada.ca. April 05, 2016. Accessed October 02, 2018. https://www.canada.ca/en/revenue-agency/services/tax/technical-information/income-tax/income-tax-folios-index/series-5-international-residency/folio-1-residency/income-tax-folio-s5-f1-c1-determining-individual-s-residence-status.html.

86   "Make a Will Week." Province of British Columbia. August 29, 2018. Accessed October 02, 2018. https://www2.gov.bc.ca/gov/content/life-events/death/wills-estates/make-a-will-week.

87   "Wills in Alberta." Alberta.ca. Accessed October 02, 2018. https://www.alberta.ca/wills-in-alberta.aspx.

88   Government of Ontario. "Wills, Estates and Trusts" Ministry of the Attorney General. Accessed October 02, 2018. https://www.attorneygeneral.jus.gov.on.ca/english/justice-ont/estate_planning.php.

89   Government of Manitoba. *A Guide to Farm Estate Planning in Manitoba*. Accessed October 02, 2018. https://www.gov.mb.ca/agriculture/farm-management/business-management/pubs/farm-estate-planning.pdf

90   Financial Consumer Agency of Canada. "Making a Will and Planning Your Estate." Canada.ca. June 22, 2018. Accessed October 01, 2018. https://www.canada.ca/en/financial-consumer-agency/services/estate-planning/will-estate-planning.html.

91   "Make a Will Week, 8 April to 14 April 2018." The Society of Notaries Public of B.C. Accessed October 02, 2018. https://www.notaries.bc.ca/resources/showContent.rails?resourceItemId=41184.

92   "Home." Pro Bono Students Canada. Accessed October 02, 2018. https://www.probonostudents.ca/.

93   "Death Notifications Receive Digital Makeover." PressReader.com - Connecting People through News. February 26, 2018. Accessed October 02, 2018. https://www.pressreader.com/canada/ottawa-citizen/20180226/281771334680806.

94   Canada Revenue Agency. "Types of Trusts." Canada.ca. May 29, 2018. Accessed October 02, 2018. https://www.canada.ca/en/revenue-agency/services/tax/trust-administrators/types-trusts.html#mutual.

95   Canada Revenue Agency. "T3 Trust Guide – 2017." Canada.ca. April 10, 2018. Accessed October 02, 2018. https://www.canada.ca/en/revenue-agency/services/forms-publications/publications/t4013/t3-trust-guide-2016.html.

96   Canada Revenue Agency. "Types of Trusts." Canada.ca. May 29, 2018. Accessed October 02, 2018. https://www.canada.ca/en/revenue-agency/services/tax/trust-administrators/types-trusts.html.

97   Waters, D. W. M., Mark R. Gillen, and Lionel D. Smith. *Waters Law of Trusts in Canada*. Toronto, ON: Carswell, 2012, 3.

98   STEP. *Trusts Explained.* Accessed October 02, 2018.

https://www.step.org/sites/default/files/Comms/leaflets/Trusts_Explained_2016.pdf.

99   Canada Revenue Agency. "Types of Trusts." Canada.ca. May 29, 2018. Accessed October 02, 2018. https://www.canada.ca/en/

revenue-agency/services/tax/trust-administrators/types-trusts.
html.

100　Ontario *Trustee Act*, R.S.O. 1990, c. T.23; Manitoba *The Trustee Act*, C.C.S.M. c. T160.

101　Cooperberg, Chaya. "The Truth about Family Trusts." The Globe and Mail. July 21, 2010. Accessed October 02, 2018. https://www.theglobeandmail.com/globe-investor/personal-finance/household-finances/the-truth-about-family-trusts/article615586/.

102　Canada Revenue Agency. "Types of Trusts." Canada.ca. May 29, 2018. Accessed October 02, 2018. https://www.canada.ca/en/revenue-agency/services/tax/trust-administrators/types-trusts.html#ltr. See section on Alter Ego Trusts.

103　Canada Revenue Agency. "Types of Trusts." Canada.ca. May 29, 2018. Accessed October 02, 2018. https://www.canada.ca/en/revenue-agency/services/tax/trust-administrators/types-trusts.html#joint. See section on Joint Spousal or Common-Law Partner Trusts.

104　Canada Revenue Agency. "Types of Trusts." Canada.ca. May 29, 2018. Accessed October 02, 2018. https://www.canada.ca/en/revenue-agency/services/tax/trust-administrators/types-trusts.html#spousal. See section on Spousal or Common-Law Partner Trusts.

105　Canada Revenue Agency. "Types of Trusts." Canada.ca. May 29, 2018. Accessed October 02, 2018. https://www.canada.ca/en/revenue-agency/services/tax/trust-administrators/types-trusts.html#RESP. See section on RESP Trusts.

106　Canada Revenue Agency. "Types of Trusts." Canada.ca. May 29, 2018. Accessed October 02, 2018. https://www.canada.ca/en/revenue-agency/services/tax/trust-administrators/types-trusts.html#QDT. See section on Qualified Disability Trust (QDT) Trusts.

107　Canada Revenue Agency. "Tax Changes Announced in January 2016 for Certain Trusts and Loss Restriction Events." Canada.ca. June 16, 2016. Accessed October 02, 2018. https://www.canada.ca/en/revenue-agency/programs/about-canada-revenue-agency-cra/federal-government-budgets/budget-2016-growing-middle-class/tax-changes-announced-january-2016-certain-trusts-loss-restriction-events.html.

108　Financial Consumer Agency of Canada. "Being an Estate Representative and Settling the Estate." Canada.ca. September

07, 2017. Accessed October 02, 2018. https://www.canada.ca/
en/financial-consumer-agency/services/estate-planning/estate-
representative.html.

109 Canada Revenue Agency. "Legal Representative." Canada.ca.
January 05, 2018. Accessed October 02, 2018. https://www.
canada.ca/en/revenue-agency/services/tax/individuals/life-events/
what-when-someone-died/legal-representative.html.

110 Northwest Territories Justice. *Questions and Answers about wills
in Northwest Territories*. Accessed October 02, 2018. https://www.
justice.gov.nt.ca/en/files/estate-administration/Questions%20
and%20Answers%20about%20Wills.pdf.

111 *"Frequently Asked Questions* about Estates." Ministry of
the Attorney General. August 2012. Accessed October 02,
2018. https://www.attorneygeneral.jus.gov.on.ca/english/estates/
estates-FAQ.php.

112 "The Role of Liquidators (Executors)." Éducaloi. January 17, 2017.
Accessed October 02, 2018. https://www.educaloi.qc.ca/en/
capsules/role-liquidators-executors.

113 "Your Duties as Executor." CBA British Columbia. April
2017. Accessed October 02, 2018. https://www.cbabc.org/
For-the-Public/Dial-A-Law/Scripts/Wills-and-Estates/178.

114 Financial Consumer Agency of Canada. "Provincial and Territorial
Resources on Estate Law." Canada.ca. September 12, 2018.
Accessed October 02, 2018. https://www.canada.ca/en/financial-
consumer-agency/services/estate-planning/resources-estate-law.
html.

115 Financial Consumer Agency of Canada. "Being an Estate
Representative and Settling the Estate." Canada.ca. September
07, 2017. Accessed October 02, 2018. https://www.canada.ca/
en/financial-consumer-agency/services/estate-planning/estate-
representative.html.

116 "Request a Clearance Certificate." Canada.ca. March 20,
2018. Accessed October 02, 2018. https://www.canada.ca/en/
revenue-agency/services/tax/individuals/life-events/what-when-
someone-died/clearance-certificate.html; Financial Consumer
Agency of Canada. "Being an Estate Representative and Settling
the Estate." Canada.ca. September 07, 2017. Accessed October
02, 2018. https://www.canada.ca/en/financial-consumer-agency/
services/estate-planning/estate-representative.html.

117   Canada Revenue Agency. "Trusts: Amount Payable." Canada.ca. September 05, 2002. Accessed October 02, 2018. https://www. canada.ca/en/revenue-agency/services/forms-publications/publications/it286r2/archived-trusts-amount-payable.html.

118   Public Guardian and Trustee of Manitoba. *Deceased Estate Handbook*. Accessed October 02, 2018. https://www.gov.mb.ca/ publictrustee/pdf/deceased_estate_handbook.en.pdf. See section called "What is Not an Asset of an Estate?"

119   "Search for Policy of a Deceased." OLHI – OmbudService for Life & Health Insurance. Accessed October 02, 2018. https://www.olhi. ca/insurance/search-for-lost-policy/.

120   Canada Revenue Agency. "Employers' Guide – Payroll Deductions and Remittances." Canada.ca. June 15, 2018. Accessed October 02, 2018. https://www.canada.ca/en/revenue-agency/services/ forms-publications/publications/t4001/employers-guide-payroll-deductions-remittances.html.

121   "Estate Administration." Public Guardian and Trustee of British Columbia: Estate and Personal Trust Services *Frequently Asked Questions*. Accessed October 02, 2018. http://www.trustee. bc.ca/services/estate-and-personal-trust-services/Pages/estate-administration.aspx.

122   "The Office of the Public Guardian and Trustee (OPGT)." Ministry of the Attorney General. Accessed October 02, 2018. https://www. attorneygeneral.jus.gov.on.ca/english/family/pgt/.

123   "The Office of the Children's Lawyer." Ministry of the Attorney General. Accessed October 02, 2018. https://www.attorneygeneral.jus.gov.on.ca/english/family/ocl/.

124   "Estate Administration." Public Guardian and Trustee of British Columbia: Estate and Personal Trust Services *Frequently Asked Questions*. Accessed October 02, 2018. http://www.trustee. bc.ca/services/estate-and-personal-trust-services/Pages/estate-administration.aspx. See section called "Naming the PGT as Your Executor."

125   People's Law School. *Being an Executor*. Accessed October 02, 2018. https://www.peopleslawschool.ca/file/286/ download?token=o4I8vxGZ.

126   Speak Up. *Frequently Asked Questions*. Accessed October 02, 2018. http://www.advancecareplanning.ca/wp-content/

uploads/2015/09/acp_faq_8.5x11_final-web_aug8-12.pdf. See section called "What is advance care planning?"

127 "Representative Agreement." Seniors First BC. Accessed October 02, 2018. http://seniorsfirstbc.ca/resources/legal-research-articles/representative-agreement-article/.

128 "Legal Capacity Standards." Seniors First BC. Accessed October 02, 2018. http://seniorsfirstbc.ca/for-professionals/capacity/legal-capacity-different-transactions/.

129 British Columbia *Healthcare (Consent) and Care Facility (Admission) Act*, R.S.B.C. 1996, c. 181, s. 16 (Temporary substitute decision makers).

130 Public Guardian and Trustee of British Columbia. *Information about Temporary Substitute Decision Makers Authorized by the Public Guardian and Trustee*. Accessed October 02, 2018. http://www.trustee.bc.ca/documents/STA/Information%20for%20Temporary%20Substitute%20Decision%20Makers%20Authorized%20by%20the%20Public%20Guardian%20and%20Trustee.pdf.

131 British Columbia *Healthcare (Consent) and Care Facility (Admission) Act*, R.S.B.C. 1996, c. 181, s. 12 (Exception — urgent or emergency health care).

132 R.S.B.C. 1996, c. 349.

133 British Columbia *Public Guardian and Trustee Act*, R.S.B.C. 1996, c. 383.

134 The Office of the Public Guardian and Trustee (OPGT)." Ministry of the Attorney General. Accessed October 02, 2018. https://www.attorneygeneral.jus.gov.on.ca/english/family/pgt/.

135 Ministry of Attorney General. *Powers of Attorney*. Accessed October 02, 2018. https://www.attorneygeneral.jus.gov.on.ca/english/family/pgt/poa.pdf.

136 Ontario Securities Commission. "7 Signs of Financial Elder Abuse." GetSmarterAboutMoney.ca. Accessed October 02, 2018. https://www.getsmarteraboutmoney.ca/fact-cards/7-signs-financial-elder-abuse/.

137 "Brochures and Factsheets." CNPEA. Accessed October 02, 2018. https://cnpea.ca/en/tools/brochures-and-factsheets.; ComThmonwealth Bank of Australia Customer Advocate. *Safe & Savvy: A Guide to Help Older People Avoid Abuse, Scams and*

Fraud. Accessed October 02, 2018. https://cnpea.ca/images/safe-and-savvy-preventing-the-financial-abuse-of-seniors.pdf.

138 "Home." Canadian Anti-Fraud Centre. September 28, 2018. Accessed October 02, 2018. http://www.antifraudcentre-centreantifraude.ca/index-eng.htm; Government of Canada, Royal Canadian Mounted Police. "Scams and Fraud." Biology Services - Royal Canadian Mounted Police. June 14, 2017. Accessed October 02, 2018. http://www.rcmp-grc.gc.ca/scams-fraudes/index-eng.htm; Government of Canada, Royal Canadian Mounted Police. "Identity Theft and Identity Fraud." Biology Services - Royal Canadian Mounted Police. December 04, 2015. Accessed October 02, 2018. http://www.rcmp-grc.gc.ca/scams-fraudes/id-theft-vol-eng.htm.

139 Government of Manitoba. *A Legal Information Guide for Seniors*. April 2014. Accessed October 02, 2018.

http://www.gov.mb.ca/publictrustee/pdf/legal_guide_seniors.pdf.

140 Public Legal Information Association of Newfoundland and Labrador. *Seniors and the Law in Newfoundland and Labrador*. Accessed October 02, 2018. http://www.cssd.gov.nl.ca/seniors/pdf/seniors_law.pdf.

141 "Home." Legal Information of Nova Scotia. Accessed October 02, 2018. https://www.legalinfo.org/fr/i-have-a-legal-question/wills-and-estates-law/#representative-decision-making-for-an-adult-representative-guardian.

142 Government of Ontario. "Wills, Estates and Trusts" Ministry of the Attorney General. Accessed October 02, 2018. https://www.attorneygeneral.jus.gov.on.ca/english/justice-ont/estate_planning.php.

143 Community Legal Information Association of PEI. *An Introduction to Putting Your Affairs in Order at Any Age*. Accessed October 02, 2018. http://www.cliapei.ca/sitefiles/File/publications/PLA5.pdf.

144 Public Legal Education and Information Service of New Brunswick. When You Can't Manage Your Affairs...Who Will? March 2018. Accessed October 02, 2018. http://www.legal-info-legale.nb.ca/en/uploads/file/pdfs/When_You_Cant_Manage_Your_Affairs_EN.pdf.

145 "Your Money and Your Possessions." Québec Ministère de la Justice. Accessed October 02, 2018. https://www.justice.gouv.qc.ca/en/your-money-and-your-possessions/.

146 Centre for Public Legal Education Alberta. *Making a Power of Attorney in Alberta*. Accessed October 02, 2018. http://p.b5z. net/i/u/10086419/f/MakingAPowerOfAttorney.pdf.

147 "Dementia Numbers in Canada." Alzheimer Society of Canada. August 24, 2018. Accessed October 02, 2018. http://alzheimer.ca/ en/Home/About-dementia/What-is-dementia/Dementia-numbers.

148 British Columbia *Power of Attorney Act*, R.S.B.C. 1996, c. 370, Part 2; Ontario *Substitute Decisions Act, 1992*, S.O. 1992, c. 30 (Continuing *Powers of Attorney* for Property).

149 Ontario *Powers of Attorney* Act, R.S.O. 1990, c. P.20.

150 "Preparing your mandate in three steps." Le Curateur Public Du Québec. Accessed October 02, 2018. https://www.curateur.gouv. qc.ca/cura/en/outils/publications/mon_mandat.html.

151 Saskatchewan *The Powers of Attorney Act, 2002*, S.S. 2002, c. P-20.3.

152 Saskatchewan *The Powers of Attorney Act, 2002*, S.S. 2002, c. P-20.3.

153 Ontario *Substitute Decisions Act, 1992*, S.O. 1992, c. 30.

154 British Columbia Power of Attorney Act, R.S.B.C. 1996, c. 370, ss. 10, 11. [Note: every province has a different word for POA, I used the B.C. term in brackets (for "financial affairs")].

155 *"Powers of Attorney."* Ministry of the Attorney General. Accessed October 02, 2018. https://www.attorneygeneral.jus.gov.on.ca/ english/family/pgt/incapacity/poa.php; *My Voice: Expressing My Wishes for Future Health Care Treatment: Advance Care Planning Guide*. Victoria, B.C.: Ministry of Health, 2013. Accessed October 02, 2018.

   http://www.health.gov.bc.ca/library/publications/year/2013/ MyVoice-AdvanceCarePlanningGuide.pdf.

156 *"Powers of Attorney."* Ministry of the Attorney General. Accessed October 02, 2018. https://www.attorneygeneral.jus.gov.on.ca/ english/family/pgt/incapacity/poa.php.

157 Alberta *Personal Directives Act*, R.S.A. 2000, c. P-6.

158 *My Voice: Expressing My Wishes for Future Health Care Treatment: Advance Care Planning Guide*. Victoria, B.C.: Ministry of Health, 2013. Accessed October 02, 2018.

http://www.health.gov.bc.ca/library/publications/year/2013/
MyVoice-AdvanceCarePlanningGuide.pdf.

159 R.S.B.C. 1996, c. 405.

160 "Advance Care Planning Interactive Workbook." Speak Up.
     Accessed October 02, 2018. http://www.myspeakupplan.ca/.

161 "Making an Advance Care Plan." Dying With Dignity Canada.
     Accessed October 02, 2018. http://www.dyingwithdignity.ca/
     download_your_advance_care_planning_kit.

162 Kessler, David. *The Needs of the Dying*. New York:
     HarperPaperback, 2007.

163 Okun, Barbara F., and Joseph Nowinski. *Saying Goodbye: How
     Families Can Find Renewal through Loss*. New York: Berkley
     Books, 2011.

164 Statistics Canada. *Table 13-10-0715-01: Deaths, by place of death
     (hospital or non-hospital)*. CANSIM table 102-0509 (database).
     October 02, 2018. Accessed October 02, 2018. https://www150.
     statcan.gc.ca/t1/tbl1/en/tv.action?pid=1310071501.

165 Government of Canada. "Options and Decision-Making at
     End of Life." Canada.ca. May 31, 2017. Accessed October 03,
     2018. https://www.canada.ca/en/health-canada/services/options-
     decision-making-end-life.html.

166 "Home." End of Life Doula Association of Canada. Accessed
     October 03, 2018. http://deathdoulacanada.org/.

167 Canada Health. "Options and Decision-Making at End of Life."
     Canada.ca. May 31, 2017. Accessed October 03, 2018. https://
     www.canada.ca/en/health-canada/services/options-decision-
     making-end-life.html.

168 Government of Canada. "Provincial and Territorial Contact
     Information for End-of-life Care Services." Canada.ca. March 12,
     2018. Accessed October 03, 2018. https://www.canada.ca/en/
     health-canada/services/provincial-territorial-contact-information-
     links-end-life-care.html.

169 Government of Canada. "Palliative Care." Canada.ca. June 17,
     2016. Accessed October 02, 2018. https://www.canada.ca/en/
     health-canada/services/palliative-care.html.

170 Canadian Hospice Palliative Care Association. "Palliative Care
     FAQs." CHPCA. Accessed October 02, 2018. http://www.chpca.

net/family-caregivers/faqs.aspx. See section: What is the definition of hospice palliative care?

171 "Home." Canadian Hospice Palliative Care Association. Accessed October 02, 2018. http://www.chpca.net/.

172 "New on Virtual Hospice." Canadian Virtual Hospice. Accessed October 02, 2018. http://www.virtualhospice.ca/en_US/Main Site Navigation/Home.aspx.

173 S.C. 2016, c. 3, s. 241.2(1).

174 S.C. 2016, c. 3, s. 241.2(1).

175 Ministry of Health. "Expected/Planned Home Deaths." Province of British Columbia. April 13, 2017. Accessed October 03, 2018. https://www2.gov.bc.ca/gov/content/health/accessing-health-care/home-community-care/care-options-and-cost/end-of-life-care/expected-planned-home-deaths.

176 Champlain Community Care Access Centre. Expected Death in the Home Protocol: EDITH Guidelines for Implementation. May 2015. Accessed October 02, 2018. https://champlainpalliative.ca/wp-content/uploads/2017/02/Expected-Death-in-the-Home-Protocol-1.pdf.

177 Procaylo, Nick. "Seniors Care in B.C.: A Primer on the System." Vancouver Sun. June 21, 2018. Accessed October 03, 2018. https://vancouversun.com/news/local-news/caring-for-our-elders-a-primer-on-the-system.

178 "Home." Nidus Personal Planning Resource Centre and Registry. Accessed October 03, 2018. http://www.nidus.ca/.

179 "Home." The Order of the Good Death. Accessed October 03, 2018. http://www.orderofthegooddeath.com/.

180 "Welcome to Death Cafe." Death Cafe. Accessed October 03, 2018. http://deathcafe.com/.

181 "'Death Cleaning:' The New, Not-as-Morbid-as-It-Sounds Decluttering Trend." CTV News. June 26, 2018. Accessed October 03, 2018. https://www.ctvnews.ca/lifestyle/death-cleaning-the-new-not-as-morbid-as-it-sounds-decluttering-trend-1.3988406; Racco, Marilisa. "'Swedish Death Cleaning' Is the Latest Self-Help Craze." Global News. October 12, 2017. Accessed October 03, 2018. https://globalnews.ca/news/3799362/swedish-death-cleaning-is-the-latest-self-help-craze/; MacMillan, Amanda. "'Death Cleaning' Is the Newest Way to Declutter." Time. October

17, 2017. Accessed October 03, 2018. http://time.com/4985533/death-cleaning-declutter/.

182 Verde, Tom. "Aging Parents with Lots of Stuff, and Children Who Don't Want It." The New York Times. August 18, 2017. Accessed October 03, 2018. https://www.nytimes.com/2017/08/18/your-money/aging-parents-with-lots-of-stuff-and-children-who-dont-want-it.html?smid=tw-nytimes&smtyp=cur&_r=0.

183 Horton, Helena. "More People Have Died by Taking Selfies This Year than by Shark Attacks." The Telegraph. September 22, 2015. Accessed October 03, 2018. https://www.telegraph.co.uk/technology/11881900/More-people-have-died-by-taking-selfies-this-year-than-by-shark-attacks.html.

184 "Digital Assets Global Special Interest Group." STEP. Accessed October 03, 2018. https://www.step.org/digital-assets-global-special-interest-group.

185 STEP Digital Assets Special Interest Group. *What Are My Digital Assets?* Accessed October 02, 2018. https://www.step.org/sites/default/files/Digital_Assets/Digital_Assets_PUBLIC_GUIDE.pdf.

186 "Unclaimed Balances." Bank of Canada. Accessed October 03, 2018. https://www.bankofcanada.ca/unclaimed-balances/.

187 "Do You Have Money Sitting in an Unclaimed or Dormant Account?" B.C. Unclaimed Property Society. Accessed October 03, 2018. https://unclaimedpropertybc.ca/.

188 Uniform Law Conference of Canada. *Uniform Access to Digital Assets by Fiduciaries Act (2016).* August 2016. Accessed October 02, 2018. https://www.ulcc.ca/images/stories/2016_pdf_en/2016ulcc0006.pdf.

189 STEP Digital Assets Special Interest Group. *What Are My Digital Assets?* Accessed October 02, 2018.

190 Griffith, Eric. "Two-Factor Authentication: Who Has It and How to Set It Up." PC Mag. February 16, 2018. Accessed October 03, 2018. https://www.pcmag.com/feature/358289/two-factor-authentication-who-has-it-and-how-to-set-it-up; "Two-factor Authentication for Apple ID." Apple Support. September 27, 2018. Accessed October 03, 2018. https://support.apple.com/en-ca/HT204915.

191 "Turn on 2-Step Verification - Android." Google. Accessed October 03, 2018. https://support.

google.com/accounts/answer/9096865?co=GENIE.
Platform&hl=en&visit_id=636741250530333308-283613254&rd=1.

192 "About Two-Step Verification." Microsoft Support. August 16, 2018. Accessed October 03, 2018. https://support.microsoft.com/en-us/help/12408/microsoft-account-about-two-step-verification.

193 Henry, Alan. "The Difference Between Two-Factor and Two-Step Authentication." Lifehacker. October 06, 2016. Accessed October 03, 2018. https://lifehacker.com/the-difference-between-two-factor-and-two-step-authenti-1787159870; Elliott, Matt. "Two-factor Authentication: How and Why to Use It." CNET. March 28, 2017. Accessed October 03, 2018. https://www.cnet.com/how-to/how-and-why-to-use-two-factor-authentication/.

194 "Google Authenticator - Apps on Google Play." Google. Accessed October 03, 2018. https://play.google.com/store/apps/details?id=com.google.android.apps.authenticator2.

195 Financial Consumer Agency of Canada. "Digital Currency." Canada.ca. January 19, 2018. Accessed October 11, 2018. https://www.canada.ca/en/financial-consumer-agency/services/payment/digital-currency.html.

196 Sagar, Leigh. *The Digital Estate*. London: Sweet & Maxwell, 2018.

197 Uniform Law Conference of Canada. *Uniform Access to Digital Assets by Fiduciaries Act (2016)*. August 2016. Accessed October 02, 2018. https://www.ulcc.ca/images/stories/2016_pdf_en/2016ulcc0006.pdf.

198 If you are looking for further information on the fiduciary differences between the U.S. and Canada, see Rhoads Perry, Shelley and Cunningham, Kathleen. "Access All Areas?" *STEP Journal* 26 (2018).

199 Uniform Law Commission: The National Conference of Commissioners on Uniform States Law. Fiduciary Access to Digital Assets Act, Revised (2015). Accessed October 02, 2018. http://www.uniformlaws.org/Act.aspx?title=Fiduciary%20Access%20to%20Digital%20Assets%20Act,%20Revised%20(2015).

200 Canada Revenue Agency. "What You Should Know about Digital Currency." Canada.ca. December 03, 2014. Accessed October 03, 2018. https://www.canada.ca/en/revenue-agency/news/newsroom/fact-sheets/fact-sheets-2013/what-you-should-know-about-digital-currency.html.

201 Canada Revenue Agency. "Digital Currency." Canada.ca. March
     07, 2018. Accessed October 11, 2018. https://www.canada.ca/en/
     revenue-agency/programs/about-canada-revenue-agency-cra/
     compliance/digital-currency.html; Ligaya, Armina. "If You Sold
     or Used Bitcoin Last Year, Canada Revenue Agency Wants Its
     Due." Financial Post. February 01, 2018. Accessed October 11,
     2018. https://business.financialpost.com/technology/blockchain/
     if-you-sold-or-used-bitcoin-last-year-the-cra-needs-to-collect-
     its-due; Bruno, Jessica. "How to Report Digital Currency to CRA."
     Advisor. March 27, 2015. Accessed October 11, 2018. https://
     www.advisor.ca/advisor-to-client/tax-advisor-to-client/
     how-to-report-digital-currency-to-cra/.

202 "66 Ways to Protect Your Privacy Right Now."
     Consumer Reports. February 21, 2017. Accessed
     October 03, 2018. http://www.consumerreports.org/
     privacy/66-ways-to-protect-your-privacy-right-now/.

203 Service Canada. "Cyber Security." Canada.ca. October 01, 2018.
     Accessed October 03, 2018. https://www.canada.ca/en/services/
     defence/cybersecurity.html.

204 "What Will Happen to My Facebook Account If I Pass Away?
     Facebook Help Center. Accessed October 03, 2018. https://www.
     facebook.com/help/103897939701143?helpref=search&sr=4&quer
     y=memorialization.

205 "About Inactive Account Manager." Google. Accessed October 03,
     2018. https://support.google.com/accounts/answer/3036546.

206 "Choose a Legacy Contact." Facebook Help Center. Accessed
     October 03, 2018. https://www.facebook.com/help/991335594313
     139/?helpref=hc_fnav.

207 Rubenking, Neil J. "The Best Password Managers of 2018." PC
     Mag. July 12, 2018. Accessed October 03, 2018. https://www.
     pcmag.com/article2/0,2817,2407168,00.asp; Ansaldo, Michael.
     "Best Password Managers: Reviews and Buying Advice."
     PCWorld. May 04, 2018. Accessed October 03, 2018. https://www.
     pcworld.com/article/3207185/software/best-password-managers-
     reviews-and-buying-advice.html; Gewirtz, David. "11 Best
     Password Managers to Keep Your Life Secure." CNET. February
     16, 2018. Accessed October 03, 2018. https://www.cnet.com/
     news/the-best-password-managers-directory/.

208 "Powerful Tools and Features." Dashlane. Accessed October 03,
     2018. https://www.dashlane.com/features.

209 "Setting up Emergency Access." Password Boss. Accessed October 03, 2018. https://support.passwordboss.com/hc/en-us/articles/115001354387-Setting-up-Emergency-Access; "What Is Emergency Access?" LastPass Awareness. Accessed October 03, 2018. https://lastpass.com/support.php?cmd=showfaq&id=9972.

210 "Best Secure Online Password Manager & Digital Vault." Keeper Blog. Accessed October 03, 2018. https://keepersecurity.com/.

211 "1Password 7 for Mac." 1Password Support. Accessed October 03, 2018. https://support.1password.com/explore/whats-new-mac/.

212 Golombek, Jamie. "You Might Have to Pay Tax on That - What Uber, Airbnb and Bitcoin Could Affect Your Return." Financial Post. April 26, 2018. Accessed October 11, 2018. https://business.financialpost.com/personal-finance/uber-drivers-airbnb-hosts-and-bitcoin-buffs-heres-what-you-need-to-know-to-do-your-taxes-this-year.

213 Canada Revenue Agency. "Barter Transactions." Canada.ca. September 06, 2002. Accessed October 03, 2018. https://www.canada.ca/en/revenue-agency/services/forms-publications/publications/it490/archived-barter-transactions.html.

214 Canada Revenue Agency. "Personal-Use Property." Canada.ca. January 03, 2018. Accessed October 03, 2018. https://www.canada.ca/en/revenue-agency/services/tax/individuals/topics/about-your-tax-return/tax-return/completing-a-tax-return/personal-income/line-127-capital-gains/completing-schedule-3/personal-use-property.html.

215 Golombek, Jamie. "You Might Have to Pay Tax on That - What Uber, Airbnb and Bitcoin Could Affect Your Return." Financial Post. April 26, 2018. Accessed October 11, 2018. https://business.financialpost.com/personal-finance/uber-drivers-airbnb-hosts-and-bitcoin-buffs-heres-what-you-need-to-know-to-do-your-taxes-this-year.

216 Lakhan, Dwarka. "Bitcoin: Currency, Commodity or Payments?" Investment Executive. October 22, 2015. Accessed October 11, 2018. https://www.investmentexecutive.com/newspaper_/news-newspaper/bitcoin-currency-commodity-or-payments/.

217 Financial Consumer Agency of Canada. "Digital Currency." Canada.ca. January 19, 2018. Accessed October 11, 2018. https://www.canada.ca/en/financial-consumer-agency/services/payment/digital-currency.html.

218 R.S.C. 1985, c. 1 (5th Supp.).

219 "You're Already out of Time to Read the Income Tax Act before Filing Deadline: CTF." Taxpayer. Accessed October 03, 2018. https://www.taxpayer.com/news-releases/you-re-already-out-of-time-to-read-the-income-tax-act-before-filing-deadline--ctf; "Time to Slash Income Tax Act." Toronto Sun. May 05, 2014. Accessed October 03, 2018. https://torontosun.com/2014/05/05/time-to-slash-income-tax-act-2/wcm/2e549a31-c946-4725-8328-562c33577d27.

220 Canada Revenue Agency. "Disposing of Personal-use Property." Canada.ca. January 03, 2018. Accessed October 03, 2018. https://www.canada.ca/en/revenue-agency/services/tax/individuals/topics/about-your-tax-return/tax-return/completing-a-tax-return/personal-income/line-127-capital-gains/you-have-a-gain-loss/disposing-personal-use-property.html.

221 Canada Revenue Agency. "T4037 Capital Gains 2017." Canada.ca. January 03, 2018. Accessed October 03, 2018. https://www.canada.ca/en/revenue-agency/services/forms-publications/publications/t4037.html.

222 British Columbia *Probate Fee Act*, S.B.C. 1999, c. 4.

223 Ontario *Estate Administration Tax Act, 1998*, S.O. 1998, c. 34, Sched.

224 Prince Edward Island *Probate Act*, R.S.P.E.I. 1988, c. P-21; "New Brunswick Courts - Probate Court." Government House - Lieutenant Governor of New Brunswick. Accessed October 03, 2018. https://www.gnb.ca/cour/05Prob/index-e.asp.

225 Ministry of Government and Consumer Services. "Central Forms Repository." Service Ontario. Accessed October 03, 2018. http://www.forms.ssb.gov.on.ca/mbs/ssb/forms/ssbforms.nsf/FormDetail?OpenForm&ACT=RDR&TAB=PROFILE&SRCH=&ENV=WWE&TIT=9955&NO=9955E.

226 Alberta Judicature Act Surrogate Rules, Alta. Reg. 130/1995, Sch. 2 (Court Fees).

227 British Columbia *Probate Fee Act*, S.B.C. 1999, c. 4, s. 2 (Probate fee).

228 Manitoba The Law Fees and Probate Charge Act, C.C.S.M. c. L80.

229 Nova Scotia *Probate Act*, S.N.S. 2000, c. 31.

230 Ontario *Estate Administration Tax Act, 1998*, S.O. 1998, c. 34, s. 2(6) (Amount, certificate sought after June 7, 1992).

231 "Wills. What Is a Notarial Will?" Éducaloi. May 25, 2018. Accessed October 02, 2018. https://www.educaloi.qc.ca/en/capsules/wills.

232 *"Estate Administration Tax Calculator." Ministry of the Attorney General. Accessed October 03, 2018. https://www.attorneygeneral.jus.gov.on.ca/english/estates/calculate.php.*

233 Ministry of Justice. "Probating a Will." Province of British Columbia. Accessed October 03, 2018. https://www2.gov.bc.ca/gov/content/life-events/death/wills-estates/probating-a-will; "Estate Administration Tax." Ministry of Finance: Government of Ontario. Accessed October 03, 2018. https://www.fin.gov.on.ca/en/tax/eat; Public Guardian and Trustee of Manitoba. *Deceased Estate Handbook*. Accessed October 02, 2018. https://www.gov.mb.ca/publictrustee/pdf/deceased_estate_handbook.en.pdf.

234 "Your Duties as Executor." CBA British Columbia. April 2017. Accessed October 02, 2018. https://www.cbabc.org/For-the-Public/Dial-A-Law/Scripts/Wills-and-Estates/178.

235 Wilson, Mary-Jane. *British Columbia Probate Kit*. North Vancouver, B.C.: Self-Counsel Press, 2015.

236 "About Us." Self-Counsel Press. Accessed October 02, 2018. http://www.self-counsel.com/about-self-counsel-press.

237 "Ten Reasons Why Joint Ownership May Be Problematic." The Globe and Mail. May 15, 2018. Accessed October 03, 2018. https://www.theglobeandmail.com/globe-investor/personal-finance/taxes/ten-reasons-why-joint-ownership-may-be-problematic/article24922693/.

238 "In Estate Planning, Know the Hazards of Joint Ownership." The Globe and Mail. May 03, 2018. Accessed October 03, 2018. https://www.theglobeandmail.com/globe-investor/personal-finance/in-estate-planning-know-the-hazards-of-joint-ownership/article627136/.

239 Canada Revenue Agency. "Deemed Disposition of Property." Canada.ca. January 03, 2018. Accessed October 03, 2018. https://www.canada.ca/en/revenue-agency/services/tax/individuals/life-events/what-when-someone-died/deemed-disposition-property.html.

240 Canada Revenue Agency. "Do You Have a Gain or Loss?" Canada.ca. January 03, 2017. Accessed October 03, 2018. https://www.

canada.ca/en/revenue-agency/services/tax/individuals/topics/
about-your-tax-return/tax-return/completing-a-tax-return/per-
sonal-income/line-127-capital-gains/you-have-a-gain-loss.html;
Canada Revenue Agency. "Disposing of Canadian Securities."
Canada.ca. January 03, 2018. Accessed October 03, 2018. https://
www.canada.ca/en/revenue-agency/services/tax/individuals/
topics/about-your-tax-return/tax-return/completing-a-tax-return/
personal-income/line-127-capital-gains/you-have-a-gain-loss/
disposing-canadian-securities.html.

241 Canada Revenue Agency. "T4037 Capital Gains 2017." Canada.
ca. January 03, 2018. Accessed October 03, 2018. https://www.
canada.ca/en/revenue-agency/services/forms-publications/publi-
cations/t4037.html.

242 Canada Revenue Agency. "5000-S3 T1 General 2017 - Schedule
3 - Capital Gains (or Losses) in 2017 - Common to All." Canada.
ca. January 04, 2018. Accessed October 03, 2018. https://www.
canada.ca/en/revenue-agency/services/forms-publications/tax-
packages-years/general-income-tax-benefit-package/5000-s3.
html.

243 Canada Revenue Agency. "Reporting the Sale of Your Principal
Residence for Individuals (other than Trusts)." Canada.ca. August
15, 2018. Accessed October 03, 2018. https://www.canada.ca/en/
revenue-agency/programs/about-canada-revenue-agency-cra/
federal-government-budgets/budget-2016-growing-middle-class/
reporting-sale-your-principal-residence-individuals.html.

244 Canada Revenue Agency. "T4037 Capital Gains 2017." Canada.
ca. January 03, 2018. Accessed October 03, 2018. https://www.
canada.ca/en/revenue-agency/services/forms-publications/publi-
cations/t4037.html.

245 Caldwell, Penny. "Have You Had the Talk?" *Cottage Life*.

246 Canada Revenue Agency. "Which Gains Are Eligible?" Canada.
ca. January 03, 2018. Accessed October 03, 2018. https://
www.canada.ca/en/revenue-agency/services/tax/individuals/
topics/about-your-tax-return/tax-return/completing-a-tax-return/
deductions-credits-expenses/line-254-capital-gains-deduction/
which-gains-eligible.html.

247 Canada Revenue Agency. *Preparing Returns for Deceased
Persons 2017*. Accessed October 03, 2018.

https://www.canada.ca/content/dam/cra-arc/formspubs/pub/
t4011/t4011-17e.pdf.

248   Canada Revenue Agency. "Death of an RRSP Annuitant." Canada. ca. April 18, 2018. Accessed October 03, 2018. https://www. canada.ca/en/revenue-agency/services/tax/individuals/topics/ rrsps-related-plans/death-rrsp-annuitant-a-prpp-member.html.

249   Canada Revenue Agency. "Death of a RRIF Annuitant." Canada. ca. May 29, 2018. Accessed October 03, 2018. https://www. canada.ca/en/revenue-agency/services/tax/individuals/topics/ registered-retirement-income-fund-rrif/death-a-rrif-annuitant.html.

250   Canada Revenue Agency. "Death of an RRSP Annuitant." Canada. ca. April 18, 2018. Accessed October 03, 2018. https://www. canada.ca/en/revenue-agency/services/tax/individuals/topics/ rrsps-related-plans/death-rrsp-annuitant-a-prpp-member.html.

251   Canada Revenue Agency. "Death of a RRIF Annuitant." Canada. ca. May 29, 2018. Accessed October 03, 2018. https://www. canada.ca/en/revenue-agency/services/tax/individuals/topics/ registered-retirement-income-fund-rrif/death-a-rrif-annuitant.html.

252   Canada Revenue Agency. "Registered Disability Savings Plan." Canada.ca. April 17, 2018. Accessed October 03, 2018. https:// www.canada.ca/en/revenue-agency/services/forms-publications/ publications/rc4460/registered-disability-savings-plan.html. See section called "What happens if the beneficiary dies?"

253   Cestnick, Tim. "Don't Forget Your RESP in Your Will." The Globe and Mail. May 03, 2018. Accessed October 03, 2018. https://www. theglobeandmail.com/life/parenting/dont-forget-your-resp-in-your- will/article623000/; Heath, Jason. "What Happens to an RESP When You Die". MoneySense. July 31, 2018. Accessed October 03, 2018. https://www.moneysense.ca/save/financial-planning/ estate-planning-what-happens-resp-die/.

254   Canada Revenue Agency. "Chart 1 - Returns for the Year of Death." Canada.ca. January 03, 2018. Accessed October 03, 2018. https://www.canada.ca/en/revenue-agency/services/tax/ individuals/life-events/what-when-someone-died/chart-1-returns- year-death.html.

255   Canada Revenue Agency. "Marital Status." Canada.ca. January 03, 2018. Accessed October 03, 2018. https://www.canada.ca/ en/revenue-agency/services/tax/individuals/topics/about-your- tax-return/tax-return/completing-a-tax-return/personal-address- information/marital-status.html.

256   Canada Revenue Agency. "Update Your Marital Status with the Canada Revenue Agency." Canada.ca. April 17, 2018. Accessed

October 03, 2018. https://www.canada.ca/en/revenue-agency/services/child-family-benefits/update-your-marital-status-canada-revenue-agency.html.

257 Canada Revenue Agency. "T4011 *Preparing Returns for Deceased Persons 2017*." Canada.ca. January 03, 2018. Accessed October 03, 2018. https://www.canada.ca/en/revenue-agency/services/forms-publications/publications/t4011.html.

258 "Que Faire Lors D'un Décès." Gouvernement Du Québec. Accessed October 03, 2018. https://www.quebec.ca/services-quebec/deces/; Blades, Elaine. "Don't Take These Shortcuts." Advisor. August 24, 2018. Accessed October 03, 2018. https://www.advisor.ca/tax/estate-planning/dont-take-these-shortcuts/; Templeton, Wendy D. "Estate Planning for Fractured Families: Cross Canada Complexities." Estate Planning for Fractured Families: Cross Canada Complexities. February 9, 2013. Accessed October 2, 2018. http://www.cbapd.org/DocViewer.aspx?id=6649&region=NB.

259 Canada Revenue Agency. "T4011 *Preparing Returns for Deceased Persons 2017*." Canada.ca. January 03, 2018. Accessed October 03, 2018. https://www.canada.ca/en/revenue-agency/services/forms-publications/publications/t4011.html.

260 Canada Revenue Agency. "Individuals – Executors." Canada.ca. September 04, 2012. Accessed October 03, 2018. https://www.canada.ca/en/revenue-agency/services/forms-publications/forms-publications-listed-client-group/individuals-executors.html.

261 Canada Revenue Agency. "T4011 *Preparing Returns for Deceased Persons 2017*." Canada.ca. January 03, 2018. Accessed October 03, 2018. https://www.canada.ca/en/revenue-agency/services/forms-publications/publications/t4011.html.

262 Canada Revenue Agency. "Legal Representative." Canada.ca. January 05, 2018. Accessed October 03, 2018. https://www.canada.ca/en/revenue-agency/services/tax/individuals/life-events/what-when-someone-died-legal-representative.html.

263 "Dealing With a Death." Revenu Québec. Accessed October 03, 2018. https://www.revenuquebec.ca/en/citizens/your-situation/dealing-with-a-death/.

264 Canada Revenue Agency. "T4011 *Preparing Returns for Deceased Persons 2017*." Canada.ca. January 03, 2018. Accessed October 03, 2018. https://www.canada.ca/en/revenue-agency/services/forms-publications/publications/t4011.html.

265   Canada Revenue Agency. "T4011 *Preparing Returns for Deceased Persons 2017.*" Canada.ca. January 03, 2018. Accessed October 03, 2018. https://www.canada.ca/en/revenue-agency/services/forms-publications/publications/t4011.html.

266   Canada Revenue Agency. "T4013 T3 Trust Guide 2017." Canada.ca. April 10, 2018. Accessed October 03, 2018. https://www.canada.ca/en/revenue-agency/services/forms-publications/publications/t4013.html.

267   Canada Revenue Agency. "T3RET T3 Trust Income Tax and Information Return." Canada.ca. August 20, 2018. Accessed October 03, 2018. https://www.canada.ca/en/revenue-agency/services/forms-publications/forms/t3ret.html.

268   Canada Revenue Agency. "Graduated Rate Taxation of Trusts and Estates and Related Rules." Canada.ca. May 26, 2016. Accessed October 03, 2018. https://www.canada.ca/en/revenue-agency/programs/about-canada-revenue-agency-cra/federal-government-budgets/budget-2014-road-balance-creating-jobs-opportunities/graduated-rate-taxation-trusts-estates-related-rules.html.

269   Canada Revenue Agency. "T4011 *Preparing Returns for Deceased Persons 2017.*" Canada.ca. January 03, 2018. Accessed October 03, 2018. https://www.canada.ca/en/revenue-agency/services/forms-publications/publications/t4011.html.

270   "Request a Clearance Certificate." Canada.ca. March 20, 2018. Accessed October 02, 2018. https://www.canada.ca/en/revenue-agency/services/tax/individuals/life-events/what-when-someone-died/clearance-certificate.html

271   Canada Revenue Agency. "Individuals – Executors." Canada.ca. September 04, 2012. Accessed October 03, 2018. https://www.canada.ca/en/revenue-agency/services/forms-publications/forms-publications-listed-client-group/individuals-executors.html.

272   Canada Revenue Agency. "Tax Treaties." Canada.ca. June 05, 2013. Accessed October 03, 2018. https://www.canada.ca/en/revenue-agency/services/tax/international-non-residents/tax-treaties.html; "Some Nonresidents with U.S. Assets Must File Estate Tax Returns." Internal Revenue Service. January 25, 2018. Accessed October 03, 2018. https://www.irs.gov/individuals/international-taxpayers/some-nonresidents-with-us-assets-must-file-estate-tax-returns; TaxTips.ca. "US Estate Tax May Be Payable by Canadians with US Assets." TaxTips.ca - Canada's Federal

Personal Income Tax Rates. August 29, 2018. Accessed October 03, 2018. https://www.taxtips.ca/personaltax/usestatetax.htm.

273 Canada Revenue Agency. "Legal Representative." Canada.ca. January 05, 2018. Accessed October 03, 2018. https://www. canada.ca/en/revenue-agency/services/tax/individuals/life-events/ what-when-someone-died/legal-representative.html.

274 Statistics Canada. "Spotlight on Canadians: Results from the General Social Survey Charitable Giving by Individuals Spotlight on Canadians: Results from the General Social Survey Charitable Giving by Individuals." Women and Paid Work. December 16, 2015. Accessed October 03, 2018. https://www150.statcan.gc.ca/ n1/pub/89-652-x/89-652-x2015008-eng.htm.

275 Statistics Canada. "Spotlight on Canadians: Results from the General Social Survey Charitable Giving by Individuals Spotlight on Canadians: Results from the General Social Survey Charitable Giving by Individuals." Women and Paid Work. December 16, 2015. Accessed October 03, 2018. https://www150.statcan.gc.ca/ n1/pub/89-652-x/89-652-x2015008-eng.htm; Statistics Canada. "General Social Survey - Giving, Volunteering and Participating (GSS GVP)." Government of Canada, Statistics Canada. August 31, 2018. Accessed October 03, 2018. http://www23.statcan. gc.ca/imdb/p2SV.pl?Function=getSurvey&SDDS=4430.

276 Canada Revenue Agency. "Line 349 - Donations and Gifts." Canada.ca. January 03, 2018. Accessed October 03, 2018. https:// www.canada.ca/en/revenue-agency/services/tax/individuals/ life-events/what-when-someone-died/final-return/complete-final- return-steps/common-types-income-a-final-return/federal-non- refundable-tax-credits/line-349-donations-gifts.html.

277 Canada Revenue Agency. "Estate Donations - Deaths after 2015." Canada.ca. December 10, 2015. Accessed October 03, 2018. https://www.canada.ca/en/revenue-agency/programs/about- canada-revenue-agency-cra/federal-government-budgets/budget- 2014-road-balance-creating-jobs-opportunities/estate-donations- deaths-after-2015.html; Canada Revenue Agency. "Estate Donations by Former Graduated Rate Estates." Canada.ca. June 16, 2016. Accessed October 03, 2018. https://www.canada.ca/en/ revenue-agency/programs/about-canada-revenue-agency-cra/ federal-government-budgets/budget-2016-growing-middle-class/ estate-donations-former-graduated-rate-estates.html.

278 Canada Revenue Agency. "Gifts of Shares, Stock Options, and Other Capital Property." Canada.ca. January 03, 2018. Accessed

October 03, 2018. https://www.canada.ca/en/revenue-agency/
services/tax/individuals/topics/about-your-tax-return/tax-return/
completing-a-tax-return/personal-income/line-127-capital-gains/
gifts-shares-stock-options-other-capital-property.html.

279 Canada Revenue Agency. "Charities and Giving." Canada.ca. May
08, 2018. Accessed October 03, 2018. https://www.canada.ca/en/
services/taxes/charities.html.

280 Canada Revenue Agency. "Non-profit Organizations." Canada.ca.
April 28, 2017. Accessed October 03, 2018. https://www.canada.
ca/en/revenue-agency/services/tax/non-profit-organizations.html.

281 Canada Revenue Agency. "Charitable Purposes." Canada.ca. April
20, 2018. Accessed October 03, 2018. https://www.canada.ca/
en/revenue-agency/services/charities-giving/charities/registering-
charitable-qualified-donee-status/applying-charitable-registration/
charitable-purposes.html.

282 Canada Revenue Agency. "What Is the Difference between a
Registered Charity and a Non-profit Organization?" Canada.ca.
June 23, 2016. Accessed October 03, 2018. https://www.canada.
ca/en/revenue-agency/services/charities-giving/giving-charity-
information-donors/about-registered-charities/what-difference-
between-a-registered-charity-a-non-profit-organization.html.

283 "Sector Impact." Sector Source. Accessed October 03,
2018. http://sectorsource.ca/research-and-impact/sector-
impact; "Key Statistics on Canada's Charity and Non-profit
Sector." CIDA - Canadian International Development
Agency | Global Philanthropy. May 17, 2018. Accessed
October 03, 2018. https://www.globalphilanthropy.ca/blog/
key_statistics_on_canadas_charity_and_non_profit_sector.

284 "Canadian Nonprofit News, Jobs, Funding, Training."
CharityVillage. Accessed October 03, 2018. https://charityvillage.
com/app/volunteer-listings.

285 Computer Systems Group, CSG, and University of Waterloo
/ VolunteerAttract. "Volunteer Centres - I Want to Volunteer -
Volunteer Canada." Engaging Volunteers - Volunteer Canada.
October 02, 2018. Accessed October 03, 2018. https://volunteer.
ca/index.php?MenuItemID=332.

286 "Home." Canadian Board Diversity Council (CBDC). Accessed
October 03, 2018. https://boarddiversity.ca/cbdc/.

287 "Home." Giving Tuesday. Accessed October 03, 2018. https://givingtuesday.ca/.

288 "Home." Pets and Friends. Accessed October 03, 2018. http://www.petsandfriends.org/; "Therapy Dog Program – Sponsored by Subaru Canada." St. John Ambulance. Accessed October 03, 2018. https://www.sja.ca/English/Community-Services/Pages/Therapy Dog Services/default.aspx.

289 "Home." Canadian Association of Gift Planners (CAGP). Accessed October 03, 2018. https://www.cagp-acpdp.org/.

290 "Home." GIV3: Feel Great Giving. Accessed October 03, 2018. http://giv3.ca.

291 "Home." Philanthropic Foundations Canada. June 15, 2018. Accessed October 03, 2018. https://pfc.ca/.

292 CAPG, Giv3 and Philanthropic Foundations Canada. *A Guide for Professional Financial Advisors: The Philanthropic Conversation.* 2016. Accessed October 03, 2018. https://www.cagp-acpdp.org/sites/default/files/media/a_guide_for_professional_financial_advisors.pdf.

293 "Leave a Legacy." CAGP. Accessed October 03, 2018. https://www.cagp-acpdp.org/en/leave-a-legacy.

294 Henze, Lawrence. *Transitional Giving for Building Strong Fundraising Pyramids.* Blackbaud. April 2011. Accessed on October 03, 2018. https://www.blackbaud.ca/files/resources/downloads/Whitepaper_TargetAnalytics_FundraisingPyramids.pdf; Kihlstedt, Andrea. "Use the Donor Pyramid to Focus Your Attention in the Right Places." Capital Campaign Masters. December 18, 2015. Accessed October 03, 2018. https://capitalcampaignmasters.com/use-the-donor-pyramid-to-focus-your-attention-in-the-right-places/.

295 "Check Charity before You Give This Season, Watchdog Says." CBC News. December 07, 2016. Accessed October 03, 2018. https://www.cbc.ca/news/canada/british-columbia/check-charity-before-you-give-this-season-watchdog-says-1.3883854.

296 Canada Revenue Agency. "List of Charities." Canada.ca. May 31, 2018. Accessed October 03, 2018. https://www.canada.ca/en/revenue-agency/services/charities-giving/charities-listings.html.

297 Brown, Mark. "Canada's Top-rated Charities 2017." MoneySense. November 29, 2016. Accessed October 03,

2018. https://www.moneysense.ca/save/financial-planning/
canadas-top-rated-charities-2017/.

298 "About Us." How Does a Canadian Charity Determine Appropriate
     Compensation for an Executive of the Charity? - Canadian Charity
     Law. Accessed October 03, 2018. https://www.canadiancharity-
     law.ca/about_us_2.

299 "Charity Search Results" Charity Data. Accessed October 03,
     2018. https://www.charitydata.ca/search/.

300 "Home." Charity Intelligence Canada. Accessed October 03,
     2018. https://www.charityintelligence.ca/.

301 "Home." Canadian Donor's Guide. Accessed October 03,
     2018. http://www.donorsguide.ca/.

302 "Home." Canadian Donor's Guide. Accessed October 03,
     2018. http://www.donorsguide.ca/.

303 "Home." Community Foundations of Canada. Accessed October
     03, 2018. http://communityfoundations.ca/.

304 "About Us – Sharing What We Have Changes the World,
     and It Changes Us." CHIMP. Accessed October 03, 2018.
     https://chimp.net/about; "How to Donate Cryptocurrency
     to Charity with CHIMP." CHIMP. January 09, 2018.
     Accessed October 03, 2018. https://chimp.net/blog/
     donate-cryptocurrency-charity-chimp/.

305 "CanadaHelps – Donate to Any Charity in Canada." CanadaHelps.
     Accessed October 03, 2018. https://www.canadahelps.org/;
     "Donate Securities." CanadaHelps. Accessed October 03,
     2018. https://www.canadahelps.org/en/donate/donate-securities/.

306 Canada Revenue Agency. "Gifts of Shares, Stock Options, and
     Other Capital Property." Canada.ca. January 03, 2018. Accessed
     October 03, 2018. https://www.canada.ca/en/revenue-agency/
     services/tax/individuals/topics/about-your-tax-return/tax-return/
     completing-a-tax-return/personal-income/line-127-capital-gains/
     gifts-shares-stock-options-other-capital-property.html.

307 Canada Revenue Agency. "Determining Fair Market Value of
     Gifts in Kind (non-cash Gifts)." Canada.ca. November 16, 2016.
     Accessed October 11, 2018. https://www.canada.ca/en/revenue-
     agency/services/charities-giving/charities/operating-a-registered-
     charity/issuing-receipts/determining-fair-market-value-gifts-kind-
     non-cash-gifts.html.

308 Canada Revenue Agency. "Ecologically Sensitive Land." Canada. ca. September 03, 2003. Accessed October 11, 2018. https://www.canada.ca/en/revenue-agency/services/charities-giving/charities/policies-guidance/summary-policy-e05-ecologically-sensitive-land.html.

309 Canadian Heritage. "Information for Donors of Certified Cultural Property." Canada.ca. October 24, 2017. Accessed October 11, 2018. https://www.canada.ca/en/canadian-heritage/services/certification-cultural-property/donors.html.

310 "Home." Vancouver Historical Society. Accessed October 03, 2018. http://www.vancouver-historical-society.ca/.

311 "Home." Toronto Public Library. Accessed October 03, 2018. https://www.torontopubliclibrary.ca/torontoreferencelibrary/.

312 "Home." The Ontario Genealogical Society. Accessed October 03, 2018. https://ogs.on.ca/.

313 Treasury Board of Canada Secretariat. "Organizational Project Management Capacity Assessment Tool." Canada.ca. May 01, 2013. Accessed October 03, 2018. https://www.canada.ca/en/treasury-board-secretariat/services/information-technology-project-management/project-management/organizational-project-management-capacity-assessment-tool.html.

CPSIA information can be obtained
at www.ICGtesting.com
Printed in the USA
LVHW031408290919
632593LV00003B/18